Fundamentals of Contract Law

SECOND EDITION

Jean Fitzgerald and Laurence Olivo

2005
EMOND MONTGOMERY PUBLICATIONS LIMITED
TORONTO, CANADA

We acknowledge the financial support of the Government of Canada through the Book Publishing Industry Development Program (BPIDP) for our publishing activities.

The events and characters depicted in this book are fictitious. Any similarity to actual persons, living or dead, is purely coincidental.

Acquisitions editor
Sarah Bartsch

Copy editor
Anita Levin

Production editor
Jim Lyons, WordsWorth Communications

Interior designers
Shani Sohn / Tara Wells, WordsWorth Communications

Typesetter and Proofreader
Cindy Fujimoto, WordsWorth Communications

Indexer
Paula Pike, WordsWorth Communications

Cover designer
Darrach Design

**Library and Archives Canada
Cataloguing in Publication**

Fitzgerald, Jean
　　　Fundamentals of contract law / Jean Fitzgerald and Laurence Olivo. — 2nd ed.

Includes index.
ISBN 978-1-55239-161-7

　　　1. Contracts — Ontario — Textbooks.
2. Contracts — Canada — Textbooks.
I. Olivo, Laurence M., 1946-　　II. Title.

KEO299.F57 2005　　　346.71302　　　2005-901390-7
KF801.F57 2005

*In memory of Josef Stavroff (1942–2005),
my friend and colleague and a gifted teacher,
too soon gone from us. — L.M.O.*

Contents

Preface

The feedback we received on the first edition of this text has been gratifying; instructors and students generally found the material to be clear and comprehensible, the text user-friendly. But, as with all law texts, we captured a moment in time when the first edition was published. As time and the law have moved on, there have been changes in consumer legislation, the law governing contract formalities, limitation periods, and some of the case law. To keep our students current, a new edition seemed to be warranted.

In addition, technological changes have resulted in new commercial realities that require consideration for the impact they are likely to have on the law. The expansion of e-commerce, for example, is having a major impact on the law defining offer and acceptance. While at this time it is not clear how this will pan out, we need to bring these issues to our students' attention.

It also became clear from teaching a basic contracts course, and from the detailed feedback we received from our colleagues in the School of Legal and Public Administration at Seneca College, that a user-friendly text would become more so if we reorganized the presentation of contract law to students. We had followed an organizational scheme that made some sense from an academic consideration of the development of contract law, but did not necessarily aid a student's understanding of practical applications. Consequently, we have eliminated chapter 3, Form and Writing, and incorporated formality requirements into chapter 2, Formation of a Contract, where it is a more logical fit. Parol evidence and rectification become part of a new chapter 6, Contract Interpretation. This chapter also includes discussions of other topics located elsewhere in the first edition: exclusion and penalty clauses, representations, terms, conditions, and warranties. We have also eliminated chapter 7, Mistake and Frustration, and incorporated mistake, part of a new chapter 4, Contractual Defects, which also includes duress, undue influence, misrepresentation, and unconscionability. We are confident that this reorganization will make it easier for students to understand and connect the dots in what otherwise might be a more confusing picture of contract law.

Jean Fitzgerald
Laurence Olivo
February 2005

Acknowledgments

We would like to thank our students and colleagues for sharing their ideas about how this text could be improved. Professors Mary Ann Kelly, Jo Ann Kurtz, and Liz Thoms provided detailed feedback and suggestions about how the contents should be organized, and, trusting to their extensive experience in teaching contracts courses, we have adopted almost all their suggestions. In particular, Liz Thoms was extraordinarily helpful in providing us with some of her updated teaching materials, including fact situations, questions, and examples. Her material on the law of mistake, always an area to trap the unwary, was a model of clarity and lucidity. We incorporated this into the text with enthusiasm and thanks.

Jean Fitzgerald
Laurence Olivo

CHAPTER 1

Introduction to the Law of Contracts

WHAT IS A CONTRACT?

Contracts are agreements made between two or more persons that the law recognizes and will enforce.

Contracts are not simply long documents written in legalese and covered in ribbons and seals. They are part of everyday life in our society, where economic exchange is an essential part of getting things done. For example, buying a bus token, paying a parking fee, buying a cup of coffee, using a credit card to buy a jacket, leasing an apartment, and buying this textbook all involve agreements between you and someone else where you agree to do something (pay money) in exchange for the other person doing something (giving you a parking space for your car, a cup of coffee, or a book). These common, everyday contracts can be in writing, or they can be oral; they can be explicit, like an apartment lease that spells out in writing the details of what was agreed to, or they can be implicit, like buying a cup of coffee where you serve yourself and hand over money, and no one exchanges a word.

FEATURES OF LEGALLY ENFORCEABLE CONTRACTS

Not all agreements are recognized by the law as contracts. For example, if you invite me to dinner and I agree to come but then fail to show up, I have breached the rules of good manners, but not the law. The law would define our agreement as a social agreement rather than as an enforceable contract primarily because certain things that make an agreement a contract appear to be missing. For example, an intention to create legally binding relations is missing, as is a promise from me to do something for you of legally recognizable value in exchange for the invitation, other than just showing up and eating your food.[1]

---

1   Where parties promise to exchange something of recognizable value, there is said to be *valuable consideration*. Because of the commercial origins of contract law, the courts look for an exchange of promises involving things of monetary cost or value, although consideration need not be money or even be reduced to a specific dollars and cents amount. Consideration is discussed in more detail in chapter 2, Formation of a Contract.

Some Basic Terms

- The terms **contract** and **agreement** are used interchangeably to refer to the same thing: a binding contract.

- In the bargaining process that precedes making the contract or agreement, the promisor may be referred to as the **offeror** and the person to whom the offer is made may be referred to as the **offeree**.

- A party to a contract or agreement who undertakes to do something is sometimes referred to as a **promisor**. The party who receives the benefit of the promise made by the promisor is sometimes referred to as the **promisee**.

contract/agreement
an agreement made between two or more persons that the law recognizes and will enforce; a binding contract

offeror
a person who, during the bargaining process that precedes making a contract, agrees to do something for the other party; once the offer is accepted, the bargain is concluded and the parties have made an agreement

offeree
a person to whom an offer is made during the bargaining process

promisor
the party to a contract who undertakes to do something

promisee
the party to a contract who receives the benefit of a promise made by another party to the contract

offer
a promise to do something or give something of value to another person; if the other accepts the offer, a binding contract exists

acceptance
when there has been acceptance of an offer made by one party in the bargaining process, the parties are assumed to have reached an agreement on contract terms, and a binding contract exists from that time

Agreements that the law recognizes as contracts have certain features in common, described below.

Agreement Between the Parties

One party must offer to do something, and the other party must promise to accept that offer. This exchange of promises in contract law is referred to as **offer** and **acceptance**. To constitute an agreement, the mutual exchange of promises that constitutes an offer and acceptance must relate to acts that are performed at the time the agreement is made, or acts to be performed in the future. However, an offer may be followed by a counteroffer rather than acceptance, and this exchange, or bargaining behaviour, may go on for some time until the parties reach an agreement. When the parties have reached an agreement there is said to be, in the words of older cases, *consensus ad idem* (a "meeting of minds"), and the parties may be referred to as being *ad idem*. The concept of agreement is discussed in more detail in chapter 2, Formation of a Contract.

Intention To Create Legally Binding Relations

The parties to an agreement must each intend that the promises they make to each other will be legally binding. This means that if one party breaks a promise, the other may ask the courts to enforce the contract by remedying the breach. Generally, the courts have held that social agreements (such as a dinner invitation), agreements between family members, and moral vows (such as a vow to join a religious order or to give to charity) are not legally enforceable. In deciding whether an agreement is legally binding, the courts have taken two different approaches. In some cases, the courts have taken a subjective approach, examining the evidence of what the parties actually thought they were doing or said they were doing to determine whether they intended to create legally binding rules to govern their behaviour. In other cases, the courts have taken an objective approach, determining the intention of the parties not by what they thought they said they intended, but by what a "reasonable person" would think they intended, considering the surrounding social context. Much of the case law on this issue uses the objective method. This has resulted in an approach where a fictional "reasonable person" relying on an understanding of social norms and values in our society would simply "know" that a dinner invitation was a social agreement and outside of the law of contract.

Exchange of Valuable Consideration

Although there are some exceptions, both parties must promise something of value to the other. Usually this takes the form of payment or giving something of value in exchange for some goods or services of value. For example, when you park your car in a parking lot, the lot owner is promising a parking space for your car as valuable consideration, and you accept the offer by promising to pay an agreed price for the space. What constitutes valuable consideration is discussed in more detail in chapter 2, Formation of a Contract.

Legal Capacity To Contract

Not everyone is eligible to enter into a contract. Generally, for a contract to be enforceable, the parties are assumed to be roughly equivalent in bargaining power and must meet minimum standards of intelligence, rationality, and maturity. More important, they must meet these standards to have the contract enforced against them if they fail to keep the promises they made. For this reason, minors and persons under certain types of mental disability may not have to honour their contractual obligations in whole or in part. This is discussed in more detail in chapter 3, Protecting Weaker Parties.

Compliance with Legal Formality Requirements

Not every agreement where the parties have the capacity to enter into a contract, where there is an agreement to enter into legal relations, and where valuable consideration has been given will result in a legally binding contract. An agreement may meet all of these requirements and still be held to be unenforceable because it fails to meet formality requirements. While many contracts may be based on an exchange of oral promises, some contracts—such as contracts for the sale of land—must be in writing. Others must be in writing *and* be witnessed, have seals attached, or meet other formal requirements to be enforceable. Formality requirements are discussed in more detail in chapter 2, Formation of a Contract.

HOW CONTRACT LAW DEVELOPED

You may wonder why some agreements are recognized as binding contracts while others are not, why some people are eligible to enter into contracts but others are not, or why there must be valuable consideration for an agreement to be a valid contract. An understanding of how contract law developed can help to answer some of these questions.

Canadian contract law outside Quebec is based on English common law. While there are some minor differences in contract law in England and Canada, the main

consensus ad idem
when there has been acceptance by the offeree of an offer, the parties have reached an agreement on terms, and they have an intention to be bound by those terms; they are said to have reached a *consensus ad idem* (a "meeting of the minds"); sometimes a shorter form is used, and the parties are said to be *ad idem*

ad idem
see *consensus ad idem*

elements are derived from English law. Before the 16th century, there was no law of contracts as we now know it in England and Canada. However, from the late Middle Ages on, there did exist the tort of owing a debt and failing to repay it.[2] Here the law focused on the wrongful act of failing to repay money owed on a debt. If the agreement involved an exchange of services or goods, it was not enforceable under this rule of law. The lack of a modern law of contract was not important as long as commercial transactions were primarily simple and local. But in the early modern period, trade and commerce expanded and became more complex, and a national economy began to develop. As commercial transactions became more complex, the law evolved to permit merchants and others to enter into complex legal arrangements to govern their activities, and to provide remedies when parties found themselves in a commercial dispute. In *Slade's Case*[3] in 1602, the law finally broke away from enforcing only monetary debts to enforcing other kinds of commercial promises. From this point, the common law began to enforce all kinds of commercial bargains where there was valuable consideration, and began to evolve on a case-by-case basis to the kind of contract law we have now.

Case Law and Statute Law

Contract law arose from attempts by judges to solve individual commercial disputes brought before them on a case-by-case basis. Over several centuries, the principles of contract law were derived from the reasons for judges' decisions in cases. Very little contract law came from statute law.

When legislatures have passed statutes that create new rules or principles of contract law, they have usually focused on several areas:

- *Consumer protection* provides consumers, who have weaker bargaining power, with some protection from sophisticated and powerful sellers. Consumer protection is discussed in more detail in chapter 9, Consumer Protection.

- *Prevention of fraud* provides for formality requirements and the protection of persons who lack full capacity to enter into contracts.

- *Rationalization of the common law* creates uniform rules in areas where the common law has become confused or chaotic, as, for example, with respect to legislation in the 19th century governing the sale of goods.

Developing contract law on a case-by-case basis had certain advantages: real rather than theoretical commercial problems could be resolved in a practical way, and legal principle derived from one case could evolve and change in subsequent cases to meet changing commercial realities. But there were some disadvantages, too. Because judges were resolving specific, narrow problems, they did not always focus on establishing clear principles to guide changes in the law so that the law could develop in a rational and coherent way. In some cases, judges following **precedents** where the rationale for a decision is not clear have applied the law

precedent
an essential doctrine of common law that requires judges to follow the rule in a previously decided case when that case deals with similar facts or issues to the case currently being decided

2   For a more detailed discussion on the tort origin of contract law, see G.H.L. Fridman, *The Law of Contract in Canada*, 3d ed. (Scarborough, ON: Carswell, 1994), 8.

3   (1602), 4 Co. Rep. 91.

rigidly and mechanically, relying strongly on the similarity of facts in the cases rather than on the legal principles that may lie below the surface. For example, the law of contract determining what happens when parties are mistaken about the terms of the contract often seems to focus on classifying the type of mistake rather than on whether it was reasonable to make the mistake in question. The result, in the view of some observers, has been that the law on the issue of mistake has become confused, although courts in England and Canada have recently taken steps to sort out some of the confusion.

POSITIVISM VERSUS JUDICIAL INTERVENTIONISM

Another factor that contributes to difficulties in interpreting case law on contract issues is the tension in the courts between two points of view about how the law should be interpreted. Under the **positivist** approach, judges take the position that it is not up to them to impose their own interpretation of a contract on the parties. Judges who take this view try to give a dictionary or literal meaning to the words used in a contract, regardless of the outcome. These judges assume that parties to the contract have equal bargaining power and are free to bargain as they wish without the court meddling in the process. The judges will often say that it is not their job to remake a bad bargain or rewrite a badly written contract. Underlying this view is the idea that governments in general, and courts in particular, should not interfere in private persons' economic affairs.

Under the **judicial interventionism** approach, judges may look at the economic forces surrounding the making of a contract, at notions of fundamental fairness, and at other contextual facts as a background to interpreting the language of a contract. This approach is more likely to be used when there is an inequality of bargaining power between the parties—for example, in consumer contracts. However, some judges take this interpretive approach where the parties are equal in bargaining power but in the judge's view the likely outcome is socially or economically undesirable.

The positivist approach has been the principal, and older, approach to interpreting contract law in England, Canada, and the rest of the common law world up to the mid-20th century. As judicial interventionism or judicial activism has become more commonly used in Canadian courts in general, it has also had an increasing impact on modern contract law. To some extent, this approach is the source of some of the differences in contract law between Canada and England today, since Canadian courts tend to be more interventionist than English courts. However, the differences should not be overstressed. The basic law of contract is very similar in both jurisdictions, and Canadian judges have tended to be sparing in their use of an interventionist approach to contract law.

positivism
an approach to the interpretation of law that states that the meaning to be given to the words in legal rules should be the ordinary, dictionary meaning without resorting to social, economic, or political values to aid in interpretation

judicial interventionism
an approach to the interpretation of law that draws on social, economic, and political values in interpreting the meaning and application of legal rules and principles

SUMMARY

Contracts are agreements between two or more persons that the law will recognize and enforce. Not all contracts are enforceable, however. There must be an intention to create an enforceable legal relationship that the law will recognize. The law will usually enforce a contract if there is a clear agreement, an exchange of valuable consideration, the parties have the capacity to contract, and legal formality requirements have been complied with.

Contract law developed from tort law and evolved into modern contract law in the 17th century. It developed from case law as judges tried to adapt contract law to modern business practices. Very little contract law is based on statutes. Statutory contract law usually "corrects" problems arising in case law—preventing fraud, protecting consumers and other weaker contract parties, and rationalizing the case law in an area when it became confusing.

KEY TERMS

acceptance	offeree
ad idem	offeror
agreement	positivism
consensus ad idem	precedent
contract	promisee
judicial interventionism	promisor
offer	

REVIEW QUESTIONS

1. What is a contract?

2. What is the difference between a contract and an agreement?

3. What main features must a contract have to be binding?

4. What does it mean for the parties to an agreement to be *ad idem*?

5. What is the difference between a subjective and an objective approach to legal interpretation?

6. Explain what is meant by the term "valuable consideration."

7. Why do we limit the contractual rights of minors and persons who have certain types of mental disabilities?

8. Provide an example of a formality requirement in contract law, and explain its purpose.

9. How important is case law to the development of the law of contracts? How important is statute law to the development of the law of contracts?

10. What is the doctrine of precedent?

11. What are some of the advantages of having a law of contracts that is based on case law? What are some of the disadvantages?

12. How does the positivist approach affect the interpretation of contract law?

13. How does the judicial interventionist approach affect the interpretation of contract law?

DISCUSSION QUESTIONS

1. Explain whether, in the following fact situations, you could sue for breach of contract:

   a. You invite me to dinner. I agree to come, but fail to show up.

   b. Your sister promises to lend you some money because you are in debt, but later changes her mind and refuses to do so.

   c. You invite me to dinner and agree to pay me an amount of money if I praise an invention of yours to another dinner guest who is interested in investing in your invention. I agree to attend, but I fail to show up, and the other guest decides not to invest in your invention.

2. Explain why the law does not enforce all agreements.

3. How has the positivist interpretation of contract law led to increased reliance on statutes as a basis for contract law?

4. Contract law has been described as a practical response to the development of a more complex modern economy. Explain how contract law changed and developed to meet the needs of a changing economy.

CHAPTER 2

Formation of a Contract

ELEMENTS OF A VALID CONTRACT

As discussed in chapter 1, for an agreement to be a valid, binding, and enforceable contract, certain elements must be present. If any of these elements are missing or defective, the courts will not enforce the rights and duties created by that agreement. An unenforceable or defective contract is also known as a **void contract**. A void contract is no contract at all, since it has no legal force or binding effect. The parties to a void contract may have gone through some form of making a contract, but because one or more of the necessary elements were missing, no contract came into being. Hence, a void contract is one that may be "avoided" by one or both parties.

The essential elements of a contract are

- the intention to create a legal relationship,

- offer and acceptance,

- consideration, and

- legality.

void contract
a contract that does not exist at law because one or more essential elements of the contract are lacking; an unenforceable contract

INTENTION TO CREATE A LEGAL RELATIONSHIP

The parties to a contract must have intended from the beginning of their negotiations that legal obligations would result from their agreement. This is based on the premise that the contract will be the result of a meeting of the parties' minds, or *consensus ad idem*, on the terms and conditions that will form the contract.

The first requirement of a contract is the intention of the promisor to be bound by the promise he or she made. All agreements contain some kind of a promise either to do something or to refrain from doing something. All contracts contain promises, but not all promises become contracts. Some promises carry with them a moral obligation, but only a valid contract carries with it a legal obligation. The question to be determined, then, is whether the person making the promise (the promisor) intended to be bound by his or her promise. Some people make promises intending to be bound by them. Some people make promises with no intention of becoming legally obligated to fulfill them. Without the intention to be bound, a promise cannot form the basis of an enforceable contract.

Since examining intention requires finding out what was in the promisor's mind at the time the promise was made, proving intention can be difficult. As a

presumption of law
an inference in favour of a particular fact; a rule of law whereby a finding of a basic fact gives rise to the existence of a presumed fact or state of affairs unless the presumption can be rebutted, or proven false, by the party seeking to deny the presumed fact

onus
the burden of responsibility or proof

result, the courts rely on a **presumption of law** that promisors intend to be bound by the promises they make. Once this presumption has been made, the **onus**, or burden of proof, shifts to the promisor to prove that the intention did not exist. The courts look to evidence such as the conduct of the parties at the time the promise was made, the circumstances surrounding the making of the promise, the statements made by the parties, and the relationship between the parties. The test to be applied is "Would a reasonable person hearing the promise assume that the promisor intended to be bound?"

▧ EXAMPLE OF "REASONABLE PERSON" TEST

In the US case of *Higgins v. Lessig*,[1] a farmer who had a $15 harness stolen from him angrily exclaimed in front of several people, "I will give $100 to any man who will find out who the thief is!" Immediately, one of the people present named the thief and claimed the reward. The farmer refused to pay and the informer sued for the $100. The court held that the statement was "the extravagant exclamation of an angry man" and that a reasonable person would not assume that the farmer intended to be bound.

arm's-length transaction
a transaction negotiated by unrelated parties, each acting in his or her own independent self-interest; "unrelated" in this context usually means not related as family members by birth or marriage, and not related by business interests

The relationship between the parties is an important factor to be considered. If the promise occurs in an **arm's-length transaction** where the parties are "strangers" to each other or unrelated, or in commercial or business dealings, the courts assume that the promise is binding unless one or both parties can convince the court that there was no intention.

However, the courts also recognize that promises made between people who are not at arm's length may not be intended to be binding. Promises made between family members and in social situations are not assumed to be binding. In addition, the courts assume that promises to donate money to charity or to join a religious order are generally not intended to create a binding contract.

▧ EXAMPLE OF A NON-ARM'S-LENGTH TRANSACTION

Your sister promises to come to your daughter's ballet recital. You buy her a ticket but she does not show up, nor does she pay you for the ticket. It is unlikely that the courts would presume that your sister intended to be legally bound by her promise.

▧ EXAMPLE OF AN ARM'S-LENGTH TRANSACTION

You are selling tickets to your daughter's ballet recital to help raise funds for a new dance studio. A company promises to buy a block of tickets from you but never pays for them. The courts would be more likely to presume that the company intended to be legally bound by its promise, because it is at arm's length.

Advertisers also often make statements that they do not intend to be legally binding. The courts allow advertisers some latitude in their advertisements as long

---

1   49 Ill. App. 459 (1893).

as they do not mislead the public. Exaggeration is sometimes accepted by the courts as an indication that the advertiser did not intend to be bound (for example, "Come to Joe's Diner for the best wiener schnitzel in the world!"). As a general rule, the courts view advertisements as "invitations to do business" (sometimes referred to as "invitations to treat") rather than promises to the public at large. So if you sued Joe's Diner because its wiener schnitzel was not the best in the world, a court would be unlikely to find that Joe's Diner intended to be held to its promise.

However, while advertisers are not generally subject to the presumption that they intend to be bound by their promises, the courts will enforce those promises if the party seeking to rely on the promise can convince the court that the advertiser intended to be bound. To find this intent, the courts examine the advertisement carefully, applying the same "reasonable person" test.

■ EXAMPLE OF FACTORS IN DETERMINING INTENTION

The English case of *Carlill v. Carbolic Smoke Ball Co.*[2] is an example of the factors the courts examine in determining intention to be bound by a promise made in the form of an advertisement. In this case, the Carbolic Smoke Ball Co. manufactured and advertised a product that it claimed would cure or prevent influenza. In fact, it went so far as to advertise that it would pay £100 to anyone who used its product and contracted influenza. The advertisement also stated that the company intended to be bound by its promise and, as a sign of good faith, it had deposited £100 with a bank to be used for this purpose. Mrs. Carlill purchased the product, used it according to the company's instructions, and contracted influenza. The company refused to pay her the £100, claiming that it never intended to be bound by its promise and that the advertisement was a "mere puff." The court found that the words of the advertisement clearly expressed the intention to be bound and ordered the company to pay the £100 to Mrs. Carlill.

OFFER AND ACCEPTANCE

Nature of an Offer

A valid contract does not come into existence until one party, the offeror, has made an offer and the other party, the offeree, has accepted it. An offer is normally conditional—that is, the offeree must do something or give some promise in exchange. The initial offer is tentative. Once an offeree accepts and agrees to fulfill the conditions contained in the offer, the contract is formed and the promise becomes binding. To be valid, an offer must contain all of the terms of the contract, either expressly or impliedly.

■ EXAMPLE OF AN OFFER

I offer to sell you my car for $5,000. My offer is conditional on you agreeing to fulfill the condition in my offer—paying me $5,000. Once you accept my offer by agreeing to fulfill the condition, our mutual promises become binding. I must sell you my car, and you must pay me $5,000.

---

2 [1893] 1 QB 256.

An invitation to do business by displaying goods for sale or by advertising these goods does not constitute an offer. For example, a business that uses a newspaper advertisement to sell goods for a certain price is not making an offer because the business does not intend to sell its goods to every person who reads the advertisement. The supply of those goods is likely to be limited. If the advertisement was an offer, the business would be bound to sell the goods to every person who saw it and accepted the offer by agreeing to pay the price. The purpose of the advertisement is to attract potential customers. Those customers might make an offer to purchase the goods, which the merchant can accept, or the merchant can make an offer to customers once the customers express an interest in the goods, which the customers can accept. The advertisement is simply a way to start the negotiation process.

However, some advertisements have been found to be offers. For example, an advertisement stating that a store will sell a television set at a greatly reduced price to the first 10 people who arrive at the store on a certain date (a "gate-crasher special") can be interpreted as an offer. The offer of a reward for information or for the return of a lost item made to the public at large can be interpreted as an offer. However, these types of advertisements are the exception to the rule that advertisements are not offers but merely invitations to do business.

Communication of an Offer

There is no particular format in which the offer must be made, as long as it is understood by the offeree. Offers can be made verbally, in writing, or through gestures (for example, raising your hand to make a bid at an auction). A general rule is that the offer must be communicated by the offeror to the offeree before it is capable of being accepted.

This may seem self-evident, but it becomes important when offers are not made face to face. For example, if an offer was made by letter, telegram, fax, email, or other method, it is vital to know when the offeree became aware of the offer, because the offer is not valid until it is received by the offeree and the offeror is not bound by the offer until it has been accepted. No person can accept an offer of which she or he was unaware.

■ EXAMPLE OF LACK OF COMMUNICATION OF AN OFFER

A person posts a notice on his office bulletin board offering a reward of $100 for the return of his lost briefcase. A co-worker finds his briefcase and, unaware of the reward, returns it to him. If she later sees the notice, she cannot go back and demand the reward. Because she was not aware of the offer when she returned the briefcase, she cannot later accept the offer. No contract was created.

Another general rule is that only the person to whom an offer is made may accept the offer, even if others are aware of it. This prevents people from being forced to enter into contracts with persons not of their own choosing. However, if an offer is made to the public at large, it is assumed that the offeror is implying that the identity of the offeree is unimportant to the contract, and anyone may accept the offer.

EXAMPLE OF LACK OF COMMUNICATION OF AN OFFER

You leave a note for your neighbour in his mailbox that you will pay him $200 if he will cut down a tree on your property. Before he sees the note, another neighbour takes it and cuts down the tree in your absence. Upon your return, he demands payment of the $200. You are not obligated to pay him the $200, even though you benefited from his labour. The offer was not made to him, and therefore was not capable of being accepted by him. No contract was formed.

Acceptance of an Offer

Acceptance of an offer may be made verbally or in writing, or it may be inferred from the conduct of the parties. However, certain rules must be complied with before acceptance of an offer is valid.

First, acceptance must be communicated by the offeree to the offeror in the manner requested by or implied in the offer. Second, the acceptance must be clear, unequivocal, and unconditional.

Communication of the Acceptance

Communication of the acceptance is simple if the offer states the method of acceptance. An offer might state that the offer may be accepted only in writing or in person. In that case, the acceptance must be communicated in the stated manner.

However, the offer may not contain such a precise stipulation. The courts look at a number of variables to determine what may constitute a valid form of communication of an acceptance. For example, they look at the form in which the offer was made, the usual and ordinary way of doing business in a particular industry, and the history of dealings between the parties to determine whether the method of communication was valid.

While the form of acceptance must generally be positive in nature, even silence can be a valid form of acceptance if the parties have agreed in advance that silence is sufficient, or where the parties have habitually used this method in previous transactions.

EXAMPLE OF SILENCE AS ACCEPTANCE

You belong to a music club. Each month the club mails you a notice advising that it will send you that month's selection of CDs unless you mail back the notice stating that you do not want them. The agreement you have with the club states that failure to send back the notice constitutes acceptance of the CDs. In this case, then, silence constitutes acceptance.

If a person's conduct, though silent, leads the offeror to believe that the offeree has accepted the offer, especially where the person receives some benefit from the offeror, and knows that the offeror expects to be compensated for the services or goods supplied, the courts may find that a contract has been formed.

■ EXAMPLE OF SILENCE AS ACCEPTANCE

In the case of *Saint John Tug Boat Co. Ltd. v. Irving Refinery Ltd.*,[3] the plaintiff made its tug boat available for use by the defendant. The terms of the rental of the tug were never agreed upon in writing, but a verbal agreement was made and extended twice. No formal authorization was made for a further extension, but the defendant continued to make use of the tug. The defendant then tried to deny liability for all charges arising from the continued use of the tug. The court stated:

1. Liabilities are not to be forced upon people behind their backs any more than you can confer a benefit upon a man against his will.

2. But if a person knows that the consideration is being rendered for his benefit with an expectation that he will pay for it, then if he acquiesces in its being done, taking the benefit of it when done, he will be taken impliedly to have requested its being done: and that will import a promise to pay for it.

There is consumer legislation to deal with the situation that arises when sellers send unsolicited goods to members of the public. This topic will be discussed in greater detail in chapter 9, Consumer Protection.

In some cases, performance of the terms of the offer may constitute acceptance. In those cases, acceptance is complete when the offeree performs all of the terms contained in the offer. In such a case, notifying the offeror of the acceptance is unnecessary.

■ EXAMPLE OF ACCEPTANCE BY PERFORMANCE

You send a letter to a mail-order company offering to purchase some of the items in its catalogue. The mail-order company does not write back to you but responds by sending you the items requested. In this case, performance of the terms of the offer (sending you the items) can constitute acceptance.

The issue of communication of an acceptance was raised in the case of *Carlill v. Carbolic Smoke Ball Co.*, discussed above. The company raised the argument that Mrs. Carlill had not communicated her acceptance of its offer before using its product, so no contract was formed. The court did not accept this argument, holding that the offer implied that notification of acceptance was not necessary. The company had asked that its customers buy and use the product, and performance of these terms was sufficient acceptance of the offer, without communication to the company.

RULES FOR DETERMINING COMMUNICATION OF ACCEPTANCE

The moment of acceptance can be important, and rules have been established to determine when communication of an acceptance takes place.

If acceptance is to be made verbally, acceptance takes place when the words are spoken, either by telephone or in person.

---

3   [1964] SCR 614, per Ritchie J.

If acceptance may be made in writing, the "postal acceptance rule" applies. Using the mail to make and accept offers has been so common that the courts have established a rule that states that when acceptance of an offer may be validly made by mail, acceptance takes place when the properly addressed and stamped letter of acceptance is placed in the mailbox. The contract is formed at the time of mailing, even though the offeror may not be aware of the acceptance until several days later. Even if the letter is then lost or is delivered late, the contract is valid. The reasoning is that offerees who use the mail to accept an offer have done everything they must do at that point. While it can be argued that it may be harsh to expect offerors to be bound by contracts if they have no knowledge of the acceptance, an offeror who invited acceptance by mail must be prepared to accept the risk that the acceptance may be delivered late or go astray. However, an offeror may stipulate in the offer that acceptance by mail is acceptable but will only be binding when the letter is actually received by the offeror. Such a specific term in the offer overrides the postal acceptance rule.

The rule for using the telegraph is similar to the postal acceptance rule. An acceptance made by telegraph is complete when the telegram is delivered to the telegram office by the offeree.

The rules for determing when an offer and acceptance have been communicated were developed in the 19th century and contemplated 19th century means of communication. While the general fall-back rule is that an offer is accepted when it is received, the development in the late 20th century of email, fax, voice messaging, and interactive websites has complicated the determination of when an offer or acceptance has been communicated. This problem is likely to be resolved by legislation. The Ontario *Electronic Commerce Act*[4] is an example of how legislation can provide a solution. The key section affecting communications of offers and acceptance is set out below:

> 22(3) Electronic information or an electronic document is presumed to be received by the addressee,
>
> (a) if the addressee has designated or uses an information system for the purpose of receiving information or documents of the type sent, when it enters that information system and becomes capable of being retrieved and processed by the addressee; or
>
> (b) if the addressee has not designated or does not use an information system for the purpose of receiving information or documents of the type sent, when the addressee becomes aware of the information or document in the addressee's information system and it becomes capable of being retrieved and processed by the addressee.

The addressee can be receiving an offer or an acceptance from the addressor. If I indicate to you that you should reply by email, or by using my interactive website for ordering goods or services, or by fax machine, or voice mail, then when you do, and the message enters the electronic system I designated and it can be retrieved and processed by me, your communication of the offer or acceptance is complete, whether or not I open or check my email, check my interactive website, pick up my fax from the office machine, or check my voice mail. However, if I do not designate

---

4 SO 2000, c. 17.

a system for you to use, or you use a system I have, such as voice mail at home, but which I do not generally use to receive contract communication, then I am deemed to receive your communication only when I become aware of its presence in my communication system and it is in retrievable form that I can process.

■ EXAMPLE OF ELECTRONIC COMMUNICATION TO ADDRESSEE USING A DESIGNATED SYSTEM

Ahmed has been looking at new computers on the Compacto website. He sees a model V2 notebook at a good price. The website indicates that he can order online. He fills out the electronic order form and clicks on the "send" icon. The electronic order is received completely by Compacto's website within a second. The communication of Ahmed's offer to purchase is achieved as soon as it enters the addressee's system and is capable of being retrieved and acted on.

■ EXAMPLE OF ELECTRONIC COMMUNICATION TO ADDRESSEE USING A NON-DESIGNATED SYSTEM

Ahmed is having a chat with Enrique. Enrique says he has an old but useful notebook computer that he wants to sell for $1,000. He offers it to Ahmed. Ahmed says he will think about it. Enrique tells Ahmed to let him know by Wednesday whether he wants to buy the computer. Enrique does not indicate how Ahmed is to accept the offer. Enrique has a home email address, but he checks it rarely because he usually uses his email at work. Ahmed sends his acceptance by email to Enrique's home email address. Enrique doesn't get around to checking his email until Thursday. When he does he finds Ahmed's acceptance on his home system. Ahmed's offer is deemed to be communicated on Thursday, when Enrique discovers it. It is ineffective because Ahmed used a non-designated system or a system that Enrique does not normally use for this kind of transaction and failed to communicate acceptance of the offer by Wednesday, as stipulated by Enrique.

Counteroffers and Inquiries

If the acceptance of an offer is not clear, unequivocal, and unconditional, it is not an acceptance but may be a counteroffer or an inquiry. If a person, upon receiving an offer, states that she or he "thinks it is a great deal but would like to think about it," this is not an acceptance because it is not clear and unequivocal. If she or he agrees to some of the terms but not others, or wants to add or vary terms, this is not an acceptance because it is conditional. Until an offer is accepted without qualification, no contract is formed.

Offers, counteroffers, and inquiries are common in most negotiations. However, it can sometimes be difficult to determine what was an offer, what was a counteroffer, and what was an inquiry, in the midst of negotiations.

A **counteroffer** is a response by the offeree that does not unconditionally accept the terms of the offer but proposes to add to or modify the terms of the offer. By making a counteroffer, the offeree rejects the original offer and puts a new offer on

counteroffer
a response to an offer by an offeree that does not unconditionally accept the terms of the offer but proposes to add to or modify the terms

Highlights of the Electronic Commerce Act

- The Act establishes rules for commercial, consumer, and public transactions made by electronic means, including electronic agents such as computer programs that accept and store information (s. 1). The Act does not apply to wills, trusts created by wills, powers of attorney, registerable land transactions, negotiable instruments such as cheques, or to documents that are used to establish ownership, generally (s. 31).

- The Act provides for the validity of electronic signatures and seals (s. 1).

- The Act applies to public bodies and the Crown (ss. 1 and 2).

- Generally, the Act makes electronic document forms equivalent to analogous paper documents for most purposes, provided the electronic form maintains the integrity of the orginal paper document (ss. 4–8).

- Public bodies may conduct business using electronic documents, provided that the body gives express consent and provided that another statute does not prohibit the use of electronic documents (ss. 14–18).

- Offer and acceptance or other contract-related communication may be expressed by use of electronic documents or electronically transmitted information, unless the parties agree otherwise (s. 19).

- A contract is not deemed to be invalid simply because it is in electronic form (s. 19).

- An electronic transaction is not enforceable between an individual and an electronic agent if the individual makes a material error, provided that the individual promptly notifies the agent of the error and does not take advantage of any consideration received in the transaction (s. 21).

- Electronic information is deemed to be sent when it is beyond the sender's control or, if the parties are using the same system, when the information becomes capable of retrieval by the addressee. It is deemed to be received when it is capable of retrieval if the addressee has designated a system. If no system is designated or ordinarily used to communicate offer or acceptance, then it is deemed received when the addressee becomes aware of the communication and is able to retrieve it (s. 22).

- Contracts for shipping goods may be communicated electronically as can almost anything connected with the contract, for example, monitoring a shipment or signing for receipt of goods (s. 23).

the table. Note that by rejecting the original offer by making a counteroffer, the offeree cannot then go back and accept the original offer unless the offeror makes the original offer again.

An **inquiry** by the offeree as to whether the offeror will consider other terms or is willing to modify the terms of the offer does not constitute a counteroffer and will not result in rejection of the original offer. In this case, the offeree can still accept the original offer.

inquiry
questioning by the offeree as to whether the offeror will consider other terms or is willing to modify the terms of the offer; an inquiry does not constitute a counteroffer and is not a rejection of the original offer

▤ EXAMPLE OF A COUNTEROFFER

Michelle: I will sell you my motorcycle for $4,500. *(offer)*

Sanjay: I can pay you $3,500 for it. *(rejection and counteroffer)*

Michelle: I could lower the price to $4,200, just for you. *(rejection and counteroffer)*

Sanjay: Would you consider $3,800? *(inquiry)*

Michelle: Not a chance.

Sanjay: I will accept your offer to sell for $4,200, but I'll need three months to pay you. *(rejection and counteroffer)*

Michelle: I need the money now. Forget it. I can sell it to someone else. *(rejection)*

Sanjay: Don't be so hasty. I'll pay you the $4,200 now. *(fresh offer)*

In this case, no contract has been formed. Even though Sanjay's last counteroffer only added a term to Michelle's last offer (payment over time), it constituted a rejection of Michelle's offer. Once Sanjay rejected Michelle's offer, he was unable to go back and accept it. Even though he is willing to accept the terms of Michelle's last offer, his intervening counteroffer took it "off the table" and Michelle is under no obligation to accept Sanjay's fresh offer.

Lapse and Revocation of an Offer

lapse
the termination or failure of an offer through the neglect to accept it within some time limit or through failure of some contingency

revoke
to annul or make void by recalling or taking back; to cancel or rescind

nullity
nothing; something that has no legal force or effect

An offer may **lapse** or it may be **revoked**, rendering the offer a **nullity** and not capable of being accepted.

An offer may lapse under any of four conditions:

-   Either of the parties dies, declares bankruptcy, or is declared insane prior to acceptance of the offer.

-   The offeree rejects the offer or makes a counteroffer.

-   The offeree fails to accept the offer within the time period specified in the terms of the offer.

-   No time period is specified in the terms of the offer, and the offeree fails to accept the offer within a reasonable time period.

Once an offer has lapsed, it cannot be accepted even if the offeree was unaware of the lapse.

What constitutes a "reasonable time period" where no time period has been specified in the terms of the offer depends on the circumstances in each case and the nature of the anticipated contract. An offer to sell a crop of tomatoes will have a much shorter reasonable time period for acceptance than an offer to sell concrete blocks.

■ EXAMPLE OF A REASONABLE TIME PERIOD

In the Supreme Court of Canada case of *Barrick v. Clark*,[5] the court stated:

> Farm lands ... are not subject to frequent or sudden changes or fluctuations in price, and therefore ... a reasonable time for acceptance of an offer would be longer than that with respect to such commodities as shares or stock upon an established trading market. It would also be longer than in respect to goods of a perishable nature.

The offeror may revoke the offer at any time prior to acceptance. The revocation must be communicated to the offeree before the offeree accepts the offer. Generally, the offeror must communicate the revocation directly to the offeree. For direct communication, the revocation is effective when it is received by the offeree. However, the offer can also be revoked indirectly. If the offeree has actual knowledge (from a reliable source) of the revocation of the offer or of circumstances in which it would be unreasonable for the offeree to expect the offeror to stand by the offer, this knowledge may prevent the offeree from accepting the offer. The onus of proving that the offeree had this knowledge rests on the offeror.

Such circumstances might be the sale of the offered goods to another party, or the loss or destruction of the goods. However, an offeror who sells goods without revoking an outstanding offer runs the risk of the first offeree accepting the offer and thus becomes liable for **breach of contract**.

breach of contract
failure, without legal excuse, to perform any promise that forms part of a contract

■ EXAMPLE OF REVOCATION

Dawn offers to sell her horse to Maria. Maria says she needs time to think about it, and Dawn says she will keep the offer open until the end of the week. The next day, Dawn sells the horse to Miguel without revoking her offer to Maria first. The following day, Maria communicates her acceptance of Dawn's offer.

If Maria is unaware of the sale to Miguel, she is still entitled to accept Dawn's offer and a contract is formed. Dawn, of course, will be unable to fulfill the terms of the contract (delivering the horse to Maria) and will be in breach of contract.

If Maria hears from a reliable source that Dawn sold the horse to Miguel, Dawn may be able to argue that this was a form of indirect communication of the revocation of the offer and that Maria was no longer able to accept the offer once she had this information.

---

5   [1950] 4 DLR 529, per Estey J.

CONSIDERATION

gratuitous promise
a promise made by someone who does not receive consideration for it

consideration
the price, which must be something of value, paid in return for a promise

estopped
stopped or prevented

The law makes a distinction between a gratuitous promise and a contract. In a **gratuitous promise**, one party agrees to do something for free or without reward. In contrast, a contract is essentially a bargain in which each party gets something in return for his or her promise to perform the obligations in the contract. The price paid in return for the promise is called **consideration**. Without consideration there is no contract.

Consideration can take many forms. Most commonly, of course, consideration is the payment of money. However, consideration can also be the exchange of goods or services, an agreement to refrain from doing something, or the relinquishment of a right. Where a party has made a statement or a promise relinquishing a right, or refraining from doing something, the party may be **estopped** (stopped or prevented) from later repudiating the statement or promise, if the other party relied on it in good faith. Factual and promissory estoppel is discussed later in this section.

The consideration in a contract must also be legal. If the consideration is illegal (for example, paying a sum of money to a person to murder someone else), the consideration fails and the contract is unenforceable. The legality of contracts will be discussed in detail later in this chapter.

Gratuitous Promises

In most circumstances, the courts will not enforce gratuitous promises. Because they lack consideration, gratuitous promises are not contracts. However, there are some exceptions to this rule.

The promise of a donation to a charity is a gratuitous promise. The promisor who pledges to donate a sum of money to a charity receives nothing in return apart from the thanks of the charity and the knowledge of a good deed done (and possibly a tax receipt). Most people do honour their pledges to charities, and most charities would not consider legal action to try to enforce a subscriber's pledge. However, there are cases in which the courts have upheld the promise of a donation to a charity on the basis that the subscribers pledged to donate funds for a specific undertaking.

■ EXAMPLE OF A PROMISE BEING A CONTRACT

In the cases of *Sargent v. Nicholson*[6] and *YMCA v. Rankin*,[7] the charity (the YMCA in both cases), relying on the pledges received from its subscribers, committed itself to constructing new buildings. When the subscribers refused to honour their pledges, the court held that there was an implied request from the subscribers that the charity undertake the project as the "price" for the pledge. The court held that this was sufficient consideration.

Note that if the pledge constitutes only a small part of the total funds needed for the undertaking, the courts are unlikely to enforce the promise. The pledge must

---

6 (1915), 9 WWR 883 (Man. CA).

7 (1916), 10 WWR 482 (BCCA).

constitute a substantial portion of the funds needed. In addition, if the moneys are pledged not for a specific project or undertaking but for the day-to-day expenses of the charity, the courts will not enforce the promise.

A gratuitous promise that is made **under seal** will be enforced even without consideration. Originally, a seal was used on a document to prove its authenticity and to substitute for a signature at a time when few people were literate. The seal was usually wax, and a signet ring was impressed into the wax. Over time, gummed wafers were substituted, or impressions were made directly onto the paper. Even the word "seal" or "L.S." (short for *locus sigilli*, or "the place of the seal") can constitute a seal. To properly execute a document under seal, the promisor must sign the document and affix the seal at the time of signature. A document under seal is called a **deed**.

A promise made under seal does not require consideration to make it binding. The courts have traditionally viewed the seal on a document as an indication that the promisor understands the significance of his or her act and intends to be bound by the promise contained in the document.

under seal
to bear an impression made in wax, a gummed paper wafer, or an impression made directly on paper

deed
a written contract, made under seal by the promisor(s); also called a formal contract

Estoppel Based on Fact

When one person asserts as true a certain statement of fact and another relies on that statement to his detriment, the maker of the statement will be estopped from denying the truth of his original statement in a court of law, even if it turns out to have been untrue.

■ EXAMPLE OF ESTOPPEL BASED ON FACT

Alberto leased a retail shop from Ewelina. Alberto wanted to get rid of furniture at back of the shop but believed that it belonged to Ewelina. She told Alberto it had belonged to the previous tenant but it came with the lease and Alberto could do what he wanted with it. Alberto sold the furniture for a profit. Subsequently, Ewelina realized that her husband had inherited the furniture from his mother. Ewelina sued Alberto for the value of the furniture, but was unsuccessful. Ewelina was estopped from denying the truth of her statement to Alberto when they negotiated the lease, that he could do as he liked with the furniture, even though the statement was untrue. Because Alberto relied on her statement, he should not have to suffer detrimental consequences because he acted in good faith on what Ewelina had told him.

Promissory Estoppel

Another exception to the rule that most gratuitous promises cannot be enforced occurs in cases involving **promissory estoppel** (also known as equitable estoppel). Once a party makes a promise or representation to the other party, and the other party relies on this statement of fact to his or her detriment, the statement or promise cannot later be denied. The party is estopped from denying the promise previously made. In other words, the party who relied on the promise can "raise estoppel" against the party who made the statement to ensure that he or she fulfills the promise.

promissory estoppel
a rule whereby a person is prevented from denying the truth of a statement of fact made by him or her where another person has relied on that statement and acted accordingly

Five elements must be present to constitute promissory estoppel:

1. There must be an existing legal relationship between the parties at the time the statement on which the estoppel is founded was made.

2. There must be a clear promise or representation made by the party against whom the estoppel is raised, establishing her or his intent to be bound by what she or he has said.

3. There must have been reliance, by the party raising the estoppel, on the statement or conduct of the party against whom the estoppel is raised.

4. The party to whom the representation was made must have acted on it to her or his detriment.

5. The promisee must have acted equitably.[8]

Promissory estoppel usually involves an assurance by one party that it will not enforce its legal rights with the intention that the assurance be relied on and acted on by the other party.

▦ EXAMPLE OF PROMISSORY ESTOPPEL

In the English case of *Central London Property Trust, Ltd. v. High Trees House, Ltd.*,[9] a landlord gratuitously promised to reduce the rent on a long-term lease because of the difficulties the tenant was experiencing due to the war. After the war, the landlord's representative sued the tenant for the full amount of the rent owing. Clearly, no consideration passed from the tenant to the landlord in exchange for the promise to reduce the rent. However, the tenant relied on the promise to his detriment. The court stated:

> [A] promise was made which was intended to create legal relations and which, to the knowledge of the person making the promise, was going to be acted on by the person to whom it was made, and which in fact was so acted on. In such cases the courts have said that the promise must be honoured.

Adequacy of Consideration

The courts insist that the consideration exchanged have some value to the parties, but will not examine the adequacy of the consideration to determine whether the promise and the consideration are of equal value. The adequacy of the consideration is a matter of personal judgment. As long as consideration is present, the requirement is satisfied. The consideration may be as little as one dollar or even one cent, or may take the form of an item that has value or significance to no one apart from the parties to the contract, such as a book or a photograph.

If a party agrees to a contract in which he or she receives grossly inadequate consideration for his or her promise, the courts will nevertheless enforce the contract. However, this lack of interference occurs only where both parties are

---

8   G.H.L. Fridman, *The Law of Contract in Canada*, 3d ed. (Scarborough, ON: Carswell, 1994), 129-35.

9   [1947] KB 130.

equally capable of looking after their own interests and there is no evidence of **fraud**, undue influence, or duress. If one party can prove that the consideration in the contract was grossly inadequate *and* can prove the existence of some form of fraud, undue influence, or duress, the court may hold that the contract is unenforceable. This is dealt with in more detail in chapter 4, Contractual Defects.

fraud
false or misleading allegations for the purpose of inducing another to part with something valuable or to give up some legal right

Past Consideration

Consideration must be something that is to be received at the instant the promise is made (*present consideration*) or at a later date (*future consideration*). It cannot be something that the person has received before the promise was made (**past consideration**). Even if a person promises to reward another who has previously done an act gratuitously, the promise is not binding because past consideration is no consideration at all. To be a valid and enforceable contract, the promise and the consideration must be exchanged for each other. This is not the case when the act is done first and the promise is made later.

past consideration
an act done or something given before a contract is made, which by itself is not consideration for the contract

▣ EXAMPLES OF PRESENT, FUTURE, AND PAST CONSIDERATION

- Fazil purchases a book from Margaret. Margaret gives him the book and Fazil pays the money immediately. The act (Margaret giving Fazil the book) and the promise (Fazil will pay for the book) occur at the same time. This is *present consideration*.

- Fazil purchases a book from Margaret on credit and agrees to pay her for it in a month. The act (Margaret giving Fazil the book) occurs in the present and the promise (Fazil will pay for the book) is made at the same time as the act, although it will occur at a later date. This is *future consideration*.

- Margaret gives Fazil a book as a gift (a gratuitous act). A few months later, Fazil finds out that it is a valuable first edition and offers to pay Margaret for it but later changes his mind and refuses to pay. The act (Margaret giving Fazil the book) occurred before the promise was made (Fazil promising to pay for the book). This is *past consideration*, and Fazil's promise to pay Margaret cannot be enforced.

Existing Legal Obligation

The promise to do something that a party is already obligated to do under another contract or under a statute cannot be consideration. If an existing contract obligates one party to perform a certain act for another party, that same act cannot form the consideration for another contract. There must be *fresh consideration* for a new promise. Otherwise, the promise is gratuitous.

▣ EXAMPLE OF EXISTING LEGAL OBLIGATION

Bruce and Patrice enter into a contract whereby Bruce agrees to build a backyard deck for Patrice. Patrice needs to have the deck completed by a certain date, and Bruce agrees to this term. However, Bruce later finds that he cannot complete the deck on time without hiring extra workers. He tells Patrice that he will need an additional $5,000 if she wants the deck completed by the date specified. Patrice agrees to pay the extra $5,000, and Bruce then completes the deck on time. However, Patrice refuses to pay Bruce the additional $5,000.

Bruce cannot enforce Patrice's promise to pay the additional $5,000 because Patrice received no consideration for her promise to pay. The only thing Bruce offered her in exchange for the additional $5,000 was the completion of the deck by a certain date, something he was already obligated to do in the original contract. Patrice received no fresh consideration for her promise. However, if Bruce had offered her fresh consideration (such as offering to stain the deck as well), Patrice's promise to pay would have been enforceable because it would have been supported by consideration. Bruce could also have had the agreement to pay the additional $5,000 executed under seal, which would have made fresh consideration for the promise to pay the additional $5,000 unnecessary.

Similarly, if a party has an obligation under a statute to perform certain duties, agreeing to perform those duties cannot be consideration for another contract. This applies to persons who have obligations to perform public duties, such as police officers.

Debtor–Creditor Relationships

While the requirement for fresh consideration for a promise makes good sense in most instances, it can lead to unfair results in others, particularly in debtor–creditor relationships. In a debtor–creditor relationship, the debtor is obligated to pay to the creditor a certain sum of money. The debtor's obligations are discharged when the full amount of the debt is paid in accordance with the terms of the contract (loan, credit card, financing agreement, and so on). However, it is common practice, especially where a debtor has defaulted in payment, for debtors and creditors to enter into an agreement to allow the debtor to pay a lesser amount than the total owed.

For example, Marcel, a debtor, owes $10,000 and offers to pay $9,000. The creditor, Su Mei, agrees to accept the sum of $9,000 in full and final settlement of the $10,000 debt. For many reasons, Su Mei may find that it is to her benefit to accept the lesser amount rather than to pursue Marcel through the courts for the full amount. In addition, Marcel ought to be able to rely on Su Mei's promise that she will take the lesser amount in full satisfaction for the debt. However, the requirement of fresh consideration makes the agreement to accept the lesser amount unenforceable. Because Marcel was already obligated to pay that sum of money (and more), Su Mei received no fresh consideration for the promise to pay the lesser amount. Su Mei would then be free to sue Marcel for the outstanding sum of $1,000.

To address this problem and to allow debtors and creditors to enter into such arrangements with the knowledge that they are enforceable, many provinces in Canada have passed legislation that states that a creditor who accepts a lesser sum in satisfaction of a debt will not later be allowed to claim the balance. In Ontario, such a provision is found in the *Mercantile Law Amendment Act*.[10] However, where

---

10 RSO 1990, c. M.10, s. 16.

the creditor agrees to accept a lesser amount, he or she can change his or her mind at any point before receiving the lesser sum.

Quantum Meruit

It is not unusual for one party to request goods or services from another and for that person to deliver such goods or services without a price being discussed. This is not a situation of a gratuitous promise. Even though the consideration is not specifically mentioned in the request, an agreement of this type will not fail for lack of consideration. The law will imply a promise to pay in a request for goods or services.

Quantum meruit is a concept that is relied on by someone whose occupation is to provide services or goods in a situation where payment is understood and expected.

Where there is no mention of price, the implied promise is for payment of what the services are reasonably worth, or payment for *quantum meruit*. Parties who have negotiated a contract that contains a term as to the price to be paid for the goods or services cannot later rely on the doctrine of *quantum meruit* to get a better price. *Quantum meruit* can be relied on only when the contract is silent as to the amount (or *quantum*) of the consideration, in circumstances where payment is clearly required.

In determining what goods or services are reasonably worth, the courts look to the prices charged by similar suppliers and fix the contract price accordingly. *Quantum meruit* also applies to situations where there has been substantial performance, although performance is not complete. To prevent one party from getting some benefit for the work done without having to pay would be unfair. Where there has been substantial performance, the court therefore will try to determine the value of the work that has been done and award compensation for that work. *Quantum meruit* in connection with substantial performance is discussed in more detail in chapter 8, Breach of Contract and Remedies.

quantum meruit
an equitable doctrine that states that no one should unjustly benefit from the labour and materials of another; under those circumstances, the law implies a promise to pay a reasonable amount, even in the absence of a contractual term for price; loosely translated as "as much as is deserved"

INTRODUCTION TO LEGALITY

In order to be binding and enforceable on the parties, a contract must have a legal purpose. To have a legal purpose, a contract cannot violate any statute, and it cannot violate public policy. If, for either reason, the contract is found to have an unlawful purpose, the courts will not enforce it and will declare it to be void, or illegal, or both.

The distinction between a contract that is merely void for having an unlawful purpose and one where the contract has an unlawful purpose and is illegal as well, is important. If the contract is merely void for being unlawful, the court may grant some remedies to parties who entered into a contract by attempting to restore them to their original positions. For example, if money and goods have changed hands but the contract is unlawful, the court may order the goods and the money returned.

However, if the contract is not only unlawful but also illegal, the court will not grant any remedies to any party who knowingly entered into an illegal contract. Remedies are discussed in more detail in chapter 8, Breach of Contract and Remedies.

■ EXAMPLE OF EFFECTS OF ILLEGALITY

In the case of *Archbolds (Freightage), Ltd. v. Spanglett, Ltd.*,[11] the court stated:

> The effect of illegality upon a contract may be threefold. If at the time of making the contract there is an intent to perform it in an unlawful way, the contract, although it remains alive, is unenforceable at the suit of the party having that intent; if the intent is held in common, it is not enforceable at all. Another effect of illegality is to prevent a plaintiff from recovering under a contract if in order to prove his rights under it he has to rely upon his own illegal act. ... The third effect of illegality is to avoid the contract ab initio [void from the time it is made] and that arises if the making of the contract is expressly or impliedly prohibited by statute or is otherwise contrary to public policy.

Contracts That Violate Statute Law

It is important to look closely at the wording of the statute in question to determine whether a contract that violates the statute is void or void and illegal.

- Some statutes impose certain requirements on certain activities. A contract that provides for activities that do not comply with those requirements has an unlawful purpose by implication.

- Some statutes expressly prohibit certain activities and may describe contracts that provide for such activities and the activities themselves as "unlawful" and "illegal" and may impose criminal penalties, such as a fine or imprisonment. Such contracts have an unlawful purpose and may be illegal as well.

- Some statutes prohibit certain kinds of agreements; only a few will be discussed here.

A contract to commit any act prohibited by the *Criminal Code*[12] is both void and illegal. This includes, for example, any agreement to commit murder, rob, assault, or kidnap. The courts will not enforce such a contract and will not provide any remedies to parties who enter into the contract. Because it is a criminal offence to conspire to commit a crime, entering into a contract to commit a crime is a form of conspiracy and a crime in itself. Even if the crime is not carried out, the parties to the illegal contract can be charged with conspiracy.

The *Competition Act*[13] prohibits business practices that are contrary to the public interest and unduly restrict business, such as an agreement to fix prices, eliminate competition, allocate markets, or create monopolies. Such business practices represent forms of **restraint of trade**. The Act renders illegal any contract entered into whose purpose is to engage in the prohibited practices. It is possible to

restraint of trade
practices that are designed to artificially maintain prices, eliminate competition, create a monopoly, or otherwise obstruct the course of trade and commerce

---

11 [1961] 1 QB 374 (CA).

12 RSC 1985, c. C-46, as amended.

13 Formerly the *Combines Investigation Act*, RSC 1985, c. C-34; now the *Competition Act*, SC 1986, c. 26.

obtain governmental approval to enter into contracts to engage in such practices (such as for mergers) to avoid violating the Act. However, without approval, such contracts are void and illegal.

The *Workplace Safety and Insurance Act, 1997*[14] prohibits any agreement between employers and employees that attempts to deprive employees of the protection of the Act. For example, a contract in which an employee agrees not to make any workplace injury claims if he or she is injured on the job is void, although it is not illegal. Contracts to sell land that violate the provisions of the *Planning Act,*[15] and in which the parties do not obtain approval from the government, are void but not illegal. The *Customs Act*[16] prohibits contracts to smuggle, and such contracts are both void and illegal. The *Bankruptcy and Insolvency Act*[17] renders void, but not illegal, any contract a person enters into in which that person transfers property either as a gift or for inadequate compensation within one year before declaring bankruptcy.

Various statutes and bylaws require tradespeople and professionals to be licensed before they can offer services to the public. If an unlicensed tradesperson or professional enters into a contract for services she or he is not licensed to provide, such a contract is void but not illegal. However, this generally applies only to the services provided, not to any goods provided. An unlicensed plumber, then, could not enforce that part of the contract for payment for the work she or he did, but could enforce that part of the contract that provided for the supply of goods, such as pipes and fittings. However, this issue cannot be raised as a defence by the unlicensed tradesperson to the enforcement of the contract by the other party. If the unlicensed plumber did shoddy work and caused damage, the plumber could be sued for breach of contract by the customer. The plumber could not then claim that she or he incurred no liability under the contract because of being unlicensed. This is an application of the general principal that a party may not rely on her or his own wrongdoing to gain an advantage in court.

Contracts That Violate Public Policy

Contracts that violate public policy are void and may be illegal as well. These contracts are contrary to the public good.

Such contracts include those designed to interfere with the administration of justice (for example, paying a witness to give a certain kind of evidence in court), injure the public service (for example, giving "kickbacks" to a public official), promote unnecessary litigation (for example, paying someone to start a lawsuit to generate publicity), or suppress evidence of a crime (for example, entering an agreement not to report a theft if the wrongdoer pays back the money). Note that while most contracts that violate public policy are merely void, statute law may be in place that makes them illegal as well (for example, bribing a public official).

Other contracts may be void because they involve an agreement to commit a dishonest or immoral act. For instance, contracts for loans that charge an uncon-

---

14 SO 1997, c. 16, sched. A.

15 RSO 1990, c. P. 13.

16 SC 1986, c. C-1.

17 RSC 1985, c. B-3.

scionably high rate of interest are void. Contracts for loans that charge an interest rate higher than 60 percent are also illegal. Contracts that involve prostitution are void. Some contracts that involve gambling are void. However, societal mores change, and some acts that may once have been considered immoral by the courts are no longer illegal.

■ EXAMPLE OF CHANGE IN SOCIETAL MORES

In the case of *Prokop v. Kohut*,[18] the court stated that it would not enforce an agreement made between a man and a woman that granted the woman a half interest in the man's estate based on the couple's commitment to live together as a married couple. Despite the fact that the couple lived together for 16 years, the court dismissed the woman's claim, stating that any such contract would be "void as having been made for an illegal consideration and the plaintiff can recover nothing." However, the more recent case of *Chrispen v. Topham*[19] dismissed the traditional approach, stating, "In my opinion, it cannot be argued that the [cohabitation agreement] between the plaintiff and the defendant was made for an immoral purpose, and therefore, [is] illegal and unenforceable. Present day social acceptance of common-law living counters that argument."

restrictive covenant
a provision in a contract that prohibits certain activities or uses of property

Business contracts can be challenged as void for containing **restrictive covenants** that constitute a restraint of trade. While these contracts may not violate the *Competition Act*, discussed above, they nonetheless may be void for violating public policy. There is a presumption at law that all restrictive covenants that constitute a restraint of trade are void. However, this presumption can be rebutted by the party wishing to enforce the contract.

When a business is sold, the purchasers usually want to ensure that the vendors do not engage in a business that would compete with them. The parties often include a restrictive covenant in the sale agreement that the vendors will not open a competing business for a certain period of time within a certain geographical area. If the time period and the geographical area of restriction are reasonable, the courts will uphold the contract. However, if they are unreasonable, the courts will find that the restrictive covenant is a restraint of trade and will not enforce it. What is reasonable depends on the circumstances of each case and the standards of the industry or business in question.

■ EXAMPLE OF A RESTRICTIVE COVENANT

Newco Ltd. buys a dry-cleaning business in Toronto from Oldco Ltd. In the sale agreement, Newco states that it does not want Oldco opening a dry-cleaning business anywhere in the province of Ontario for a period of 25 years. The courts would likely find that such a restrictive covenant is contrary to public policy and therefore void. However, if the covenant stated that the restricted area was within a 10 km radius from the business site and for a period of four years, the courts would likely uphold the restrictive covenant.

18 (1965), 54 DLR (2d) 717 (BCSC).

19 (1986), 28 DLR (4th) 754 (Sask. QB).

Contracts between employers and employees that unreasonably restrict the employee's right to compete with the employer or to work for a competitor after the employment agreement terminates can also be void for restraint of trade. However, if the time period and geographical area are reasonable, the courts may enforce the contract. It is harder to enforce a contract of this nature than a contract for the sale of a business, since the courts are reluctant to restrict an individual from earning a living. However, if the restraint is reasonable and necessary, it will not offend the public interest and will be enforced.

FORM AND WRITING REQUIREMENTS

Formal and Simple Contracts

Contracts can be classed in terms of form or appearance as either **formal contracts** or **simple contracts**. Formal contracts, also called deeds, are in writing and sealed by the promisor. Deeds were the first type of contract to be recognized as valid, enforceable contracts. The early common law did not recognize most promises, whatever the form, for the purpose of enforcement. However, if a contract was written and sealed by the promisor, the formal act of applying a seal to the document was seen as evidence of a serious intention to make and keep a promise. If the promise was broken, it raised a serious issue of moral wrongdoing, which might bring the promise breaker before the church courts or local manorial courts to enforce the promise. By the late Middle Ages, the king's common law courts began to assume jurisdiction and enforce some contracts if they were in writing and made under seal, on the basis that the seal was evidence of a serious intention. At first, only contracts under seal were enforced; the courts would not recognize oral or unsealed written contracts as worthy of enforcement.

formal contract
a contract that is in writing and sealed by any party who is a promisor (which may be one or both parties); formal contracts are also called "deeds," and in English law are sometimes referred to as "covenants"

simple contract
a contract that can be oral or in writing and that is not a formal contract

---

Types of Contracts

Formal contracts (deeds) must be in writing and under seal. A seal is required to enforce a promise made if there is no consideration. For example, if I promise to give you my car as a gift, there is no consideration, because you are not required to do anything to obtain the car. For this gift to be enforceable by you, I must make the gift in writing and under seal. This type of contract is enforceable because of its form, regardless of its contents.

Simple contracts

- *may* be oral agreements,

- *may* be in writing,

- if required by the *Statute of Frauds* or other legislation, *must* be in writing and signed by the parties who have made promises that are meant to be enforced if breached.

Contracts that are not formal contracts are called simple contracts. "Simple" does not refer to the complexity of the contract. A simple contract can be very complicated and may go on for pages. It may be oral or in writing. In the medieval period, the common law courts would not recognize simple contracts as worthy of enforcement, although church and manorial courts might enforce them in some limited circumstances, as they did for formal contracts, provided there was some evidence of serious intention—for example, a deal confirmed by a handshake made in public. However, while the king's courts began to enforce formal contracts on evidence of a breach of the promise made by a party, they did not enforce simple contracts on the basis of a breach of the promise made. Instead, if one party performed his or her obligations but performed them badly, the other party could sue in **tort** for damages resulting from the other party having performed the promise poorly. Here, liability rested on a legally recognized civil wrong or tort rather than on the contractual basis of the breach of a promise. However, if the promisor did nothing at all to fulfill his or her obligation, he or she was not liable in tort to the promisee for the omission. This problem was solved not by recognizing contractual rights but by creating the tort of deceit, which made those who did nothing to fulfill a promise liable for damages. However, by the beginning of the 17th century, as modern contract law began to develop, the common law began to enforce simple contracts as contracts rather than as parts of tort law. In fact, by the end of the 17th century the law was well on its way to enforcing all simple contracts and abandoning prescribed formality requirements altogether. Today, simple contracts do not depend on any particular ceremony or prescribed form to be enforceable. However, there are some areas of contract law where enforceability depends on some formality requirements having been met.

As you will see in this chapter, contracts of certain types and covering certain subject matter must be in writing and signed by the party or parties to be bound to be valid and enforceable. As well, when a contractual promise is made by one party to another without any valuable consideration, a seal is required. In the absence of consideration, the seal is still seen as evidence of a serious intention to create legal relations.

tort

a civil wrong done by one party to another for which the law awards damages; the law of torts is much older than the law of contracts, and it is from tort law that modern contract law developed

The Statute of Frauds

The *Statute of Frauds* was enacted in England in 1677[20] and was adopted during the colonial period in Canada and the United States. It is still part of the law in most Canadian provinces, except for British Columbia, Quebec, and Manitoba, and in some American states. It requires that certain types of contracts be in writing and be signed by the parties who are to be bound by their promises. Such contracts do not necessarily have to be made under seal unless there is an absence of consideration. The Statute was originally passed in the wake of the English civil war and other upheavals that began in 1640 and was designed to introduce order and stability to the law, particularly with respect to fraudulent claims concerning long-term leases and other land rights (which had required deeds or formal contracts). It also covered situations that are now dealt with by simple contracts, although because of the Statute, these contracts must be in writing.

---

20 *An Act for the Prevention of Frauds and Perjures*, 29 Car. II, c. 3.

The Statute has long been regarded as an anachronism and has been repealed in England. Sections 1–4 are relevant to the law of contract today in most parts of Canada. The Statute was amended in Ontario,[21] and the Ontario Statute is the basis for discussion in this chapter. Some parts of the original Ontario *Statute of Frauds* have found their way into other statutes. The content of s. 17 of the Statute is now found as part of sale of goods legislation in most provinces. It requires contracts for the sale of goods in excess of a stated price to be in writing unless the existence of the contract is established in other ways: by part payment or by acceptance of some of the goods. Similarly, the requirement that marriage contracts be in writing, formerly part of s. 4, is now found in s. 52 of the Ontario *Family Law Act*[22] and in the family law legislation of other provinces.

CONTRACTS THAT MUST BE IN WRITING AND SIGNED

Under the *Statute of Frauds*, certain types of contracts must be in writing and signed by the person to be bound:

- contracts by an executor of an estate to pay debts of the estate from personal funds (s. 4),

- contracts by a person to guarantee the debts of another or be responsible for the *tort* obligations of another (s. 4),

- contracts for the sale of land or affecting any interest in land except for leases of less than three years (ss. 3 and 4), and

- contracts made after attaining the age of majority to ratify debt obligations incurred as a minor (s. 7).

Contracts by a Trustee of an Estate To Pay Estate Debts

If the trustees of an estate decide to pay the debts of the estate out of their own personal funds, their promise to do so must be put in writing if they are to claim from the estate what they paid out to third parties. This might happen if an estate debt is pressing and penalty or interest is accumulating on the debt. The estate trustee might pay the debt out of personal funds to prevent the estate from losing money. Then, when estate funds later become available, she or he may claim from the estate the amount paid.

■ EXAMPLE OF PAYMENT OF ESTATE DEBTS FROM PERSONAL FUNDS

Sandra is the trustee of her mother's estate. Her mother had a personal loan at the time of her death and owned some bonds. There is interest running against the personal loan, which is now a debt of the estate. Sandra would like to pay off the loan as soon as possible to avoid further interest charges against the estate. The bonds are assets of the estate and

---

21 RSO 1990, c. S.19.

22 RSO 1990, c. F.3.

could be used to pay off the loan, but the estate would lose money if the bonds are cashed in now. Sandra pays off the personal loan out of her own money. She sets out in a document the fact that she is acting as the estate trustee and paying off the personal loan, setting out the amount and the recipient, and that she is entitled to be reimbursed from the estate. She signs and dates the document, and has a friend witness her signature. She also obtains an acknowledgment and receipt from the creditor to show that the payment has been received. Both of these documents will be necessary to prove that Sandra is entitled to be reimbursed from the estate assets when they become available if she is challenged by other beneficiaries of the estate.

Contracts To Assume the Liabilities of Another

Contracts where a third party promises to perform the obligation of another person must, under the Statute, be in writing and be signed by the third party. If the promise is not in writing, it cannot be enforced against the third party. The Statute describes two contractual situations where third parties agree to assume another's liability: guarantees and assumed liability for torts.

guarantee

a promise by a third party to pay the debt of another person if that person fails to pay the debt when it is due

guarantor

a third party who gives a guarantee to the creditor of another person

Guaranteeing Debt   A **guarantee** arises where the **guarantor** promises to pay the debt of another person if that other person fails to pay the debt when it is due. In this situation there are two levels of liability. The original debtor is primarily liable to pay the debt. Only after the original debtor fails to pay the debt does the liability of the guarantor arise. The guarantor's liability in this situation depends on the principal debtor's failure to pay the debt when it is due and extends only to the terms of the original guarantee. If the primary debtor and the creditor agree to change the terms, the guarantor is released from his or her obligation to pay the debt unless the guarantor also agrees in writing to the new terms.

Examine loan agreements carefully to see if the terms indicate that a person is a guarantor of payment by the principal debtors or primarily liable along with other debtors to pay the debt. A person who co-signs a loan or accepts joint liability with another to pay a debt is primarily liable along with that other debtor. A guarantor, on the other hand, is liable only when the principal debtor defaults on payment when the debt is due. If a guarantor pays a debt for the primary debtor, the guarantor has a right to demand payment of the amount of the debt from the primary debtor. Guarantees are sometimes confused with indemnity agreements. An indemnifier is assuming or sharing primary liability on the debt, whether the other debtor fails to pay or not. An indemnity agreement need not be in writing.

Creditors who are lending to someone who is a poor credit risk often ask the debtor to find someone who has a good credit rating to guarantee repayment. In this situation, if the creditor wishes to enforce the guarantee, it must be in writing and signed by the guarantor. In some jurisdictions, the guarantor may also be required to sign a document indicating that the responsibilities of a guarantor have been explained to her or him, and that the guarantor understands those responsibilities. The amount of consideration, however, does not have to be in writing.[23]

---

23 RSO 1990, c. S.19, s. 6.

■ EXAMPLE OF GUARANTEE OF A DEBT

Johann wants to borrow money from the Caring Bank. The bank manager knows that Johann doesn't have a full-time job, has few assets, and is a poor credit risk. The bank manager says the bank will lend Johann the money if Johann can find someone to guarantee the loan. Johann asks his friend Antonio to act as guarantor. Antonio goes to the bank and gives his guarantee in writing, signing the guarantee. A few weeks later, Johann misses a payment installment. On default, the manager calls Antonio and tells him that the bank is looking to him to repay the loan and will be relying on the signed guarantee to enforce Antonio's obligation.

Assuming Responsibility for Tort   If a third party promises to pay the damages that may be found to be owing by another person to a tort victim, the third party must give this promise in writing and sign the document if she or he is to be held liable for the torts of another. If there is no signed, written document, a mere oral promise is unenforceable.

■ EXAMPLE OF GUARANTEEING DAMAGES FOR ANOTHER'S TORT

Jocasta's son Oedipus drove his car into Tiresias's parked van. Jocasta, who owns the insurance policy on her son's car, does not want to have to pay a higher insurance premium as a result of the accident. She promises Tiresias that she will pay for the damage to his van out of her own pocket if he agrees not to notify the insurance company. Tiresias, having read this text, insists that she set out her promise in writing and place her signature on it so that he can enforce the agreement if she tries to back out of it.

Contracts for the Sale of Land or Affecting Any Interest in Land

Contracts in which one person gives an interest in land to another must be in writing under the terms of the Statute. In addition, in various jurisdictions in Canada, transfers of interests in land must meet other formality requirements, including the use of a prescribed form, seals, and other mandatory information. "Interest in land" includes not only the sale of the freehold interest but also the transfer of interests that are less than freehold: leases for more than three years, **life estates**, and **easements**, but probably not most **licences**, which the courts usually see as a right to a particular use of land without any interest in it being transferred. For example, your right to occupy a space in a parking lot is usually seen as an occupational licence rather than the transfer of an interest in the space itself. Deciding whether you are dealing with an interest in land is important, since oral agreements to convey an interest in land are not enforceable, subject to some exceptions discussed later in this section.

The rules requiring written agreements for transfers of interests in land have given rise to two problems. First, the courts have had great difficulty in determining what kinds of agreements are concerned primarily with land and not something else. Second, where an agreement is unenforceable because it is not in writing, the courts have had to decide what remedies can be provided where one person performed his or her part of the bargain, relying on the agreement, and the

life estate
a transfer of interest in land for a term of years measured by the life of the transferee or by the life of another person; when the person dies, the life estate ends, and the property goes back to the transferor or other persons designated to receive the interest in land

easement
an interest in land that permits certain uses without interruption or interference by the person who has legal title to the land

licence
a grant of a right; in real property law, a grant of a right to some use of land that does not amount to a grant of an interest in the land

other was using the technical requirements of the Statute to unfairly get out of the deal by getting the benefit of the other's part performance without having to do anything in return.

Determining What Constitutes a Contract Regarding Any Interest in Land The vagueness of the Statute regarding a definition of "any interest … concerning [land]"[24] has caused great confusion in the case law. The courts have had to develop some principles by which they can sort claims into two categories: contracts that are concerned primarily with the sale of land or the transfer of some interest in land, and contracts that may have involved a transfer of an interest in land but are also concerned with other things. The Statute requires contracts that are concerned primarily with land transfers to be in writing to be enforceable; contracts that are about land but also about something else may not have to be in writing.

◼ EXAMPLE OF CONTRACT CONCERNED WITH A TRANSFER OF
   AN INTEREST IN LAND

Cain promises to sell Canaan to Abel for $10. For Abel to enforce this agreement, it must be in writing and signed by Cain because it is primarily concerned with the transfer of an interest in land.

◼ EXAMPLE OF CONTRACT CONCERNED WITH A TRANSFER OF
   AN INTEREST IN LAND AND SOMETHING ELSE

Vivaldi wishes to hire Offenbach to play in his orchestra. Vivaldi offers Offenbach a large salary and promises that if Offenbach stays with the orchestra Vivaldi will also transfer a parcel of land to him. The contract may not need to be in writing to be enforceable by Offenbach because it is primarily about something other than the transfer of a parcel of land.

One of the reasons that so much attention has been focused on deciding whether a contract is primarily a land transaction is because the courts have wanted to limit the application of the Statute requiring land contracts to be in writing. Situations arise where it would be unfair to enforce the conveyance of an interest in land where the conveyance is not in writing. For example, Abelard promises Eloise that he will convey his house to her on his death if she accepts only room and board and looks after him as a housekeeper until his death. If Eloise performs her part of the bargain, it seems unfair to allow Abelard or his heirs to avoid conveying the land to Eloise solely because the agreement is not in writing. The courts have met this problem by sometimes classifying the contract as having to do with something other than land, thus taking it outside the Statute so that an oral agreement can be enforced. The court can also accept that the contract falls within the Statute but use the equitable doctrine of part performance to achieve a fair result. Part performance is discussed below.

---

24 RSO 1990, c. S.19, s. 4.

The Doctrine of Part Performance A contract that involves the transfer of an interest in land may be enforceable through the equitable doctrine of part performance, even if the contract is not in writing, if the promisee performs some acts in reliance on the promisor's oral offer to convey land. However, the doctrine of part performance in Canada has received a narrow interpretation. A person arguing against the requirement that the contract be in writing must come within all of the following four requirements:

1. The party claiming part performance must show that the acts performed are done only with respect to the promise to convey a specific parcel of land. If part performance is related to something other than the conveyance of land, or if the acts are not in respect of the specific land itself, the doctrine cannot be successfully invoked.

■ **EXAMPLE OF PERFORMANCE DIRECTLY RELATED TO LAND**

Artemis promises to sell Swamp Acre to Chloe for $10. The offer is oral, and Chloe accepts it. She moves onto the land and begins to build a house. Artemis then says that she is backing out, and since the agreement is not in writing, there is no contract. Here there is a promise to convey and part performance by Chloe, who builds a house. Part performance is exclusively based on the agreement to convey land. Without the promise to convey, Chloe would never have built the house. Further, the acts done are with respect to the land itself, so that Chloe can rely on part performance.

2. The party claiming part performance must show that enforcing the statutory requirement of a written contract would defraud the party relying on the promise and cause hardship.

■ **EXAMPLE OF ENFORCEMENT OF STATUTE DEFRAUDING A PARTY**

If the contract could not be enforced, then Chloe, who relied on the promise, would be defrauded of the cost of building a house and of the house itself. She would also have suffered hardship from losing a substantial sum of money.

3. The party claiming part performance must show that the agreement involves an interest in land. Something less than a legally defined interest does not suffice.

■ **EXAMPLE OF AGREEMENT PRIMARILY ABOUT AN INTEREST IN LAND**

The promise was clearly a conveyance of the freehold to Chloe, which is an interest in land.

4. The party claiming part performance must show that, aside from the requirement of writing, there is a valid and enforceable oral agreement. There

must be cogent and persuasive oral evidence to support the existence of the agreement.[25]

EXAMPLE OF VALID AND ENFORCEABLE AGREEMENT

Chloe and Artemis have a valid contract: an offer, an acceptance, and valuable consideration that would support the existence of a valid oral agreement. Cogent evidence of the agreement might include a receipt for $10 or a cancelled cheque, witnesses present when the agreement was reached, the building of the house without interference by Artemis, or any other rational explanation for undertaking such work.

The case of *Deglmann v. Guarantee Trust Co. of Canada*[26] demonstrates some of the difficulties in relying on the doctrine of part performance to overcome the requirement of a written agreement. In this case, Deglmann lived with his aunt in her house while he attended a course. She also owned the property next door (property X). During this time, the aunt said that if Deglmann was good to her and would do such services for her as she might request during her lifetime, she would make adequate provision for him in her will and, in particular, she would leave him property X. While he lived with her, Deglmann did chores around her house and property X. Afterward he did odd jobs on both buildings, ran other errands for her, and took her on trips and drives. He never lived on property X and only lived on her other property for six months. When she died, he received nothing from her estate and never received property X. Deglmann sued her estate, claiming enforcement of the oral agreement for the transfer of land.

The court, in reviewing the evidence, held that none of the numerous acts done for the aunt were "by their own nature, unequivocally referable to" property X, so the doctrine of part performance could not be invoked. The court did go on to hold, on other grounds, that there was some kind of contractual relationship that justified some payment to Deglmann.

A more flexible approach that expanded the application of the doctrine of part performance was followed in England by the House of Lords in *Steadman v. Steadman*.[27] In this case, a husband and wife had separated. The husband was in arrears in his support payments. The husband and wife orally agreed that she would release her half-interest in the house if he paid £1500 and £100 in arrears of maintenance. He paid the arrears, but the wife refused to transfer her interest, arguing that the promise to convey was not in writing and there was no part performance because the payment of the arrears was not specifically referable to the land itself. The House of Lords took the view that if the husband paid the arrears, this could be used to prove the existence of the agreement to convey the property and his reliance on it. If so, looking at all the circumstances, to require the husband's acts to be with respect to the property itself was too narrow an approach. Acts to improve the property, for example, certainly provided evidence of his reliance on the agreement, the existence of the agreement, and the expectation

---

25 J.A. Willes, *Contemporary Canadian Business Law*, 4th ed. (Toronto: McGraw-Hill Ryerson, 1994), 196-97.

26 [1954] SCR 725.

27 [1976] AC 536 (HL).

of the property being transferred to him, but they were not the only evidence that could prove the existence of the agreement. If there was other cogent evidence of the existence of the agreement to transfer the property, and his reliance on it, then that should be sufficient. In this case, his payment of the arrears constituted acceptable evidence of the existence of the agreement and his reliance on it. This approach is broader than the Canadian approach, but it is consistent with the idea that the Statute should be used to prevent fraud, not to escape one's obligations on a technicality.

Ratification of Minors' Contracts

If a minor incurs a debt before reaching the age of majority, and the debt is not related to necessities, the contract cannot be enforced against the minor once he or she has reached the age of majority unless the individual ratifies the contract in writing. The effect of minority status on contract enforcement is discussed in chapter 3, Protecting Weaker Parties.

Technical Requirements for Written Contracts

The Statute requires that an agreement be in writing. Whether required by the Statute or generally, the following considerations apply. A formal document drafted by lawyers is not necessarily required. The contract can consist of written notes on the back of a menu or on a restaurant tablecloth, or an exchange of letters, faxes, or emails. Whatever the form, a written agreement, whether it is one document or several letters between the parties, should

- identify the parties to the contract by name or by description,

- identify the terms of the contract, including the offer that has been accepted and the consideration to be given,

- be signed by the party whose promise is being enforced; it is not necessary to have other parties' signatures if the agreement is not being enforced against them, and

- include a printed or stamped signature, which may suffice in place of an actual signature. But an actual signature is preferable if there is an issue about whether a party actually "signed" an agreement.

Formal contracts (deeds) must be in writing and under seal. This means that the document should be signed by the persons being bound, with a gummed paper seal or a wax impression attached next to the signature. Drawing a circle next to the signature and labelling it "L.S." (*locus sigilli* or "legal seal") is sufficient evidence that the document is meant to be under seal. It is also usual for the document to be signed by a person who witnessed the promisor signing and affixing the seal to the document.

Signatures are not legally required in theory, but are invariably present because seals are usually gummed and do not by themselves identify the person to be bound. When contract law was developing, seals were usually made by impressing a signet ring with a person's identifying sign or coat of arms into hot wax applied to the document. This is obviously no longer done, since most people don't have signet rings or seals or carry around hot wax.

The existence of the seal indicates that the party signing the document intends to be bound by the agreement even when he or she receives no consideration from other parties, as in cases where the promisor is promising a gift to someone. This can be important if, as in tax cases, it matters that a conveyance of something is to be seen to be a gift and not something else.

Must the seal be affixed for the contract to be enforceable? The fact that a person has gone to the trouble of affixing a seal is, in theory, evidence of serious intent, so that validity and enforceability arise from the solemn form of the agreement itself. In most cases, if there is evidence that the document was intended to be sealed, that will suffice to make it a deed and have it enforced as if it were a deed. However, there are still cases where some evidence that seals were affixed (even if they later fell off) is required.[28]

If a corporation or other legal "person" who is not an individual, such as a government department, is a signatory to a contract, it usually will execute an agreement using a corporate seal that identifies the corporation by name. Some statutes require that a signing officer of the corporation sign his or her name next to the seal. Often, the seal alone or the signature of a corporate officer is sufficient. Legislation governing business corporations in many jurisdictions no longer requires a corporation to have and use a seal.

affidavit of execution
a sworn statement in writing, signed by the witness to a contract, stating that the witness was present and saw the person signing the contract actually sign it; the affidavit can be used to prove that a party to a contract actually signed it

Generally, most contracts need not be witnessed unless there is some statutory requirement. But it is a good idea to have the signatures witnessed so that if proof of a signature on a contract is required it can be more readily obtained. For some deeds, witnesses are required, and an **affidavit of execution** by the witness may also be required in which the witness swears that she or he was present and saw the party sign the document. In this situation, the affidavit of execution itself becomes evidence that a party to the contract signed it.

SUMMARY

A contract is an agreement that is enforceable at law. A contract that is not enforceable is a void contract. For a contract to be enforceable, the essential elements of a contract must be present. The parties must have the intent to create an agreement that is legally binding. An offer, or a promise, must be made by the offeror and communicated to the offeree. The offer must not lapse or be revoked. The offeree must communicate his or her unequivocal acceptance to the offeror. The contract must include consideration, or an exchange of something of value between the parties. An agreement without consideration is a gratuitous contract and will not be enforced unless it is under seal. The purpose of the contract must be legal, and any agreement that violates statute law or public policy is void and may be illegal as well.

In considering formality requirements, contracts are either formal or simple contracts. Formal contracts, also called deeds, are in writing and under seal. Simple contracts may be oral or in writing but are not formal contracts, usually because they are not under seal. While many oral contracts are enforceable, some contracts must be in writing and in some cases must be under seal as well.

---

28 See *Township of South-West Oxford v. Bailak* (1990), 75 OR (2d) 360; 73 DLR (4th) 411 (Gen. Div.), per Meisner J.

The *Statute of Frauds* requires that certain contracts involving estate debts, guarantees for third parties, and the transfer of interests in land must be in writing. To prevent rigid and unfair application of this rule requiring written contracts, the courts have developed some exceptions where there has been part performance by one party.

KEY TERMS

affidavit of execution	life estate
arm's-length transaction	licence
breach of contract	nullity
consideration	onus
counteroffer	past consideration
deed	presumption of law
easement	promissory estoppel
estopped	*quantum meruit*
formal contract	restraint of trade
fraud	restrictive covenant
gratuitous promise	revoke
guarantee	simple contract
guarantor	tort
inquiry	under seal
lapse	void contract

REVIEW QUESTIONS

1. How do the courts determine whether the parties to an agreement intended to create a legal relationship?

2. What is the "presumption of law" with respect to the intention to create a legal relationship?

3. Explain why an offer must be communicated before it can be accepted.

4. When does an offer lapse?

5. How may an acceptance be communicated? When does silence constitute acceptance?

6. What is the "postal acceptance rule"?

7. Consider whether acceptance has been communicated and a contract formed in the following examples:

   a. Allan emails Betty on Monday and offers to sell her his car for $3,000. She emails him back the same day and accepts his offer. Allan does not check his email.

   b. Allan phones Betty and offers to sell her his car for $3,000. She tells him that she will get back to him. She emails him the same day, accepting his offer. He only uses his email for work and doesn't check it. Betty doesn't phone him back, so he sells the car to Charles.

   c. Allan meets Betty and offers to sell her his car for $3,000. She cannot decide immediately, so Allan tells her to email him before Wednesday, although he usually only uses his email address for work. On Tuesday Betty emails him her acceptance.

8. What distinguishes a counteroffer from an inquiry?

9. What effect does a counteroffer or an inquiry have on an offer?

10. How may an offer be revoked, and when is such revocation effective?

11. "The courts are not concerned with the adequacy of consideration." What does this mean, and what is an exception to this statement?

12. Under what conditions will a court enforce a gratuitous promise?

13. What is promissory estoppel?

14. What is estoppel based on fact?

15. Explain the differences among past, present, and future consideration.

16. What conditions must be present for the courts to enforce a claim of *quantum meruit*?

17. What is the difference between a contract that has an unlawful purpose and a contract that is illegal?

18. Describe two instances where a contract would be void for violating a statute.

19. Describe two instances where a contract would be void for violating public policy.

20. What is a restrictive covenant?

21. When is a restrictive covenant enforceable?

22. What are the formality requirements for a contract that is a deed?

23. What are the formality requirements for a simple contract?

24. In what circumstances must a deed be used if a contract is to be enforceable?

25. What kinds of contracts does the *Statute of Frauds* require to be in writing and signed by the parties to be enforceable?

26. When does the *Statute of Frauds* require that a written contract be a formal document? When is a seal required? When is a pen and ink signature required?

27. Is a guarantor bound if, after she or he signs a guarantee, the creditor and the debtor alter the terms of the credit agreement between them by changing the interest rate? Explain.

28. How does a guarantor's liability differ from a joint debtor's liability?

29. John has orally agreed to pay for repairs to a tavern that his son Jacob wrecked in a barroom brawl if the tavern agrees not to sue Jacob. The tavern sends the repair bill to John, who refuses to pay. Can the tavern make John do what he agreed to do?

30. What is an "interest in land" that would bring a contract within the *Statute of Frauds*?

31. What hardships might arise if courts always refused to enforce oral agreements that provided for the transfer of an interest in land?

32. Suppose Alberto promises to convey his land to Hamish if Hamish looks after Alberto in his old age. There is no written agreement. Hamish looks after Alberto. Alberto dies and leaves his land to be turned into a bird sanctuary. Can Hamish enforce Alberto's oral promise? Explain. Would Hamish's chances improve if he had made some repairs to the buildings on the property at his own expense while Alberto was alive? Explain.

33. What must you show to prove that a contract that must be sealed is under seal?

34. What advantages to having a contract under seal are not available for a simple contract?

35. If its seal falls off, is a contract enforceable? Does it make a difference to your answer if the seal was meant to be applied but never was?

36. Is it a good idea to have a signed contract witnessed? Why or why not?

DISCUSSION QUESTIONS

1. Extreme Skiing Company, a company that specializes in ski trips, offers a heli-skiing trip that involves a helicopter ride to a remote mountain slope. The price of $1,000 per person, which includes hotel, meals, and helicopter transportation, is advertised in a skiing magazine. In response to the advertisement, Allyson calls Extreme Skiing and agrees over the telephone that she and Matthias will join the trip. Extreme Skiing's representative says he will mail the enrollment forms to Allyson and Matthias. Allyson agrees that she and Matthias will meet the trip operators at the hotel the day before the trip. Two weeks before the trip date, Allyson and Matthias receive and complete the enrollment forms. They mail the forms back to Extreme Skiing along with the payment price. These are received by the company one week before the trip.

Allyson and Matthias go to the designated hotel the day before the trip. As they and the other eight participants assemble in the hotel lobby, the trip operators hand out forms entitled "Standard Release and Waiver of Liability" and ask each participant to sign one. The form states that Extreme Skiing is not responsible for any losses or damages suffered by the participants for any reason, including negligence on the part of the company.

Allyson and Matthias are reluctant to sign the form but are told that unless they do so they will not be allowed to go on the trip. Finally they sign the form. The next day, all the participants are taken by helicopter to the ski slope.

During the course of the ski trip, there is an avalanche and Allyson suffers a broken leg as a result. Matthias also loses all of his ski equipment. An investigation reveals that there had been an avalanche warning about the area into which the participants were flown, and that Extreme Skiing ought to have been aware of this warning.

What contract issues arise in this fact situation?

2. Willie the electrician receives a telephone call late at night from Colin. Colin explains that he has just come home and his house has no power. Colin insists that Willie come over immediately because it is the middle of winter and he is without heat. Willie explains that he charges extra for emergency calls, but no actual price is ever discussed over the phone. Willie arrives at Colin's house. He finds that the house has no power because Colin tripped the main circuit breaker by plugging in too many appliances. Willie simply turns the main circuit breaker back on and leaves. He sends a bill to Colin for $400. Is Colin obliged to pay this amount? Explain.

3. Sharri places an advertisement in the paper offering to sell her piano for $4,000. Aaron writes to Sharri in response to the advertisement and offers to buy her piano for $3,000. Sharri receives Aaron's offer on January 3 and telephones him to ask if he will consider increasing his offer. Aaron tells her he will think about it. Mary writes to Sharri, offering to buy her piano for $3,200. Sharri receives the letter on January 5. She writes to Mary the same day and tells her she will sell the piano for $3,500. Mary receives the letter on January 7, and writes back the same day advising Sharri that she accepts the offer to buy the piano for $3,500. Unfortunately, the letter is lost in the mail, and Sharri never receives it. Aaron writes to Sharri on January 5 stating that he will pay her $4,000 for her piano by paying her $3,000 now and $1,000 in one month. Sharri receives Aaron's letter on January 8 and telephones Aaron the same day to confirm that the payment terms are acceptable. Sharri then receives a telephone call from Mary on January 9 in which she learns of Mary's acceptance by letter dated January 7. Sharri then tells Mary she now wants $4,000 for the piano. Is Sharri bound to sell her piano to either Mary or Aaron? Why or why not?

4. Sara needs her car repaired before she leaves for a business trip on December 15. She takes it to Speedy Repair, where she agrees to pay $500, and they agree to have her car ready for December 14. On December 12, Speedy Repair telephones Sara to tell her that the repairs are behind schedule and they do not think they can have the car ready by December 14 as promised. Sara is frantic and offers them an additional $500 to have the car ready for December 14. Speedy Repair agrees and offers to throw in a car wash and wax "for good business relations." Speedy Repair's mechanics work overtime and the car is ready by December 14, as well as being shiny and clean. Sara then refuses to pay the extra $500. Is Speedy Repair entitled to the additional $500? Explain.

5. Upon his death, Phillippe left his entire fortune in trust to his daughter, Danielle. Because she was a child when he died, Elizabeth was appointed Danielle's guardian. When Danielle turns 21, she is entitled to her inheritance. However, under the terms of the trust, Danielle cannot access the trust moneys until then. Elizabeth spends a great deal of money on Danielle's education, sending her to expensive private schools and to university. Elizabeth incurs personal debt as a result of Danielle's educational costs. When Danielle turns 21, she gets her inheritance and promises to repay Elizabeth for the money Elizabeth spent on her education. Danielle fails to repay Elizabeth. Can Elizabeth enforce Danielle's promise? Why or why not?

6. Viktor owns a movie theatre that shows unusual and little-known movies. He wants to generate publicity to attract audiences to a movie he is showing that is particularly violent and frightening. He enters into an contract with Louise whereby Louise will come to his theatre and pretend to faint during the movie. She is then to sue him, claiming damages for nervous shock and stress. Viktor agrees to pay her expenses for the lawsuit and an additional $5,000. Louise fulfills her part of the contract. The lawsuit is well publicized, and even though Louise loses her lawsuit, people flocked to see the movie in droves. Viktor never pays Louise the $5,000. Can she enforce this contract? Explain.

7. Diego owns an automobile repair business. He also owns the land on which the business operates. Dorion has worked for Diego as a mechanic. Diego is interested in retiring and suggests that Dorion buy the business as an ongoing operation. Diego offers to sell for $100,000. Dorion says he doesn't have that kind of money and doesn't have the kind of credit that would allow him to get a loan. Diego says that is no problem. If Dorion can raise $25,000, Diego will give him a mortgage on the garage property for $75,000 at a very low rate of interest. Dorion agrees to this proposal provided, he says, that he can raise the $25,000 downpayment. Diego says that's fine. The agreement is entirely oral. Dorion raises the $25,000 and pays it to Diego. Before he can make the first mortgage payment, Diego dies. Diego's executors find out about these arrangements but refuse to honour them, claiming there was no enforceable contract. Assess the likelihood that the executors will be able to resist Dorion's claim.

8. Maupassant Developments obtained planning permission to build a subdivision in Boresville in 1990. As part of the permission process, Maupassant promised to set aside some of the land as parkland or to pay green space fees to the municipality. This document was required by provincial legislation to be by way of a formal deed. In 2000, the municipality of Boresville discovers that Maupassant has neither set aside parkland nor paid the green space fees. The typed document was sealed by the municipality with its municipal seal. Maupassant's name was typed in, but there is no evidence that a seal was ever applied or that he signed it. What is the likelihood of the municipality being able to enforce this agreement?

CHAPTER 3

Protecting Weaker Parties

From the 17th century on, the development of modern contract law was driven by the needs of an expanding trading, manufacturing, and banking economy. These needs included a legal system that would enforce commercial agreements without interfering with the bargaining process that led to them. The common law met these needs by interpreting commercial agreements and then enforcing them. The courts rarely inquired into the process that led to forming a contract; they assumed that in commercial agreements, businesspeople were roughly equal in bargaining power and could look after themselves. If a party made a bad bargain because he or she was not as sharp or clever as the other party, that was his or her misfortune.

While this "hands-off" approach is the one usually taken in contract law, the courts do sometimes intervene where parties are clearly unable to protect themselves in the bargaining process. Sometimes this is because one party lacks the intellectual capacity to protect herself or himself, the other party acts dishonestly during the bargaining process or takes advantage of a position of trust, or the other party has expert knowledge of the subject matter of the contract that the weaker party cannot have and takes unfair advantage of that knowledge. This chapter explores some of the circumstances in which the courts protect weaker parties where the capacity of a party to enter into a contract is at issue.

LEGAL CAPACITY TO CONTRACT

Not everyone is legally entitled to enter into contracts. Some persons, by their status, are presumed not to have the ability to enter into contracts or have limited rights to contract. The purpose here is to protect the weaker party from the stronger and more able party. This class of persons who lack or have limited capacity to contract include **minors** and **persons under mental disability**.

There are other situations where the capacity of a party to contract is based on the nature of the contracting entity or on public interest or public policy issues, and not on the strength or weakness of the parties' bargaining power. Enemy aliens, for policy reasons, do not have the capacity to contract, and their contracts in Canada are void and unenforceable by them unless they hold a licence from the Crown. Corporations, as artificial entities, may enter into contracts but do not have the capacity to enter into ones that deal with subject matter that is entirely outside the corporate purposes and objects set out in the company's articles of

minor
at common law, an individual under the age of 21; minority status has also been defined by statute law, lowering the age of majority to 18 or 19 in most provinces

persons under mental disability
a general term that includes persons who are delusional and insane so as to be a danger to themselves and others, and those who, while not insane and dangerous, lack the ability to manage their own affairs

incorporation or corporate charter, or where the corporation has been created by statute, outside the powers granted by the statute. Trade unions, which can act like corporations for some purposes and are certified under labour legislation, cannot usually sue or be sued as legal entities absent enabling legislation. Bankrupts may not enter into any contract except for necessaries until they are discharged from bankruptcy. The discharge from bankruptcy relieves the bankrupt of personal liability under contracts entered into before the bankruptcy occurred, except where the bankrupt engaged in fraud or breach of trust.

MINORS

The general rule is that minors may not enter into contracts. At common law, a minor is an individual who is under 21 years of age. The common law definition of age has been replaced by statutory definitions in most provinces, where, as in Ontario, the age of majority is now 18 for the purposes of entering into contracts.[1] The reason for this rule is that minors are presumed to be naive, inexperienced, and easily taken advantage of, so some protection is required.

Contract Rights and Obligations Generally

While the general rule is that minors may not enter into contracts, contracts for necessaries of life made by a minor are enforceable, but other contracts are not if the minor repudiates them. The reason for enforcing contracts for necessaries is that some minors may have to meet some of their basic needs themselves; if a seller could not enforce a contract against a minor in these circumstances, the seller might choose not to sell at all rather than risk not being able to collect the debt. Because this might leave a minor in a position of not being able to purchase food or shelter, these contracts are enforceable and minors may not repudiate them. Because minors may be taken advantage of, the law creates various opportunities for them to treat contracts for non-necessaries that provide some benefit as **voidable** by allowing minors to repudiate them, in some cases even after the age of majority has been reached. If the contract is prejudicial or of no benefit, it may be treated by the courts as **void *ab initio***. This means the court will treat the contract as invalid from the beginning and of no force or effect. No rights can ever arise under such a contract, and the minor gets no choice as to whether it is enforceable against him or her or not.

If the contract is voidable, the minor may enforce it if she or he chooses, or repudiate it and recover money paid under it, or the minor may use it as a defence to enforcement by the other party. However, until the minor does what is required to treat the contract as voidable, unless the contract is void *ab initio*, it is presumed to be valid and enforceable.

voidable contract
a contract that may be avoided or declared void at the option of one party to the contract; once it is declared invalid no further rights can be obtained under it, but benefits obtained before the declaration are not forfeit

void *ab initio*
a contract that is invalid from the beginning; no rights can arise under it

---

1   In some provinces the age of majority is 19. There are also other statutes that grant rights on the basis of age. For example, an individual in Ontario can enter into contracts as someone of full age and capacity at 18 but cannot buy alcoholic beverages until the age of 19. See *Age of Majority and Accountability Act*, RSO 1990, c. A.7.

Enforceable Contracts: Purchases of Necessaries

As in most provinces, the Ontario *Sale of Goods Act*[2] provides that a minor is liable to pay a reasonable price for goods that are necessaries that have been sold and delivered to the minor. It follows from this that a minor may be able to repudiate a contract for the sale of goods if it is an **executory contract**. An executory contract is one where the obligations are performed after the contract is made. Thus a minor may repudiate a contract for the sale of necessary goods between the time the minor agreed to purchase the goods but before they are delivered. If the contract is partly performed—for example, goods are delivered but not yet paid for—the minor is bound. If the minor borrows money to purchase necessaries and the money is used for that purpose, then the debt is enforceable against the minor. The Act also describes necessaries as goods "suitable to the conditions in life of the minor" and as goods actually required when ordered. This means that if the goods are necessaries and they are ordered and delivered when the minor is amply supplied with such goods, then the minor may be able to repudiate the contract on the grounds that they were not actually required when ordered.

As to what goods are actually necessaries "suitable to the conditions in life of the minor," the case law indicates that the context determines what is suitable given the minor's "conditions in life" or social and economic class. The necessaries for a minor from a wealthy family may be luxuries for a minor from a less wealthy family. How goods are used may also determine whether they are necessaries. If a minor buys clothes so that he or she will be "cool," they may be seen as non-necessaries, but if the minor buys clothes, even expensive ones, to be properly dressed at work, they may be classed as necessaries because they are used in connection with earning a living. Even where a contract is binding because it is for necessaries, the law will not make the minor pay more than a reasonable price. Thus, a merchant suing a minor on a contract for necessaries may find recovery of the purchase price limited to what the court thinks is a reasonable price.

It is also clear that contracts for necessary services are binding on a minor. Medical and dental services and, in some cases, contracts for training for employment have been classed as necessaries.[3] An executory contract for necessary services, unlike the situation for the sale of goods, is probably not voidable by the minor.[4]

executory contract
a contract between a buyer and seller in which full payment is not made at the time of the contract; a contract to buy on credit

▩ EXAMPLES OF CONTRACTS FOR NECESSARIES

- Tamar, age 17, moves into a dormitory at school because she is far from home. She signs a rental contract. She also decides to rent a TV. Both of these are executory contracts. A month later, Tamar decides to move back home and tries to repudiate both contracts. She may be held to the dorm rental contract, since this was for necessary services. The TV is arguably

---

2 RSO 1990, c. S.1.

3 G.H.L. Fridman, *The Law of Contract in Canada*, 3d ed. (Scarborough, ON: Carswell, 1994), 144. The scheme for analyzing the enforceability of contracts on minors is taken from Fridman because it is a rational and sensible analytic scheme.

4 Ibid.

not a necessary; she may be able to avoid this contract by pleading her minority status and get her money back, and be relieved of future rental charges. She will also have to return the TV.

- Stanislaus, age 16, orders a new winter coat, although he already has three others. Before the coat is delivered, he changes his mind and repudiates the contract. The coat is a necessary item, but it has not been delivered at the time of repudiation, so he can repudiate the agreement. Stanislaus could also argue that the coat is not a necessary because he has three others and is amply supplied with winter coats.

Enforceable Contracts: Employment

Generally, minors who enter into employment contracts, formal or informal, are bound by their terms unless the terms are not beneficial to the minor. Presumably, minors accept employment to meet their needs, so an employment contract could be viewed as a contract for necessaries. However, just as an article of clothing can be a luxury or a necessity, depending on what it is for, so can a job be classed that way. A minor who works because her or his needs would not be met otherwise is in a different position from a minor who works to acquire spending money for luxuries. However, the case law does not focus on whether work is a necessity; rather, it accepts a service contract as enforceable by both parties unless the contract does not benefit the minor. "Benefit" has been held by the courts to include an appropriate salary, but also may include consideration of whether there was a general advantage for the minor in acquiring skills and satisfying aims or desires, and whether the minor was taken advantage of. It has also been suggested that the test of "benefit" may be whether a "prudent and informed parent" would have approved this contract for his or her minor child.[5]

EXAMPLE OF MINOR EMPLOYMENT CONTRACTS

Arturo, age 16, is hired to work in a factory. He is paid less than the minimum wage and has to sign a form that he will not make a workers' compensation claim if he is injured on the job. He quits without notice and repudiates the contract. The employer will have difficulty enforcing the contract since these conditions appear to be detrimental to Arturo, and a prudent and informed parent would not likely permit a child to work under these conditions.

Contracts for Non-necessaries

Where a minor has entered into a contract for non-necessaries, the contract is always enforceable by the minor, but the minor may be able to avoid enforcement of the contract against him or her.

If the contract is not fully executed, as was the case for contracts for necessaries, the minor may avoid the contract. If the minor as a buyer repudiates the contract, he or she must return the goods, whatever state they are in. He or she will

---

5 See *Toronto Marlboro Major Junior "A" Hockey Club v. Tonelli* (1979), 23 OR (2d) 193 (CA), especially the dissent of Zuber JA.

not be liable for the wear and tear to the goods but may be liable for damage to them that goes beyond reasonable wear and tear. If the minor is the seller, he or she must be able to return the money if the minor wishes to repudiate and have the goods returned to him or her.

If the contract has been fully executed so that goods and money have changed hands, the contract cannot be set aside. However, the court may order a refund to the minor of the difference between the price actually paid and a court-determined price, as would be the case for necessaries.

If the contract is ongoing, as, for example, if the minor has joined a monthly CD or book club, she or he can repudiate any future liability, but she or he cannot recover money spent for benefits already received.

If the creditor has loaned money for non-necessaries to a minor, the creditor cannot recover the debt if the minor chooses not to pay.

Effect of Reaching the Age of Majority on Minors' Contracts

Where a contract is for necessaries, the liability continues. However, if the contract is for non-necessaries and has not been repudiated by the minor, the contract has to be classified as to type. For this purpose there are two types.

1. *Contracts that are valid unless the minor repudiates them.* These are contracts that confer ongoing or continuous benefits that are made while an individual is a minor, and which carry on after the age of majority has been reached. The contract will continue to bind the individual unless he or she, before or shortly after reaching the age of majority, does something that constitutes repudiation of the agreement.

2. *Contracts that are invalid unless ratified by the minor.* These are contracts that confer a one-time benefit, for example, where goods are ordered while the individual is a minor but are not to be delivered to complete contract performance until the minor has reached the age of majority. These contracts must be ratified in writing by the minor during his or her minority or shortly thereafter. If the minor does not ratify the contract, the seller must return the deposit.

Voidable Ongoing Benefit Contracts for Non-necessaries: Valid Unless Repudiated

Where a minor acquires by contract permanent property that carries some obligations for the minor, the contract is presumed to be valid and enforceable unless the minor repudiates it during her or his minority or shortly after reaching the age of majority. "Shortly after" appears to be measured in weeks or months rather than years.[6] The classes of contracts affected are contracts that transfer shares to a minor, partnership agreements, and marriage contracts. If

---

6   *Foley v. Canada Permanent Loan and Savings Society* (1883), 4 OR 38; *Whalls v. Learn* (1888), 15 OR 481 (CA).

the minor, after reaching the age of majority, acts to accept the contract, she or he cannot repudiate it.[7] If she or he does repudiate it, no special form of repudiation is required.[8] It can be written, oral, or inferred from an act. Repudiation is an all-or-nothing affair: the minor cannot repudiate the non-beneficial parts of the contract and hold the other party to the rest of the agreement.[9]

■ EXAMPLE OF CONTRACT THAT IS VALID UNTIL REPUDIATED

Luc bought 80 shares in a private company when he was a minor. He paid $8,000, and a further $2,000 is due when he is 22 years old. Two days after reaching the age of majority, Luc considers repudiating the contract. However, a dividend cheque arrives and he cashes it. Luc would be able to repudiate this contract since it is in a contract category—share transfers—that allows for repudiation while he is a minor or shortly thereafter; two days is certainly "shortly thereafter." However, before he repudiates the contract he engages in an act that affirms his acceptance of the contract by cashing the dividend cheque. As a result, Luc may now be barred from repudiating the contract.

CONSEQUENCES OF REPUDIATION

- Contracts are enforceable and effective until they are repudiated.

- The minor, on repudiating the contract, is relieved of future obligations and accrued but undischarged obligations.[10]

- Money paid by the minor before repudiation may not be recoverable if the adult party performed his or her obligations under the contract before repudiation by the minor.[11]

- The minor may also recover property such as goods after repudiation if the goods have not been consumed and can be restored to the minor.

Voidable One-Time Benefit Contracts for Non-necessaries: Void Unless Ratified

All other contracts for non-necessaries made by a minor must be ratified when the minor reaches the age of majority or they cease to be valid and enforceable against the minor who has now reached the age of majority. Such contracts, being for non-necessaries, also could have been repudiated by the minor before reaching the age of majority, but were presumed valid unless challenged. Their validity ceases on the age of majority being reached unless they are ratified. In Canada, the ratification must be in writing and signed by the minor.

---

7   *Re Prudential Life Co; Re Paterson*, [1918] 1 WWR 105 (Man. KB).

8   *Butterfield v. Sibbit and Nipissing Elec. Supply Co.* (1950), 4 DLR 302 (Ont. HC).

9   *Henderson v. Minneapolis Steel & Machinery Co.* (1931), 1 DLR 570 (Alta. SC).

10   *Re Central Bank and Hogg* (1890), 19 OR 7 (Ch.).

11   *Steinberg v. Scala (Leeds) Ltd.*, [1923] 2 Ch. D. 452 (CA).

■ EXAMPLE OF CONTRACT THAT MUST BE RATIFIED TO BE VALID

Michelle, age 17, decides to buy a sailboat. She pays $10,000 as a first installment and will pay the balance in June of next year. She will be 18 in April of next year. Michelle decides she doesn't want the sailboat and refuses to ratify the contract when she turns 18. Because she must ratify the contract and the sailboat is not a necessary, the contract ceases to be enforceable by the seller and is now void. Michelle is entitled to get her money back because the seller can be restored to his or her previous position.

CONSEQUENCES OF INVALIDATION FROM FAILURE TO RATIFY

- Prior to validation, the minor can enforce the contract against the adult, but not vice versa.

- A third party cannot rely on the invalidity of a contract to escape liability. For example, an adult who agrees to indemnify another for a minor's debt is still bound even if the minor fails to validate the contract by ratifying it.[12]

- If the minor does not ratify, she or he is not liable for future accrued liabilities under the contract.

- If the minor does not ratify, money can be recovered provided the minor can restore the adult to his or her pre-contract position. If the minor has paid in part and then refuses to ratify, she or he must return the goods and may lose the deposit, although she or he may recover other moneys paid.[13]

Void Contracts

In Canada, some minors' contracts have been held to be void *ab initio*. Some cases have held that a contract that is not beneficial is void without the minor having to do anything. But the better view is that to fall into the void *ab initio* category, a contract would have to be more than "not beneficial"—it would have to be clearly prejudicial or harmful, which is a more stringent requirement for holding a contract to be void.[14]

■ EXAMPLE OF CONTRACT VOID AB INITIO

Henry is a wealthy minor. He is prevailed upon by his cousin Anna to lend her a large sum of money at a very low rate of interest. Anna has been bankrupt three times and is clearly a poor credit risk. Because the interest is unreasonably low and the risk of loss of the money is very high, the contract would be prejudicial to Henry, and it is arguably void *ab initio*.

---

12 *McBride v. Appleton*, [1946] OR 17 (CA). An adult who gives a guarantee, however, is not bound, since the guarantee can apply only to a valid contract. Once the contract has been voided it is gone, and there is nothing to guarantee.

13 Fridman, supra footnote 3, at 153.

14 *Beam v. Beatty* (1902), 3 OLR 345 (HC).

CONSEQUENCE FOR VOID CONTRACTS

The minor is entitled, not being bound, to have all of her or his money or property returned, and the adult need not be restored to her or his pre-contract position.

Alternative Remedies for Void or Void Ab Initio Contracts

If a minor is immune from liability in contract because the contract is void, the adult cannot make an end run around contractual immunity by suing the minor in tort. This is certainly true for the tort of negligence, but wilful destruction of the subject matter of the contract by the minor may give rise to an action for an intentional tort such as trespass to goods.[15]

If the minor misrepresents his or her age, claiming to have reached the age of majority, at common law an action for the tort of fraudulent misrepresentation will not be permitted.[16] However, the adult may invoke equitable remedies under which the minor must restore goods purchased in a contract where the minor fraudulently misrepresented his or her age.

A practical approach for an adult who contracts with a minor is to find another adult to be jointly liable with the minor for the contractual liability. It is not a good idea to have an adult guarantee the obligation as a secondary debtor, because if the minor's contract is made void, the liability on the guarantee is also void, although an agreement by an adult to indemnify a person who contracts with the minor may survive if the minor contract is found to be void.[17]

LAW AFFECTING MINORS IN BRITISH COLUMBIA

The law affecting minors in British Columbia is somewhat different from the law in other common law provinces and Quebec. It is summarized as follows:

> A minor's contract is unenforceable against the minor unless one of these conditions is met:
>
> - the contract is enforceable under some statute,
>
> - the minor validates the contract on attaining the age of majority,
>
> - the minor wholly or partly performs the contract shortly after attaining the age of majority, or
>
> - it is not repudiated by the minor within a year of having attained the age of majority.
>
> Where a contract is invalid, the court has broad discretion to provide remedies and may discharge parties from contractual obligations, order restitution or compensation.[18]

---

15 *Burnard v. Haggis* (1863), 143 ER 360.

16 *Stocks v. Wilson*, [1913] 2 KB 235.

17 Fridman, supra footnote 3, at 155-57.

18 Ibid., at 157-58.

CAPACITY OF DRUNKARDS AND PERSONS UNDER MENTAL DISABILITY TO CONTRACT

Drunkenness

The law will intervene in some circumstances where someone who is intoxicated enters into an agreement. Intoxication alone is not sufficient, but it can be a defence to enforcement by the sober party, and the intoxicated party may void the contract on the basis of his or her own intoxication in the following circumstances:

- The intoxicated party, because of the intoxication, did not know what he or she was doing.

- The sober party was aware of the intoxicated state of the other party.

- Upon becoming sober, the intoxicated party moved promptly to repudiate the contract.[19]

The basis for this approach is not that one party is drunk but that the other party might defraud the drunkard. Thus, even where the sober party is not aware of the intoxicated state of the other party, if there is evidence of intoxication so that it may be presumed, the unfairness or one-sidedness of a contract might result in its being voided.[20] This view moves the law toward a position that an unconscionable agreement permits the court to presume that the sober party had knowledge of the intoxication of the other party once there is evidence of intoxication.

How intoxicated does a party have to be to avoid a contract? Merely being in an excited state with one's judgment somewhat impaired may not be sufficient to allow a contract to be voided. If the intoxicated party knew what the basics of the contract were and what he or she was being asked to do, that may not be enough to allow for repudiation.[21] The cases do not indicate that intoxication from substances other than alcohol would give rise to a right to repudiate a contract. Perhaps because intoxication from sources other than alcohol are often illegal, litigants on this issue have been reluctant to come forward.

■ EXAMPLE OF REPUDIATION FOR DRUNKENNESS

Melissa has had so much to drink that she cannot stand, her words are slurred, and her conversation makes little sense. Semareh has an old sofa she would like to get rid of. She persuades Melissa to buy the sofa for a price that is almost the price of a new sofa. Melissa sobers up the next morning, realizes what she has done, and calls Semareh to tell her the deal is off. Melissa was clearly very drunk; it would have been hard for Semareh to be unaware of that. It is doubtful that Melissa was coherent enough to know what she was doing when she bought the sofa. Melissa repudiates at the first reasonable opportunity once she sobers up. She will probably succeed in repudiating the contract.

---

19 *Gore v. Gibson* (1845), 153 ER 260.

20 *Black v. Wilcox* (1977), 70 DLR (3d) 192 (Ont. CA).

21 *Watmough v. Cap's Const. Ltd.*, [1977] 1 WWR 398 (Alta. Dist. Ct.).

Mental Disability

Some types of mental disability may be sufficient to allow a person to repudiate a contract in certain circumstances. Generally, the law is concerned with the lack of capacity arising from mental disability. For example, people who have schizophrenia may have delusions, but if they can manage their own daily and business affairs and look after their personal finances, they may have the capacity to enter into contracts. The mentally disabled persons that the law protects are those who are unable to manage their own affairs or are unable to appreciate the nature and consequences of their actions.

The law deals in the followings ways with those who are unable to manage their affairs:

- Provincial legislation provides that a person can be declared to be unable to manage his or her affairs. If there has been such a judicial finding, contracts made after the judicial finding are void on the grounds that there is a lack of capacity to consent to the provisions of a contract.[22] Contracts made prior to the finding may be voidable, as noted below.

- If a person lacks capacity because she or he is unable to handle her or his affairs, but there has been no judicial finding, the contracts made are voidable at the option of the person who is mentally disabled. If the contracts are not repudiated, they are presumed to be enforceable.[23]

As is the case with drunkenness, for repudiation to succeed where no judicial finding of incapacity has been made, the other party must know of the mental disability. There need not be actual knowledge if there is wilful disregard of the surrounding circumstances from which the mental state could be presumed. Thus, if the non-disabled party suspects from the other's conduct that the other might lack capacity due to mental disability, that may be sufficient knowledge.[24]

The fairness of the contract is also important because there must be evidence that the contract is fair to the mentally disabled party. Some cases go on to require that the contract must be unconscionable, although that view has been rejected in Canada and England.[25] It follows that if the contract is fair, or the other party is unaware of a mental disability that affects capacity, then the contract is enforceable and not voidable by the person who is mentally disabled.

As with minors, persons under a mental disability are liable to pay a reasonable price for necessaries, and contracts for necessaries cannot be repudiated.

▨ EXAMPLES OF MENTAL DISABILITY AS A GROUND FOR AVOIDING A CONTRACT

- François has been diagnosed with Alzheimer's disease and has been found by a court to be incompetent to handle his own business affairs. After this finding, François contracts to have aluminum siding installed on

22 *Rourke v. Halford* (1916), 37 OLR 92 (CA).

23 *Fykes v. Chisholm* (1911), 3 OWN 21 (HC).

24 *Grant v. Imperial Trust Co.* (1934), 3 DLR 660 (SCC).

25 *Archer v. Cutler*, [1980] 1 NZLR 386.

his house. His brother finds out and tells the contractor. The contractor has no right to proceed, because a contract made by a person found by a court to be incompetent is void *ab initio*.

- François's brother also discovers that François had contracted to have aluminum siding installed by another contractor two weeks before being found incompetent by the court. François has memory problems that are obvious to a casual observer, but the terms of the contract are reasonable. Because the contractor has not taken advantage of François, this contract may be difficult to repudiate. However, if there is already new or adequate aluminum siding on the house, François (through his brother) may be able to argue that the contract is unfair because it is unnecessary, and that, on the whole, the contract is inequitable.

SUMMARY

While the courts normally do not interfere with the rights of parties to contract, they will in some circumstances intervene to protect a weaker party from a stronger one where it is likely that one side will extract an unfair advantage from the other.

Some parties to a contract are protected on the basis of their status. Protective rules apply to minors, drunkards, and persons under a mental disability. Minors can be held to contracts for necessaries and to beneficial employment contracts. But if the contract is for non-necessaries, these may not be enforced against minors in most instances. If the minor accepts the contract and does not repudiate during his or her minority, the minor may be able to repudiate the contract on reaching the age of majority. In some cases, the contract must be positively ratified or affirmed by the minor on reaching the age of majority. A minor's contract that is prejudicial or harmful may be void *ab initio*.

In the case of drunkards, if intoxication results in the drunkard not knowing what he or she was doing, but the other party knew it, and on becoming sober, the intoxicated party moves to repudiate the contract, a court may well set the contract aside because of diminished capacity.

In the case of those under a mental disability, a person found by a court to lack mental capacity is unable to enter into valid contracts except for necessaries; contracts for non-necessaries are void. When the person suffers from a mental disability but has not been so declared by a court, and if the other party to the contract knew or ought to have known of the disability, the mentally disabled party may be able to avoid the contract.

KEY TERMS

executory contract

minor

person under mental disability

void *ab initio*

voidable contract

REVIEW QUESTIONS

1. Why do courts usually take a "hands-off" approach when it comes to examining the bargaining process?

2. What does the phrase "inequality of bargaining power" mean?

3. In what circumstances must minors honour their contractual obligations? In what circumstances can they escape their contractual obligations?

4. If a contract is detrimental to a minor, is the contract void *ab initio* or voidable? What is the difference between a contract that is void *ab initio* and one that is voidable?

5. If a minor orders goods that are necessaries, can she or he back out of the deal if the goods have been delivered? Does it matter if the minor already has three of what was ordered? Explain.

6. Suppose the contract made by a minor is binding. Must the minor pay the price set by the seller? Why or why not?

7. In what circumstances can a minor's contract be repudiated if it is not for necessaries and not an employment contract?

8. In what circumstances must a minor's contract that is not for necessaries and not an employment contract be validated by the minor?

9. What are the consequences of repudiating a minor's contract?

10. What are the consequences of invalidating a minor's contract by failing to ratify it?

11. What are the consequences for the parties if a minor's contract is void *ab initio*?

12. What are the consequences if a minor misrepresents his or her age when entering into a contract and presents himself or herself as having reached the age of majority?

13. In what circumstances can a drunkard avoid a contract?

14. Describe the way the law treats contracts of persons under a mental disability.

DISCUSSION QUESTIONS

1. Greta is 17 and lives with her mother, who does not earn much money. Greta needs to work part time to contribute to the family income while going to school. She gets a job in an office as a receptionist. Because she has few clothes suitable for business purposes, she buys several suits to wear to work. She gets a good price and buys them on sale. After bringing them home, Greta decides she wants to return some of them. The seller says they were sold on sale with no right of return. Can Greta argue her minority status and repudiate this agreement?

2. How can adults who wish to contract with minors protect themselves from repudiation of a contract by a minor? What will work? What will not work?

3. Compare and contrast the rights of drunkards and minors to repudiate contracts. How are their rights similar? How are they different? Do the differences in approach make sense to you? Why or why not?

CHAPTER 4

Contractual Defects

A contractual defect is a defect in one of the elements of a valid contract. In some cases, the contractual defect will render the contract void *ab initio*, and in other cases, will render the contract voidable. This chapter discusses misrepresentation, duress, undue influence, unconscionability, and mistake—factors that can affect the parties' intention to create a legal contract.

MISREPRESENTATION

Overview

A misrepresentation is a false statement that induces someone to enter into a contract. It is generally part of the bargaining process. For example, if you are considering ordering a carload of tomatoes and while you examine them you ask the seller, "Are these grade A tomatoes?" and the seller replies "Yes," then the "Yes" may be a statement made to induce you to enter into the contract. If you enter into the contract because of the answer, then the inducement is a **material inducement**. If the statement is false and the seller is not aware that it is false, it is an **innocent misrepresentation**. If the statement is false and the seller knows it is false, it is a **fraudulent misrepresentation**. If you are aware that the statement is a misrepresentation and enter into the contract anyway, or you are not influenced by the statement to enter into the agreement but enter into it for other reasons, then you may not **rescind** the contract because of the false statement because you were not induced by it to enter into the contract.

If the misrepresentation induces you to enter into the agreement but it is not related to a material fact that goes to the heart of the contract, then you may not rely on it to rescind the contract. For example, if the seller says, "Tomatoes are necessary for health," this general statement about tomatoes may be a misrepresentation (you can enjoy good health and never eat a tomato), but it is not the kind of statement that has anything directly to do with material concerns that affect buying a carload of tomatoes.

Usually failing to say anything does not give rise to rescission. If you ask the seller, "Are these grade A tomatoes?" and the seller says nothing and the tomatoes turn out not to be grade A, there is no misrepresentation, particularly if you could look at the tomatoes and decide for yourself. However, if the seller has special information that you could not reasonably know, his or her omission may amount to a misrepresentation. Some statutes, in particular those protecting consumers from sophisticated sellers, also permit rescission for an omission by a seller that amounts to a material misrepresentation.

material inducement
a statement made before a contract is made that influences a party to enter into the contract

innocent misrepresentation
a false statement made to induce a party to enter into a contract that the maker of the statement does not know is false

fraudulent misrepresentation
a false statement made to induce a party to enter into a contract that the maker knows is false

rescission
the cancellation, nullification, or revocation of a contract; the "unmaking" of a contract

A statement that is a misrepresentation must be a statement of fact and not an opinion. The words themselves do not always make it easy to decide whether a statement is a fact or statement of opinion. In our example, the seller's answer "Yes" to a question could be seen as a statement. However, if the seller had instead said, "I *think* these are grade A tomatoes," this would be his or her opinion and no more than that. The cases indicate that an opinion is not seen as sufficient to induce you to enter into a contract, because it lacks the certainty and emphasis of a statement. This may be an impractical and illogical distinction, because the opinion of a knowledgeable seller, though a misrepresentation, might very well induce you to enter into a contract.

A material misrepresentation does not make a contract void *ab initio*. It will make the contract voidable by the party who was misled by the misrepresentation (or material omission). Once the misrepresentation is discovered, the misled party should act as soon as possible to rescind the contract. In doing so, she or he must accept no further benefits under the contract, or she or he may be deemed to have affirmed the contract notwithstanding the misrepresentation, and by doing so waived the right of rescission.

A misrepresentation may not only induce you to enter into a contract, it may also become a term of the contract. For example, the seller may not only make a misrepresentation that the tomatoes are grade A, he or she may also make it a term of the contract by describing the tomatoes as being grade A. In this case, the contract is not subject to rescission for misrepresentation, but is subject to an action for breach of contract because the tomatoes described and promised to you do not meet the description in the contract itself.

Innocent Misrepresentation

This is the misrepresentation of a material fact that the person making it believes to be true, but which is discovered to be false after the contract has been made. If the innocent party can show that she or he was induced by the statement to enter into the contract and that the statement was material, she or he may ask for the equitable remedy of rescission. At common law, the injured party can obtain no remedy unless the untrue statement can be construed as a term of the contract or the untrue statement was made negligently. If it is a term of the contract, then the victim can sue for breach of what is a perfectly valid contract and obtain damages for whatever losses she or he sustained. If the false statement was negligently made, though the maker thought it was true, then while there is no contractual remedy at common law, the innocent party could sue the other party for negligent misrepresentation in tort,[1] in which case the maker of the statement would be liable for all the foreseeable damage actually sustained.

The common law, then, leaves the victim of a "pure" innocent misrepresentation without a remedy. But as is often the case when the common law has failed to provide needed remedies, equity provides relief. The victim of a pure misrepresentation may request the equitable remedy of rescission. Rescission does not yield damages for the victim's losses; however, it does revoke a voidable contract at the instance of the injured party and, as far as possible, restores the parties to their pre-

---

1   *Hedley Byrne and Co. Ltd. v. Heller and Partners Ltd.*, [1964] AC 465 (HL).

contract position. The injured party may get an indemnification for what she or he has paid on the contract and may have lost benefits restored, but if there are other consequential damages, even in equity these cannot be recovered. This means that of the three types of innocent misrepresentation, the pure type may lead to something less than full recovery of all of the losses causally connected to the contract. Consequently, it is important to classify the innocent misrepresentation further because of the different circumstances.

- If an innocent misrepresentation can be classified as a term of the contract, then this would give rise to an action for breach of the term of the contract.

- If an innocent misrepresentation is made negligently, then this would give rise to an action in tort for negligent misrepresentation.

- But if an innocent misrepresentation is classified as "pure," then this will give rise to revocation of the contract and some indemnification to restore the injured party as much as possible to his or her pre-contract position. This remedy is referred to as **restitution** or by the Latin term *restitutio in integrum*.

restitution
a remedy by which one seeks to rescind a contract; if granted, restitution restores the party, as far as possible, to a pre-contract position

There has been some question as to whether the victim can obtain more damages by suing in tort for negligent misrepresentation than by suing for breach of a term of the contract. In practical terms, there is probably little difference. It is clear that while a contract matter may give rise to a lawsuit, it does not have to be a contract suit if an action in tort is made out. The plaintiff may sue in both tort and contract.

For an innocent misrepresentation to be material, it must result in a substantial difference between what the party bargained for and what the party obtained from the contract.[2] This requirement has been narrowly interpreted. For example, if the victim bargained for land, and a misrepresentation was made that it was 5 hectares when it turned out to be 3 hectares, the victim may ask for rescission on the grounds that she or he was induced to enter into the agreement by the representation as to size. However, in one case, the court held that the victim bargained for land and he got land in the contract; the size was immaterial.[3] Rights of rescission have been further narrowed in Canada and England by cases that have had the effect of making it almost impossible to obtain rescission for innocent misrepresentation if the subject matter of the contract was real property, the transfer had been completed, and the contract had been fully executed. The reasons for protecting contracts for real property more than contracts for goods are not convincing, particularly since restitution is probably no more difficult with real property than with some goods or **intangible property**. A better approach would be to follow the English statutory solution and permit rescission on an executed contract where there has been an innocent misrepresentation unless restitution at or near the loss sustained is impossible, third parties acquired legitimate rights and would be harmed by rescission, or damages are available for negligent misrepresentation or for breach of a term of the contract.[4]

intangible property
personal property where the interest in it or its value rests in rights it confers rather than in its physical properties

---

2 *Alberta North West Lumber Co. v. Lewis*, [1917] 3 WWR 1007; *Kennedy v. Royal Mail Co. of Panama* (1867), LR 2 QB 580.

3 *Komariniski v. Marien*, [1979] 4 WWR 267.

4 G.H.L. Fridman, *The Law of Contract in Canada*, 3d ed. (Scarborough, ON: Carswell, 1994), 305-8.

■ EXAMPLES OF INNOCENT MISREPRESENTATION

- Eduardo wants to buy a vacant lot on which to build a warehouse. He asks Marlene, the seller, if the lot is zoned for a warehouse. Marlene asks the municipality and is told the land is zoned for a warehouse. She tells Eduardo this. Eduardo agrees to purchase the vacant land at an agreed price. After the contract is made but before the property is transferred to Eduardo, Marlene discovers that since she inquired, the city has changed the zoning to residential use only. She tells Eduardo, who states that he is rescinding the contract. In this case, Eduardo wanted to buy vacant land and he obtained it but the statement about the zoning was a material inducement considering what he wanted to do with the land. The statement probably is not a term of the contract, since the sale was for land, not for land zoned commercial. However, as he probably would not have bought the land if the zoning did not meet his needs, it is arguable that Marlene's statement is a "pure" misrepresentation (it is not a term and it was not made negligently, because she made inquiries). Because the contract is not fully executed (the land has not yet been transferred), the facts of the case come within the case law that allows rescission on land transfers if the contract is not fully executed.

- Assume the same facts as in the preceding example, but when asked whether the zoning is appropriate to Eduardo's purpose, Marlene says "Sure." She honestly thinks it is, but she does not check with the municipality to see if she is correct. Because Marlene may be negligent in not checking the zoning before answering the question, she may be held to have made a negligent misrepresentation on which Eduardo relied to his detriment.

- Eduardo said to Marlene, "I am looking to purchase a truck with a 10-ton capacity. I am prepared to buy your truck if it can carry 10 tons, but not otherwise." Here it could be argued that Eduardo is not just bargaining for a truck but for a truck with specific qualities, which could be seen to be a term of the agreement. In this case, Marlene's misrepresentation, because it leads to a breach of the term of the contract, gives rise to an action for breach of contract rather than an action for rescission.

Fraudulent Misrepresentation

A fraudulent misrepresentation is one in which an apparent statement of fact is made without any belief by the maker that it is true and with the intent that the person to whom it is made will act on it and be induced to enter into the contract.[5] The fact stated must be a positive misstatement of a past or present fact, although in some cases a representation of a future event may be seen as a fact about what is certain to happen rather than an opinion about what might happen. For example, you invest in a business because you are told that it will expand to all major Canadian cities within two years. The statement is known by the maker to be false, but because it is unqualified and certain in tone, it may be classed as a fraudulent misrepresentation of a fact rather than an opinion. Otherwise it could be seen as an opinion as to what is expected to happen in the future, which as mere opinion

---

5   Ibid., at 295.

could not be held to be an actionable misrepresentation. If a statement about the future is made and qualified by words such as "likely to happen," "fully expect," or "strongly anticipate," then it is likely, because of the qualifications, to be seen as a statement of opinion, not fact.[6]

If the statement of fact is one that the intended victim could check, the law normally expects the victim to look after his or her interests, and affords no remedy if she or he fails to do so. However, even where the victim could find out, if the statement is made fraudulently the law will step in, because eliminating fraud is more important than teaching contracting parties to be careful and alert.[7]

A fraudulent statement about the state of the law, as opposed to a statement of fact, however, cannot amount to a misrepresentation because everyone is presumed to know the law. In practical terms, this makes little sense, particularly where the maker of the statement is presumed to have some expert knowledge or experience so that a listener might reasonably rely on the statement.

The speaker must make the fraudulent statement with no belief in the truth. This means that the speaker knew the statement was untrue, or the speaker made the statement with reckless disregard as to whether it was true or not, but the speaker believed it to be untrue. If the speaker is reckless in making the statement but believed it to be true, it would not amount to a fraudulent statement.[8] It could of course give rise to negligent misrepresentation, for which damages are available.

For an action to succeed, the representation must be fraudulent, but it must also be made with the intent of having the intended victim act on it. Thus the statement must be material and must be made to induce the other party to enter into the contract. It must also be made or at least directed at, among others, the person who acts on it. If a knowingly false statement is made to X, who enters the contract, and X later sells to Y, who knew nothing of the statement, Y cannot sue for fraudulent misrepresentation because the statement was not directed at Y or intended by the speaker to be made to Y, and the statement did not induce Y to enter into the agreement.

If the statement must be directed to the victim, it must also influence the victim to enter into the contract. The statement cannot be material if the intended victim is not induced by it to enter into the contract. Reliance on the statement by the victim is something that must be shown. The statement does not have to be the only reason the victim enters the contract, but it does have to be an important reason.

If the victim is successful in showing that she or he was induced to enter into the agreement by a fraudulent misrepresentation, the following remedies may be available:

- Fraudulent misrepresentation is equivalent to the tort of deceit and thus gives rise to a claim in tort for damages.

- Fraudulent misrepresentation results in a contract induced by fraud that is voidable at the option of the victim. It is not, however, void *ab initio*. If

6   *Allen v. Allen* (1976), 15 Nfld. & PEIR 362 (Nfld. Dist. Ct.).

7   *Sager v. Manitoba Windmill Co.* (1913), 23 DLR 556 (SCC).

8   *Derry v. Peak* (1889), 14 App. Cas. 337 (HL).

rescission is granted, the court will attempt to restore the victim to his or her position before the contract was made. If this cannot be done, then the court will award damages. Damages for other losses not covered by rescission may also be available. If damages are awarded, they should put the victim back into the position he or she would have been in had the fraud not occurred. If the injured party wishes to rescind, he or she must not delay in making the claim and must not affirm the contract by accepting any benefits from it once he or she discovers the fraud.

■ EXAMPLE OF FRAUDULENT MISREPRESENTATION

Rory has founded a software company and is trying to sell shares to raise capital. His prospectus states that he has secured government support. He knows that in fact he has not done so, and has no idea whether he will be successful in getting it. Sonia, smelling a winner (she thinks), buys some shares. Later the government refuses to give Rory's company a cent. Sonia moves to rescind for fraudulent misrepresentation on the ground that she would not have invested if she had known the government would not support the company, and that Rory made a statement that was untrue at the time, so that he fraudulently misrepresented the situation. This gives Sonia a right to rescind the contract so that she can be restored to her pre-contract position as far as possible. In the alternative, she may sue him for the tort of deceit and claim damages for the fraudulent misrepresentation.

Misrepresentation by Omission

While silence usually cannot be interpreted as misrepresentation, in some circumstances a failure to disclose may amount to misrepresentation. If the failure to disclose has the effect of making previous statements or disclosures untrue and fraudulent, then it can give rise to an action for fraudulent misrepresentation. If the failure to disclose results in statements that are true but misleading, this does not result in a fraudulent misrepresentation unless there is a clear duty to inform.

The duty to inform is restricted to a range of contracts where "utmost good faith" is required between the parties (sometimes referred to by the Latin term as ***uberrimae fidei* contracts**). These contracts are characterized by a marked power imbalance between the parties, where one party is in the position of having to trust and rely on the other and has placed confidence and trust in the other. Many family agreements fall into this category, as do trust agreements where a trustee has ownership and control over property that she or he exercises for a beneficiary of that property. Other types of trust agreements include the lawyer–client relationship, doctor–patient relationship, partnership contracts, and corporation–corporate director contracts. Lastly, insurance contracts require full disclosure. An insurance company is absolutely dependent on the insured party disclosing all risks before the insurance rate is fixed. The insurance company has no way of knowing some of the risks unless the party who has the knowledge cooperates by providing information about these risks. For all of these "good faith" contracts there is a positive duty to disclose and not to remain silent. A knowing silence may amount to a fraudulent misrepresentation.

***uberrimae fidei* contracts** a class of contracts where full disclosure is required because one party must rely on the power and authority of another, who must behave with utmost good faith and not take advantage of the weaker party

■ EXAMPLE OF MISREPRESENTATION BY OMISSION

Sara is the trustee for her disabled sister Rachel and invests in property for the trust to earn income for Rachel. Sara decides to borrow money from the trust to invest in her own highly risky company. She fails to disclose this to Rachel. Later, Rachel finds out and rescinds the loan contract on the ground that Sara has, as trustee, a duty of the utmost good faith that requires Sara to disclose to Rachel that she is investing for her own benefit. Sara's omission, where the information is material and where Rachel relies generally on Sara to behave toward her with the utmost good faith, amounts to a misrepresentation that allows Rachel to rescind the contract.

DURESS

At common law, a party to a contract can ask that it be declared void or can defend against its enforcement on the ground that the party was induced to enter the contract by actual or threatened physical force or unlawful confinement directed against the party or his or her spouse, children, or near relatives.[9] Because **duress** can rest on threats made to immediate family, the contracting party need not be threatened, but the threat must be the reason that she or he enters the contract. Because the effect of threats is to negate real consent to enter the agreement, one can argue that if there is no consent there can be no contract so that the contract is void *ab initio*. However, the law in Canada and England treats duress like fraud by making the contract voidable.[10]

For duress to succeed, it is not always necessary for the person making the threat to be a party to the contract. If a third party threatens one of the contracting parties and the other contracting party knows of the threat and takes advantage of it, that is sufficient for a defence of duress to succeed.[11] However, since the contract is voidable, if there are grounds for a defence based on duress and the threatened party delays taking steps to void the contract or takes steps to affirm and accept the contract, the threatened party loses the right to rescind the agreement.

This doctrine of duress is very narrow and is based on tort and criminal law concepts that are older than the modern law of contract and have simply been carried over to contract law. However, the common law does expand and evolve, and courts have recognized that this narrow concept of duress may be inadequate for contract law situations. Consequently, the concept of duress has been expanded to include physical threats to property as well as to people, and also to include economic duress.[12] For example, in *North Ocean Shipping Co. v. Hyundai Construction Ltd.*, there was a contract to build a ship at a stated price. Due to currency devaluation, the price became worth less than it had been when the contract was made. The shipbuilder knew that the customer needed the ship to fulfill its own shipping contracts. The shipbuilder refused to complete the ship

duress
an unlawful threat or coercion used by one person to induce another to perform some act against his or her will

---

9 Fridman, supra footnote 4, at 314.

10 *Saxon v. Saxon*, [1976] 4 WWR 300 (BCCA); *Barton v. Armstrong*, [1975] 2 All ER 465 (PC).

11 *CIBC v. Beaudreau* (1982), 41 NBR (2d) 596 (QB).

12 Fridman, supra footnote 4, at 317-20; *North Ocean Shipping Co. v. Hyundai Construction Ltd.*, [1978] 3 All ER 1170 (QB); *Pao On v. Lau Yiu*, [1979] 3 All ER 65 (PC).

unless the customer paid more money to cover the losses from currency devaluation. In this situation, the court held that the knowledge of the customer's urgent need of the completed ship was used to pressure the customer into paying more, something it would not otherwise have done. However, no remedy was granted because the customer affirmed the contract by paying the money and accepting the ship when it was completed. The result of this expansion of the law of duress is that the courts now look not so much at the particular form duress takes but at whether

- there is commercial pressure that amounts to a coercion of the will, which negates contractual consent,

- there are alternative ways of avoiding the coercion, or

- the pressure exerted was legitimate.

This functional view of duress suggests that a variety of circumstances other than merely physical harm can give rise to the defence of duress. You should also be aware that duress in the form of threats may amount to criminal extortion, which opens up the possibility of criminal remedies as well as civil ones. In this context, however, the threat of civil proceedings to collect a debt is neither extortion nor duress provided there is a bona fide belief that there is a right to sue to collect the debt.

■ EXAMPLE OF DURESS

> Spiro has just been made an offer that he cannot refuse; Mariella has told him that if he doesn't lend her $10,000 at one-half percent interest, he might not live to attend next year's New Year's Eve party. Spiro lends her the money and then moves to rescind the contract on the grounds of duress, arguing that threats to his life caused him to enter into this disadvantageous contract.

UNDUE INFLUENCE

undue influence
persuasion, pressure, or influence short of actual force that overpowers a weaker party's judgment and free will and imposes the will of the stronger party

The common law of duress depended on a finding of physical duress to persons or property, although it has expanded to include economic duress and could well expand further. **Undue influence** developed under the law of equity to provide remedies for more subtle forms of oppressive behaviour. The doctrine can be applied in two types of contract situations: actual undue influence, which covers contracts, including gifts, where one party actually engages in conduct that results in applying moral or other undue pressure to obtain a desired contractual result; and presumed undue influence, which arises when the relationship between the parties raises a presumption of undue influence at or before the time the contract was made. In both situations the court is concerned with the same thing—the domination of one party by another so as to prevent the latter from making an independent decision. The difference between the two situations is in the onus of proof. In the case of actual undue influence, the party that is claiming undue influence must prove that the other party used undue influence to compel the first party to enter into the contract. In the case of presumed undue influence, once the relationship is shown to exist there is a presumption of undue influence. This reverses the evidentiary burden; the person alleged to have resorted to undue influence must prove that the transaction was free of its effects to escape liability.

The kinds of relationships that give rise to a presumption of undue influence include, not surprisingly, many of the relationships that give rise to the requirement of utmost good faith in contractual relations: family, solicitor–client, doctor–patient, guardian–ward, and trustee–beneficiary relationships. The Supreme Court of Canada has made it clear that the presumption is not restricted to existing categories but may extend to any other "special" relationships, such as **fiduciary** relationships, confidential relationships, or advisory relationships.[13] However, the reasoning behind this expansion is not clear. The recent cases have produced concurrent decisions with different reasons being given by different judges in the same case to explain the development of the concept of "special" relationships.[14] Where there is a "special" relationship, it is not necessary to show that the party affected by undue influence is also disadvantageously affected by the contract.

Where the presumption applies, the transaction is set aside unless the party benefiting from the contract can demonstrate that the party allegedly influenced had independent advice of some kind, often independent legal advice, so that the party allegedly influenced could be said to be entering into the contract with his or her eyes open. Independent legal advice, in particular, may be important, and it requires the adviser to do a proper and thorough job and not just go through the motions.

fiduciary
a relationship where one person is in a position of trust to another and has a duty to safeguard the other's interests ahead of his or her own interests

■ EXAMPLES OF UNDUE INFLUENCE

- Ian has befriended the elderly Enrique and does various things for Enrique, including running errands, doing chores, and generally being helpful. Enrique has become quite dependent on Ian both for help and for company. One day Ian announces that he needs money to repay a debt and unless Enrique can give him a temporary loan, Ian will have to move away to find other work. Enrique does not want to lose Ian's help and company so, against his better judgment, he lends him the money. Enrique then has misgivings and moves to rescind the loan, arguing that Ian used friendship and the dependent relationship to unduly pressure Enrique into lending him the money. If Enrique can demonstrate this, he may prove undue influence to a degree that is sufficient to void the loan agreement. It may also be a "special relationship" given Enrique's age, needs, and dependence on Ian, so undue influence would be presumed. In this case, Ian would have to rebut the presumption by showing that Enrique had independent legal advice.

- Assume the same fact situation, but suppose Enrique and Ian are father and son. Here, because the nature of the relationship falls into a category where undue influence is presumed, the burden would be on Ian to demonstrate that Enrique had independent advice sufficient to give Enrique a clear and objective view of what he was doing.

---

13 *Geffen v. Goodman Estate* (1991), 81 DLR (4th) 211. The English House of Lords has moved in the same direction: *Barclay's Bank plc v. O'Brien*, [1993] 4 All ER 417.

14 Fridman, supra footnote 4, at 323-25.

UNCONSCIONABILITY

The law of equity will relieve a party in some circumstances from the effects of unconscionable conduct by the other contracting party. The focus here is not on conduct that affects consent, as is the case for undue influence or duress. With an unconscionable transaction the focus is on the reasonableness of the contract itself and the way in which the party whose conduct is in question behaved during the bargaining process. This is very broad, and you should appreciate that not every "unfair" contract will result in a court declaring the transaction to be unconscionable when someone, through stupidity, recklessness, or foolishness, has made a bad bargain. Finding the balance between unconscionability and stupidity is not always easy, and the case law is not particularly helpful because the cases seem to turn on a judge's subjective view of particular facts. However, where an action based on undue influence or duress may fail because pressure on the victim did not interfere too much with consent by the victim, the contract may still be avoided because its terms are unconscionable or the behaviour of the other party was unconscionable. For example, where one party is illiterate or intellectually disadvantaged and the other party knows this and takes advantage by persuading the disadvantaged party that "this is a good deal" when in fact it is not, if the disadvantaged party is keen to close the deal, there may be no duress or undue influence. In fact, no pressure or coercion may have been necessary. The wrong is in one party knowing that there was a lack of bargaining power or ability by the other and taking advantage of that fact, leaving the victim with a grossly unfair and inequitable bargain.

Another approach to this issue has developed in England. In *Lloyd's Bank v. Bundy*,[15] a father placed a mortgage on his house in order to secure a loan for his son. The son was in financial difficulty, and the father was emotional, upset, and ready to do just about anything to help his son. The majority found that there had been undue influence by the bank regarding the father, its customer, who should have had but did not have independent legal advice before agreeing to what turned out to be a very bad bargain. However, Lord Denning arrived at the same result by a different route: he combined undue influence and other equitable doctrines to develop a ground for rescinding contracts on the basis of "inequality of bargaining power." This approach includes undue influence and possibly duress, where there is a lack of independent consent to the terms of the contract, as well as unconscionability, where the nature of the bargain and the state of mind of the victim in entering the contract are relevant. Where, in the circumstances, the bargain—because of its contents, the behaviour of the advantaged party, and the state of mind of the disadvantaged party—is grossly one-sided, that may be sufficient evidence of inequality of bargaining power to warrant court interference.

Whether the English "inequality of bargaining power" approach or the Canadian "unconscionability" approach is taken, the result may be the same—overturning immoral and inequitable bargains. What the case law has not developed so far is a methodology for identifying inequitable bargains that would cause the court to interfere with an individual's freedom to contract.

---

15 [1974] 3 All ER 757 (QB).

■ EXAMPLE OF UNCONSCIONABLE CONTRACTS

Derek, who has a hearing disability, thinks it would be cool to have a good stereo. He wears a hearing aid and reads lips. It is obvious to anyone talking to Derek that he is hearing impaired and that the better sound in a high-quality system would be useless to him. Derek walks into Sam's Stereo Shop and tells Sam that he wants a stereo system that is really cool. Sam notices that Derek is hearing impaired and realizes that the quality of a high-priced system would be useless to him, but he tells Derek he has a "good deal" on a cool system for $8,000. This is in fact an extremely high price. Derek eagerly puts his money down but later changes his mind and moves to rescind on the grounds that the transaction is unconscionable. Because Sam knew Derek could not derive any substantial benefit from a high-quality sound system, it may be shown that the bargain is such a poor one for Derek that it is unconscionable. The fact that the price is unduly high may be further evidence of unconscionability, but there is no evidence that Derek's disability affects his bargaining power on price—this may simply be a bad bargain and will not attract court interference. However, if the price was represented as a good price when Sam knew it was not, that may be a fraudulent misrepresentation, which would void the contract apart from the outcome on the unconscionability issue.

Unconscionability Legislation

Legislatures in common law jurisdictions have often passed legislation to protect certain classes of persons from unconscionable transactions where duress and undue influence would not necessarily offer protection, and where the application of the unconscionability principle is uncertain. This type of legislation usually tries to define unconscionability and then turns the matter over to the courts for adjudication. There are two types of such legislation in the Canadian provinces, discussed below.

UNCONSCIONABLE TRANSACTION ACTS

All provinces have legislation that permits a court to interfere with the terms of a loan where the contract is harsh and oppressive and the cost of the loan is excessive.[16] The legislation does not add significantly to the common law, except that it clearly brings loans within the reach of unconscionability doctrines. A loan is excessively expensive if it can be obtained elsewhere at a lesser rate, but this is not reliable as a test because the rate can be based on a variety of risk factors that make comparisons difficult or impossible. This is particularly so with high-risk loans, where interest rates are high, the pool of comparable lenders is small, and risk assessment is somewhat subjective. A very high interest rate will attract attention if there is an element of unfairness about the loan; for example, if the borrower is desperate and the lender knows it, a statutory remedy might be provided. By way of remedy, the court can reopen the loan and make the lender accept a fair amount, order the lender to repay any overcharges, or cancel or alter any security given by

---

16 See, for example, the *Unconscionable Transactions Relief Act*, RSO 1990, c. U.2.

the borrower to obtain the loan. This is different from the remedies available for duress, undue influence, and unconscionability, for which the usual remedies are rescission and damages.

UNFAIR BUSINESS PRACTICES

Alberta, British Columbia, Ontario, Newfoundland, and Prince Edward Island have all passed legislation that goes well beyond the common law in giving individuals remedies where a consumer transaction is unfair.[17] These acts permit consumers who have entered into contracts with business sellers on the basis of representations that are false, misleading, or deceptive to rescind those contracts and obtain damages. **Parol evidence** is admissible where at common law it would not be permitted. Most important, remedies of rescission and damages are available on proof of a misrepresentation in situations where the common law would have given no remedy. Punitive damages are also available. Sellers cannot escape the reach of this legislation: neither party can agree in a contract to exclude the operation of the act on the contract. In addition to private lawsuits to set aside contracts, an unfair practice may bring administrative proceedings before a regulatory board to ensure compliance by business sellers with the terms of the statute. These statutes are discussed in more detail in chapter 9, Consumer Protection.

> **parol evidence**
> if a contract is in writing and is clear, no other written or oral evidence is admissible to contradict, vary, or interpret the agreement

MISTAKE

Overview

Parties may negotiate all the terms of a contract and appear to come to a meeting of minds, yet fail to make an enforceable contract because they discover that they did not mean the same thing with respect to an essential element. When this happens the parties are said to be *mistaken,* so that their true intentions about something fundamental and important are not reflected in the contract. While not every mistake leads to a void or voidable contract, as a result of a mistake a contract may be declared at common law to be void *ab initio*; if equitable doctrines are invoked, it may be voidable by either party, rescinded in some cases, or rectified in others.

Traditionally, the courts have been very reluctant to terminate agreements that appear to be complete contracts on the ground that a bargain once made must be kept. A party to a contract who says, "I made a mistake, please let me out of this contract" is likely to meet with the judicial response, "Having made a bargain, you will have to live with it." On the other hand, for some mistakes the courts have ruled that it would be unjust to enforce an agreement if it does not represent what the parties were really bargaining about. What has been difficult for the courts in Canada and England to decide, whether using common law rules or equitable ones, is where to draw the line between a mistake that leaves a contract unenforceable and a mistake that does not. If you review mistake cases, you may come away with the impression that decisions turn on the court's subjective view of whether

---

17 *Business Practices Act*, RSO 1990, c. B.18; *Trade Practices Act*, RSBC 1979, c. 406; *Unfair Trade Practices Act*, RSA 1980, c. U-3; *Trade Practices Act*, RSN 1990, c. T-7; and *Business Practices Act*, RSPEI 1988, c. B-7.

enforcement would be unfair or unconscionable rather than on some universal objective test or set of criteria that could be applied to measure the nature and effect of the mistake.

Principles of the Law of Mistake

While predicting whether a mistake will give rise to relief in a particular case is difficult, the courts appear to have applied some principles in analyzing mistake cases.

- If what was offered was offered in error, it may be impossible for the other side to accept an unintended offer. Here it could be said that there was no meeting of minds and no real offer and acceptance from which to create a valid contract.[18]

- If there is a mistake that is about something fundamental in the contract, such as the existence of the thing contracted about or a term of the contract, the contract may be void or voidable or subject to rescission or rectification.[19]

- A mistake in the motive or intention for contracting is likely to be seen as irrelevant.[20]

- Unexpected and exceptional contractual consequences that stem from a mistake may well lead to a contract being declared void, voidable, or subject to rescission or rectification.

- If one party is mistaken, the other knows it and says nothing, and the mistake is about something fundamental, then the contract may be treated as void, voidable, or subject to rescission or rectification.

- If both parties are mistaken about something fundamental, the contract may be treated as void or voidable or subject to rescission or rectification.

- If the mistake was due to one party's carelessness or negligence, that party may have to live with the consequences.

- When dealing with a case of mistake, the courts tend toward upholding agreements, and when they do intervene, they are likely to try to save the contract by creating opportunities for rectification before they grant rescission or declare the contract voidable or void or treat it as voidable.

Remember that just because one or more of these principles could logically be applied to the facts of a case that involves a mistake, it does not follow that the principles will be applied or that, if applied, a court will grant a remedy. Cases about mistake with similar facts are often decided quite differently. For example,

---

18 Per Estey J in *R v. Ron Engineering and Construction (Eastern) Ltd.* (1981), 119 DLR (3d) 267, at 277 (SCC). For a detailed discussion of judicial principles used to analyze mistake cases, see Fridman, supra footnote 4, at 248-67.

19 *Bell v. Lever Bros.*, [1932] AC 161 (HL).

20 Ibid.

the Canadian and English courts have gone in quite different directions with respect to cases that involve fundamental mistake. While various theoretical reasons may be advanced to explain these differences, they may also be explained in terms of the English courts making more creative use of equitable doctrines to take a more flexible position in enforcing contracts where fundamental mistakes have been made.[21]

TREATMENT OF MISTAKE AT COMMON LAW AND EQUITY

The preceding discussion suggests that mistake cases are treated differently under common law rules from the way they are treated under equitable doctrines. At common law, a contract is valid and exists, or is invalid and does not exist. If it is valid and exists, that is the end of the matter. Equity, which is designed to introduce flexible responses to common law rigidity, takes a different approach: a contract that is not void *ab initio* may still be subjected to equitable remedies if it is inequitable or unconscionable. In equity, a contract could be treated as voidable or be subject to rescission, rectification, or relief from forfeiture. In England, and to a lesser extent in Canada, there has been a trend away from rigid and formalistic application of common law rules in mistake situations and toward increasing use of equitable doctrines; the focus is more on fairness in outcome and less on enforcing bargains regardless of fairness.[22]

Types of Mistake

Mistake cases can be categorized in terms of mistakes about particulars of the contract and in terms of the effects of the mistakes as determined by which party is mistaken.

MISTAKES OF LAW AND FACT

Mistake of Law

Generally, because everyone is expected to know the law, if either or both parties are mistaken about the law as it affects their contract, the law affords no remedy for the mistake. Because ignorance of the law is no excuse, to be ignorant is to be at the least negligent, and a negligent party cannot ask that her or his mistake, based on that negligence, be corrected.

Permitting rectification or rescission when a mistake is factual but not legal is not very satisfactory. Courts have often had great difficulty in distinguishing between a mistake of fact and one of law. Suppose, for example, that A sells land to B. A and B assume A owns the land but both are unaware that C actually owns it. This could be characterized as a mistake of law regarding the legal rights of ownership, or it could be characterized as a mistake of fact where both A and B believe as a fact that A owns the land and are unaware that in fact C owns it. It has also been argued that the rule presuming knowledge of the law is derived from criminal law that

---

21 Fridman, supra footnote 4, at 252-57.

22 Ibid., at 265.

affects citizens and the state, which may not be appropriate to law that regulates the rights of citizens among themselves.

Some jurisdictions have taken steps to counter the effect of the rule by allowing remedies for a mistake in law for contracts that concern the payment of money. The Supreme Court of Canada confronted this issue directly in 1989 in *Air Canada v. British Columbia*,[23] holding that it did not matter whether the mistake was a mistake of fact or of law in determining whether there could be recovery for a mistake. The *Air Canada* case applied to the recovery of money paid under a contract where one party claimed that the payment was made on the basis of a mistaken assumption in law that it was owing. There is no clear indication that this case necessarily applies to other types of contract, but there is no logical reason why it should not.

▓ EXAMPLE OF MISTAKE OF LAW

Bach and Handel enter into a lease agreement in which Handel rents a house from Bach. At the time, both parties mistakenly believe that a rent control law sets the rent at a lower rate than Bach would otherwise have charged. Bach discovers that the law does not apply and moves to rescind the contract on the grounds that both parties were mistaken about the amount of payment required. Depending on how narrowly the *Air Canada* case is applied, Bach may be able to rescind the contract or have it rectified.

Mistake of Fact

Identity of the Subject Matter   The focus here is on the subject matter of the contract: what it is about, the obligations involved, or what a term means. "Subject matter" is defined broadly to include the identity of the goods, land, or service; the price to be paid; and the obligations undertaken, provided that these are major or fundamental terms. If the mistake is about a minor matter or collateral term, it cannot cause a contract to be declared void, although it may result in other remedies such as rectification.

The test for determining whether there is a mistake regarding the identity of the subject matter is whether a reasonable person looking at the contract formation process and the resulting contract can determine whether the parties have identified what is fundamental to the agreement. A reasonable person need not look at the reasons or motives of the parties in deciding what is fundamental. The search is to see that important terms about the identity of the subject matter have been determined so that a reasonable person could say that the parties have reached consensus, in which case the contract is valid.

▓ EXAMPLE OF MISTAKE AS TO IDENTITY OF THE SUBJECT MATTER

Simon wanted to buy parcel A. He was induced by an error in the catalogue to buy parcel B, though he thought that he was buying parcel A. On discovering his error, he could sue to rescind the contract on the ground that

---

23 (1989), 59 DLR (4d) 161 (SCC).

there was a fundamental misunderstanding between the parties of what they were contracting for.

If there is a mistake, it must be about the identity of the subject matter, not some quality of it, unless the quality is so fundamental that it becomes part of the subject matter. The courts shy away from granting remedies when a mistake about quality is at issue, since this usually affects the value of the contract, which is perceived to raise issues about whether a party has bargained carefully. If a party has not bargained well, the courts are not likely to interfere to remake a bad bargain. Some cases have granted relief for a mistake relating to the quality of the subject matter, but only when the quality is a fundamental part of the identity of the subject matter.[24] Again, the difficulty is deciding where to draw the line between quality of the subject matter and quality assuming characteristics of identity of the subject matter. The quality of the subject matter would become part of the identity of it if a reasonable person would expect the quality to be essential to the contract. For instance, in the example below, the type of wheat (winter wheat) would become part of the identity if Karl indicated that he needed wheat for his baking operation instead of indicating just that he needed wheat. When it has been determined that there is a mistake as to the identity of the subject matter of a contract, because it is fundamental, the parties have failed to reach consensus so there is no contract, and what appears to be a contract is void *ab initio*.

◼ EXAMPLE OF MISTAKE AS TO IDENTITY/QUALITY OF THE SUBJECT MATTER

Karl wants to buy a carload of winter wheat that is suitable for making bread. He mistakenly believes that Tara has a carload of winter wheat for sale and offers to buy it. Karl says nothing to Tara about the type of wheat he wants, and Tara is unaware that Karl wants winter wheat. The wheat Tara is selling is not winter wheat. Karl completes the purchase and takes delivery. He realizes his mistake and seeks to rescind the contract on the ground that there is a mistake as to the identity of the subject matter: winter wheat versus another type of wheat.

Is this a mistake going to the identity or the quality of the subject matter? If it is the latter, there is no remedy for Karl. To answer this question, the court uses the objective test of a reasonable person analyzing the bargaining process and the final contract. In doing so, a reasonable person is likely to conclude that the parties contracted for the sale of a carload of wheat and that there was no mistake about this. There was nothing apparent in the contract or the bargaining process to indicate that the type of wheat was at issue. There was no objective evidence to alert Tara to what Karl was thinking; Karl never communicated his thoughts, and nothing he did indicated that he was thinking about winter wheat. Karl could be seen to have ideas, motives, or beliefs about the subject matter and reasons for entering into the contract. But he would have to communicate these so that a reasonable person could see and be aware that the type of wheat was fundamental and therefore that the identity of the subject matter included

---

24 *Clay v. Powell*, [1932] SCR 210.

winter wheat, not just wheat. Note that it does not matter whether Tara knew or did not know what Karl wanted—it is what a reasonable person would conclude that counts.

Existence of the Subject Matter   In this situation, the parties intend to contract about the same subject matter and there is no confusion or disagreement about what that subject matter is. However, they may be mistaken about the existence of the subject matter:

- It may never have existed.

- It may have existed but ceased to exist before the parties entered into an agreement.

- Both may think they can contract about it, but it is not something that can be the subject of a contract for legal or other reasons.

- Both may have contemplated the non-existence of the subject matter but may not have reached consensus on how to deal contractually with its non-existence.

If the parties are mistaken about the existence of the subject matter at the time of the contract, then the contract is usually void *ab initio* and both parties must be returned to their pre-contract position. The reasoning here is that the parties cannot be *ad idem* (of the same mind) over something that does not exist, so there can be no agreement.[25] It can also be argued that the existence of the subject matter is a condition precedent to the existence of a valid contract. The application of this approach illustrates a common situation in contract interpretation cases: a fact situation can be analyzed under more than one legal rule or doctrine. How a fact situation is categorized or identified may well determine the outcome of a case.

■ EXAMPLE OF MISTAKE IN EXISTENCE OF THE SUBJECT MATTER

Albert, a grain merchant, contracts to purchase from Bertha a load of grain currently being shipped to London. Unknown to both of them, the grain had spoiled en route and was sold at a distress price by the captain of the ship. In this case, the subject matter of the contract, the load of grain, had ceased to exist when the parties entered into their agreement. Consequently, they cannot reach consensus, and there is no sale.[26]

Suppose that the parties contemplate the possibility of the non-existence of the subject matter of the contract. They may assign the risk for loss or non-existence of the subject matter to one party or the other. Sale of future goods on an executory contract might give rise to this kind of arrangement. A tomato canner, for example, might enter into an agreement in spring for the purchase of field tomatoes that do not now exist but are expected to exist at the end of August. A

---

25 *Barrow, Lane and Ballard Ltd. v. Phillips & Co.*, [1929] 1 KB 574.

26 See *Couturier v. Hastie* (1856), 5 HL Cas. 673; Atiyah, "Couturier v. Hastie and the Sale of Non-Existent Goods," 73 LQR 34.

prudent party would take care to assign risk for goods that do not yet exist and are perishable and fragile. Even where the parties make no specific arrangements to cover destruction before delivery, the courts have occasionally extended the law of mistake as to existence of the subject matter to cover subject matter that did not exist when the contract was made and never existed in the form that could be delivered under the contract. A better approach might be to avoid twisting the law of mistake beyond recognition and to treat this kind of case as a contract that requires a condition precedent—the existence of the subject matter—before the contract can be valid.[27]

Identity of the Party   The common law has long held that a mistake as to the identity of a party to a contract renders the contract void. The basis for this rule is that only the person to whom an offer is made can accept it; another person has no right to the bargain. The rule has a practical basis as can be seen from the cases, many of which arise when a cheat with whom the victim would not ordinarily contract impersonates someone with whom the victim would be prepared to contract. For example, in *Cundy v. Lindsay*,[28] a person named Blenkarn fraudulently induced the respondents to sell him material. The respondents mistakenly believed that Blenkarn was Blenkiron and Co., a reputable firm with whom they would have contracted. If the respondents had known they were dealing with Blenkarn, they would not have entered into the contract. It was held that the mistake as to identity made by the respondents resulted in there being no contract, because they thought they were contracting with Blenkiron, not Blenkarn. They were not simply mistaken as to Blenkarn's attributes; they were mistaken as to his identity. They believed him to be someone other than whom he was pretending to be. Because no offer was intended to be made to Blenkarn, Blenkarn was not in a position to accept.

While a mistake about identity voids a contract, a mistake about the attributes of a party is likely to have no effect on the contract. However, it can be difficult to determine whether a mistake is about a party's identity or her or his attributes. One eminent English judge called it "a distinction without a difference."[29] If Y represents himself as a wealthy man when he is not, and X, who does not know anything about Y other than that he appears to be wealthy, deals with Y in the mistaken belief that Y is wealthy, it could be said that X was mistaken as to the identity of the party because Y was not a wealthy man. Here "wealthy man" is presumed to be the identity. But one could also argue that X thought she was dealing with someone called Y, and she did deal with Y, so there was no mistake about Y's identity, but there was a mistake about one of Y's attributes, his wealth. This is similar to the problem of distinguishing between identity of the subject matter and quality of the subject matter.

Nevertheless, the cases do distinguish between intending to contract with someone who appears to have wealth, a business, or commercial influence where there is a mistake about the person being wealthy, having a business, or having

---

27 See Fridman, supra footnote 4, at 279-81.

28 (1878), 3 App. Cas. 459 (HL).

29 *Lewis v. Averay*, [1971] 3 All ER 907, at 911 (CA), per Lord Denning.

commercial influence, and intending to contract with someone in the mistaken belief that the person is someone else. But even here, the key appears to be that the mistake in identity is fundamental. For example, B represents that he has authority to receive bonds from A. In fact, B is a thief and has no authority. A checks on B's identity and, satisfied that B is the person he says he is, delivers the bonds. Here B was who he said he was, and A was contracting with the person she thought she was contracting with. If there is a mistake, it is about B's attribute of being a thief. If there is a solution for A, it may lie in the area of fraudulent misrepresentation, not in mistake as to the identity of a party. Mistake as to identity remains limited to situations where offers are accepted by a person for whom the offer was not intended where the identity of the offeree is important or fundamental. This type of mistake can also be treated as a unilateral mistake, where one party is mistaken about something fundamental, and the other party knows it and takes advantage of the mistake. Unilateral mistake is discussed later in this chapter.

■ EXAMPLE OF MISTAKE AS TO IDENTITY OF THE PARTY

Ivan the Terrible, seeking to kill off all his enemies without making a fuss, wishes to contract with Lucretia Borgia for the purchase of poisons that do not leave a trace. Lucilla Borgia hears about Ivan's desires and, carrying a nice line of poisons herself, contacts Ivan. Thinking he is dealing with Lucretia, he purchases a variety of poisons from Lucilla. Later, in a fit of remorse after he discovers that Lucilla is not the same person as Lucretia, Ivan demands his money back, saying he was mistaken as to the identity of the person he was contracting with. Because Lucilla and Lucretia are two different people, there is a mistake in identity, not in attributes, because Ivan intended to contract with Lucretia, not Lucilla. Contracting with Lucretia may be seen as important to Ivan and fundamental, because she has a reputation for high-quality poisons, and he would not have contracted with Lucilla had he known he had mistaken her for Lucretia. The fact that Lucilla's poisons were the equal of Lucretia's is not important because this does not affect the formation of Ivan's intent to contract.

Nature of the Contract (Non Est Factum)   A party may plead as a defence to an attempt to enforce a contract that he or she made a mistake about the type of contract. For example, a party may think he or she is guaranteeing a debt when in fact he or she is becoming a principal debtor. This might happen where A is illiterate, blind, or otherwise disabled and is relying on B to prepare the agreement for signature. If B substitutes a document creating primary indebtedness for a guarantee and A signs it, A would say that this was not the type of contract he had agreed to. This defence, called the **non est factum** defence, denies that there was consent to the terms of an agreement. If there is no consent, then there is no enforceable contract.

The plea of *non est factum* is available only in certain circumstances:

- The party relying on the plea must be illiterate, unable to understand English, blind, or affected by some other disability that prevents the person from reading and sufficiently understanding the document, at least to the

non est factum
Latin for "I did not make this"; a defence used by one who appears to be a party to a contract but who did not intend to enter into this type of contract; in effect, the party is denying that he or she consented to this contract

extent of understanding the difference between the document she signed and the document she thought she was signing.[30]

- The party must not be careless or negligent in signing the document. Blindness or other disability alone is not enough. The party must make some effort to determine what the document is or to obtain assistance before signing it. The effort does not necessarily have to be successful or effective.

- The party must be entirely mistaken as to the type of transaction or contract that he or she is signing. Ignorance of the terms or confusion about the effects of the contract is not sufficient for a successful plea.

- The party relying on the plea must prove that he was mistaken as to the type of contract, that he was not negligent or careless in signing, and that he had a disability that prevented him from appreciating that the document was entirely different from what he thought it was.

- The party relying on the plea need not prove fraud, misrepresentation, or fault by the other party.

The trend in the case law in Canada and England is to narrow this defence, in particular by confining it to situations where the document signed is completely different from the one the party thought he or she was signing. Further, while the courts have been inclusive as to the types of disability that might underlie a plea of *non est factum*, they have required that the mistake go to the nature of the contract itself and that the party show some effort to try to understand the nature of the contract.[31]

■ EXAMPLE OF MISTAKE AS TO NATURE OF THE CONTRACT

Allen is an illiterate farmer. Larissa negotiates a contract to lease 40 hectares of land from Allen. Allen goes to Larissa's lawyer's office to sign the lease. He tells the lawyer he has come to sign the lease. At Allen's request, the lawyer goes over the terms with him, but by mistake she gives Allen the lease with an option to purchase attached. When Allen discovers what happened, he seeks to negate the contract and pleads *non est factum*. He may be successful, since he has a disability that prevented him from determining the true nature of the document. Allen was not careless—he asked for and received assistance. The mistake was not due to fraud or intentional misrepresentation, but that is not something Allen has to show to succeed with the plea.

The Mistaken Party

So far, we have examined mistakes about particulars of the contract, chiefly mistakes of law and fact. We now turn to an analysis of the doctrine of mistake in the context of who makes a mistake and what the consequences of the mistake are.

In many cases of mistake, it is possible to analyze the fact situation in terms of a mistake of fact or as a mistake by a party or parties. For example, where A and B

---

30 *Saunders v. Anglia Building Society*, [1971] AC 1039 (HL).

31 Ibid.; *Marvco Color Research Ltd. v. Harris* (1982), 141 DLR (3d) 577 (SCC).

are contracting over the sale of a boat and, unknown to both of them, the boat has been destroyed by fire, there is no contract. This conclusion could be based on the argument that there is a mistake about the existence of the subject matter—a mistake of fact—or it could be based on the argument that both parties have made a common mistake, since both believed that the subject matter existed when it did not. Whichever route is taken, the conclusion is the same. However, there may be cases where focusing on mistakes of fact or law may lead to different conclusions from an analysis based on which party made the mistake.

UNILATERAL MISTAKE

Unilateral mistake occurs when one party to a contract is mistaken about some fundamental element of the contract. What follows from such a mistake depends on whether the unmistaken party knew or ought to have known about the mistake.

unilateral mistake
one party to a contract is mistaken about a fundamental element of the contract

Other Party Is Unaware of the Mistake

If one party makes a mistake and the other is unaware of it and could not have reasonably been expected to know of it, then the contract is valid and cannot be rescinded or nullified.[32] This result may be explained in terms of the law that requires the mistaken party to bear the cost of his or her own negligence or carelessness. At common law, the test of the unmistaken party's knowledge is objective: what would a reasonable person who is looking at the bargaining process and contract think the unmistaken party knew or ought to have known? The equitable approach is more subjective, since it looks at the intentions of the parties.

■ EXAMPLE OF UNILATERAL MISTAKE: OTHER PARTY UNAWARE

Ravi has leased a car from 4 Wheels Ltd. He wants to buy the car at the end of the lease period. He asks 4 Wheels to quote him a buyout price, and 4 Wheels does so. Ravi agrees to the price, unaware that 4 Wheels has made a mistake and quoted a lower price than it intended. Ravi does not have the knowledge or background to know that a pricing mistake has been made and in fact has no real idea of what the market price is. Consequently, it could not be said that he knows or ought to know that 4 Wheels made a mistake, and the contract is binding on 4 Wheels.

Other Party Should Have Been Aware of the Mistake

If one party makes a mistake and the other is unaware of it but in all of the circumstances should have been aware of it, then the unmistaken party cannot rely on enforcing the contract. Although the contract may or may not be void *ab initio* at common law, it is voidable and could be rescinded in equity at the option of the party who made the mistake on the ground that it would be unconscionable to permit the unmistaken party from taking advantage of an error in offering or accepting the terms of an agreement.[33]

---

32 *Commercial Credit Corporation v. Newall Agencies Ltd.* (1981), 126 DLR (3d) 728 (BCSC).

33 *BCE Development Corp. v. Cascade Investments Ltd.* (1987), 55 Alta. LR (2d) 22 (CA).

EXAMPLE OF UNILATERAL MISTAKE: OTHER PARTY SHOULD HAVE BEEN AWARE

Marek has seen an invitation to tender on a contract to provide fuel to Elizavetta's business. He submits a tender in which he mistakenly miscalculates the unit price. Elizavetta, seeing that the price is very low, accepts the tender immediately. She suspects that Marek has made an error, but she does not know what it is and does not inquire further. Even if she does not know that there is a mistake, a reasonable person would be expected to know that the price was low and would expect the buyer to be aware of an error.

Other Party Is Aware of the Mistake

If one party makes a mistake and the other is aware of it and snaps up the bargain, the contract is voidable by the mistaken party. There is no requirement to show that the unmistaken party misled or deceived the mistaken party, and the results are the same as they would be for a situation where the unmistaken party did not know of the mistake but should have known about it. Where the unmistaken party knows of the mistake, the test is subjective, and the courts will hear evidence from the mistaken party as to what she or he actually intended to do.

EXAMPLE OF UNILATERAL MISTAKE: OTHER PARTY IS UNAWARE

In the above example, if Marek's calculation error was easily evident on the face of the tender, then Elizavetta either would have had actual knowledge of the miscalculation, or ought to have known of the miscalculation.

Remedies

The law is not entirely clear on what remedies are available in cases of unilateral mistake. In Canada, it appears that the mistaken party has a choice between rectification of the contract and rescission. If rectification is chosen, the contract is rewritten to correct the mistake. If rescission is chosen, the contract is voided and the parties are returned to their pre-contract positions.[34] This solution has been rejected in England, where rectification is the only remedy.[35] With unilateral mistake, the courts are inclined to resort to the law of equity, which allows for flexible remedies that maximize opportunities for keeping the contract alive.

MUTUAL MISTAKE

mutual mistake
both parties to a contract are mistaken but each makes a different mistake

A **mutual mistake** arises where both parties are mistaken but they each make a different mistake. The test of whether mistakes have been made is objective. If a reasonable person is of the view that the parties appear to be in agreement on the terms of the contract, then there is apparent assent to the terms of the contract,

---

34 *Devald v. Zigeuner* (1958), 16 DLR (2d) 285 (Ont. CA).

35 *Riverlate Properties Ltd. v. Paul*, [1975] Ch. D. 133 (CA).

making the contract valid. As one case put it, "[m]utual assent is not required ... only apparent manifestation of assent is required."[36] The subjective, inward secret beliefs of a mistaken party are considered to be irrelevant, which prevents the doctrine from being exploited to undo what in effect is a bad bargain by either party.

■ EXAMPLE OF MUTUAL MISTAKE

Farid is selling a second-hand mountain bike. Marsha indicates that she would like to buy it. She is looking for a new bike and thinks that Farid's, which is clean and shiny, is new. Farid is unaware that Marsha thinks she is buying a new bike—he thinks she wants to buy a second-hand one. The objective view of the reasonable person might be that the condition of the bike might provide reasonable support for the mistake Marsha made, and that there was no evidence to prevent Farid from being mistaken about Marsha's intent. If so, it might be argued that the parties did not reach consensus and there was no contract.

COMMON MISTAKE

A **common mistake** is one where both parties are mistaken and make the same mistake. They have not reached consensus on essential terms, and there is no enforceable contract. Not every common mistake yields these results—there must be a fundamental common mistake about the subject matter or a term of the contract.[37] Fact situations that give rise to analysis using the doctrine of common mistake can also be analyzed in terms of mistake as to identity, quality, and existence of the subject matter. In the end, using any of these analytic approaches, the contract may be avoided if the mistake is about something fundamental and the party appears to have received far less than what she or he had apparently contracted for.

common mistake
both parties to a contract are mistaken and make the same mistake

■ EXAMPLE OF COMMON MISTAKE

Millicent wants to sell her fur coat, which she thinks is mink. Emily agrees to buy it; she too thinks it is mink. Both intend the transaction to be about a mink coat. In fact, both are mistaken—the coat is made of some other kind of fur dyed to look like mink and is worth far less than a mink coat. Assuming that neither Millicent nor Emily is careless in failing to find the true quality on examining the coat, it appears that both have made a common mistake. Because a mink coat is perceived to be different from other kinds of coats, the mistake could be said to be fundamental and to give rise to rescission. Note that on these facts, this could also be seen as a mistake about the identity or quality of the subject matter.

---

36 *Walton v. Landstock Investments Ltd.* (1976), 13 OR (2d) 693 (CA), quoted in Fridman, *supra* footnote 4, at 258.

37 *McMaster University v. Wilchar Construction Ltd.*, [1971] 3 OR 801 (HC); aff'd. (1973), 12 OR (2d) 512 (CA).

SUMMARY

Where one party makes a statement that is a misrepresentation and induces another to enter into a contract on the basis of the misrepresentation, the law will intervene, depending on whether the statement was a term of the contract or an inducement to enter into it, and whether the misrepresentation was innocently made, negligently made, or made with the intent to defraud or deceive. Depending on the nature of misrepresentation, it can give rise to damages for breach of contract, or to rescission of the contract where the contract is voided.

The courts also will void a contract on the ground that one party was induced by duress or undue influence to enter into a contract that he or she would otherwise not have entered into. In other circumstances, where there is no apparent undue influence or duress, the court may intervene on the ground that the contract in its terms is so unfair that it is unconscionable.

When a party makes a mistake, the courts examine the situation carefully in deciding whether or not a party should be let out of his or her contractual responsibilities. If the mistake is fundamental and concerns the identity or existence of the subject matter, a term of the contract, or the nature of the contract itself, the court will often allow for rescission, rectification, or termination of the contract. The basis for these remedies is that the parties were not really in agreement about essential terms and that a reasonable person would assume that it was reasonable in the circumstances for the party or parties to have made the mistake in question.

The courts also examine mistake from the perspective of who makes the mistake and what the consequences are or should be for the mistaken party. If one party makes a unilateral mistake about a fundamental element of the contract, what happens depends on whether the other party knew or ought to have known of the mistake. One cannot take advantage of a reasonable mistake by the other party. If both parties make a mistake and it is the same one, it is a common mistake. If the mistake is fundamental, then the parties are not *ad idem* and there is no valid contract. If both parties make a mistake, but each party's mistake is different, they have made a mutual mistake. If the result is that they are not *ad idem* about something fundamental, then the contract may be avoided.

KEY TERMS

common mistake	mutual mistake
duress	*non est factum*
fiduciary	rescission
fraudulent misrepresentation	restitution
innocent misrepresentation	*uberrimae fidei* contracts
intangible property	undue influence
material inducement	unilateral mistake

REVIEW QUESTIONS

1. If a party makes a fraudulent representation to induce you to enter an agreement, and you enter it but are not influenced to do so by the fraudulent statement, can you move to rescind the contract? Explain.

2. If a seller says, "We will have zoning permission" during negotiations for the purchase of a building lot, explain whether this is a misrepresentation if

    a. the person making the statement knew permission would never be granted,

    b. the person making the statement had no idea whether permission would be granted but made the statement anyway, or

    c. the person making the statement believed permission would be granted.

3. Give an example of a situation where a misrepresentation is also a term of the contract.

4. What is the effect on the remedies available to the victim of a misrepresentation that has become a term of the contract?

5. How does an innocent misrepresentation differ from a negligent misrepresentation?

6. What determines when a misrepresentation is material?

7. Can an omission be a misrepresentation? If so, in what circumstances?

8. In what circumstances can duress be used to rescind a contract?

9. How does undue influence differ from duress in terms of circumstances where it can be used, and in terms of remedies?

10. How does unconscionability differ from duress and undue influence?

11. Why are courts reluctant to terminate or rectify a contract when a party claims that there was a mistake?

12. If an offer is made in error, in what circumstances can it be accepted?

13. Why might a court refuse to rectify a mistake if the mistake is based on the party's motive for contracting?

14. If one party makes a mistake about the subject matter of the contract and the mistake is not central or material, should a remedy be granted to the mistaken party? Why or why not?

15. Describe the role of the law of equity in dealing with cases of mistake.

16. Suppose a party to a contract makes a mistake about how the law applies to a contract. Should this mistake be treated differently from a mistake of fact? Why or why not?

17. What are the consequences if a party makes a mistake in the identity of the subject matter of a contract? How are the consequences different from

those where the mistake is about the quality of the subject matter? Is the distinction meaningful? Why or why not?

18. What are the consequences if a party makes a mistake about whether the subject matter of a contract exists? If the subject matter does not exist, does it matter if it ceases to exist before the contract is made, at the time the contract is made, and after the contract is made? Explain.

19. If the parties contemplate in a contract the possibility that the subject matter of the contract might not exist, does this automatically mean the contract is enforceable if, in fact, the subject matter turns out to be non-existent?

20. Suppose X intends to contract with Y but mistakenly contracts with Z, thinking Z is Y. In what circumstances can X void the contract? In what circumstances would she be barred from voiding the contract?

21. In what circumstances will the plea of *non est factum* succeed?

22. What are the effects of a unilateral mistake by a party to a contract if the unmistaken party is aware of the mistake or ought to be aware of the mistake? Would your answer be different if the unmistaken party has no idea that the other party has made a mistake? Why or why not?

23. Describe the kinds of mistake that constitute a mutual mistake. In what circumstances might the court grant a remedy for a mutual mistake?

24. How does a common mistake differ from a mutual mistake? How and in what circumstances are the consequences of mutual mistake different from those of common mistake?

DISCUSSION QUESTIONS

1. Compare and contrast the various remedies available for different types of misrepresentation. Comment on why some remedies are likely to be more effective for the injured party than others.

2. Duress, undue influence, and unconscionability are all treated as separate and distinct doctrines because of accidents of historical development. In fact, they could be reduced to one doctrine, inequality of bargaining power, with rescission and damages as a remedy. Discuss. (You may want to read the judgment of Lord Denning in *Lloyd's Bank v. Bundy*, [1974] 3 All ER 757 (QB).)

3. Puccini bids on a load of Edam cheese being sold by Rossini. Puccini is bidding on and requires regular Edam for his gourmet shop. Rossini has dealt with Puccini before and knows the nature of Puccini's business. Rossini is also told how to package the cheese, but he is not told precisely what grade of Edam Puccini wants. Rossini sells and delivers it. The price is quite a bit lower than the usual price for a load of Edam. On delivery, Puccini discovers that it is a grade of Edam suitable only for processing into a cheese spread. Puccini seeks to rescind the contract and get his

money back on the grounds that there was a mistake as to the identity of the subject matter.

Develop and present arguments to support Puccini's position and arguments to support Rossini's position. You may wish to share this exercise with another student, with one of you taking Rossini's position and one of you taking Puccini's.

4. Charlie, a fruit merchant, contracts with Camille to purchase from her a load of mangoes currently being shipped to Vancouver. Charlie and Camille are unaware that the mangoes spoiled along the way and were sold off very cheaply by the captain of the ship. The subject matter of the contract, the load of mangoes, ceased to exist before the parties entered into their agreement and there can be no contract. Would it make a difference if the mangoes spoiled *after* the contract was entered into? What remedies might be available to the parties in this situation? Is the law on mistake of any help here? Consider remedies for breach of contract.

5. Oscar wants to sell his piano. Leslie wants to buy a new piano and thinks Oscar's is new. Oscar doesn't know that Leslie thinks she is buying a new piano; he thinks she is looking for a second-hand one. The objective view of the reasonable person might be that the condition of the piano provides reasonable support for Leslie's mistake, and that there was no evidence to prevent Oscar from being mistaken about Leslie's intent. If so, it might be argued that the parties had not reached consensus and there was no contract.

Develop arguments to support Oscar's position and Leslie's position on the basis that the mistake is

- a unilateral mistake of Leslie's, or

- a mistake as to the identity of the subject matter of the contract.

CHAPTER 5

Contractual Rights

PRIVITY OF CONTRACT

As the term suggests, **privity** involves being privy to, or a party to, a contract. Only the parties to a contract may claim the benefits of the contract or incur any liability under the contract. This may seem self-evident, but some contracts purport to confer benefits on third parties, or third parties may wish to be substituted for one of the parties. In those cases, the third parties may wish to enforce the contract.

privity
the relationship that exists between the parties to a contract

The general rule is that a third party who is a "stranger" to the contract may not claim any benefits or incur any liability from the contract because of the lack of privity.

▦ EXAMPLES OF LACK OF PRIVITY

- Connor and Julian own adjoining properties. Connor enters into a contract with Maya whereby Maya agrees to rent Connor's property and build a motel on it. Julian would greatly benefit from this, since he owns and operates a restaurant on the adjoining property. However, Maya fails to fulfill the contract and does not build the motel. Despite the fact that Julian will suffer as a result of Maya's breach of contract, he cannot enforce the contract because he is not a party to it—he lacks privity. Only Connor can enforce the contract.

- The homeowners in a certain neighbourhood decide they want to form a residents' association. All of them enter into a contract that states that if any of the homeowners in the neighbourhood fails to cut his or her grass and lets it grow past a certain length, then any other member of the group may cut the grass and the offending homeowner will be obligated to pay a fee of $100 to the member who cut it. Some time after the contract is formed, Brian buys a house and moves into the neighbourhood. Brian doesn't cut his grass and Raffi goes over one Saturday morning and cuts it for him. Raffi then sends a bill to Brian for $100. Brian is not obligated to pay the $100 because he was never a party to the contract and cannot incur any liability under it.

The doctrine of privity can be rationalized in terms of the lack of consideration. The third party paid or received no consideration for the contract so she or he cannot enforce it, nor is bound by it. However, statutes can impose liability or confer benefits on third parties despite the lack of consideration. A few examples of statute law are as follows:

- The law of partnership states that a partner may enter into a contract on behalf of the partnership and that contract will impose liability on all the partners.

- In real property law, contracts that impose restrictions on the use of real property are binding not just on the parties to the contract but also on all subsequent owners of the property, even though they were never parties to the original contract, provided that these interests are registered on title. Such restrictions might be the granting of a right of way or a restriction on the height of any building constructed on the property.

- The parties to an insurance contract are the policyholder and the insurance company. However, many insurance contracts, or policies, such as those for life insurance, name a third party as a **beneficiary**. If the insurance company will not honour the policy, it may be enforced by the beneficiary.

beneficiary
a person who is entitled to the benefits of an agreement entered into between two or more other parties

Apart from statutory exceptions to the general rule, there are a number of other means by which third parties may assert rights under a contract.

Novation

novation
a requirement that the parties to a contract agree to substitute a new contract for an existing contract—terminating the existing contract

A third party may replace one of the parties to a contract by forming a new contract. The result of **novation** is the termination of the old contract and the substitution of the new contract. The new party has the benefits and liabilities of the contract, and the old party no longer has any rights or obligations. There is no difficulty with privity of contract with novation, because the third party becomes a contracting party. The requirements of novation are as follows:

- The new party must assume complete liability.

- The other party must accept the new party *in substitution for* the old party, not *in addition to* the old party.

- The other party must accept the new contract in substitution for the old contract.

- The other party must accept that the new contract terminates the old contract.

- The new contract must be made with the consent of the old party.

■ EXAMPLE OF NOVATION

Busy Bees Cleaners Inc. agrees to provide office cleaning services to Sharif, Wasserman, and Powell under a long-term contract. The owners of Busy Bees decide to retire and close down the business before the end of the contract. However, they recommend another company, Action Clean Ltd., to replace them. After negotiations, Sharif, Wasserman, and Powell enter into a new contract with Action Clean under the same terms and conditions as their contract with Busy Bees. In doing so, there has been novation. Busy Bees is released from its obligations under the old contract, and the new contract with Action Clean is substituted for the old contract.

Vicarious Performance

As a general rule, a party to a contract must perform her or his obligations under that contract. She or he cannot get a third party to perform those obligations without the consent of the other party. Nevertheless, there are situations in which a party might wish to have a third party do some or all of the work under a contract. This is called **vicarious performance**, and it is permissible in limited circumstances.

A party may employ a third party to perform his or her obligations when the performance required is not of a personal nature. If the work could be performed equally well by another person, the party may "contract out" the work. However, the original party to the contract remains responsible if the work is not done properly. If the work to be done is of a personal nature, the party may not hire another to perform the contract.

It is important to look at the common practices in the business or industry in question to determine whether vicarious performance is acceptable. Vicarious performance is common in a number of trades and industries, including shipping, building construction, dry-cleaning, transportation, repair of goods, and manufacturing.

vicarious performance
the performance of obligations under a contract by a third party in circumstances in which the original party remains responsible for proper performance

■ EXAMPLES OF VICARIOUS PERFORMANCE

- Saroj takes her car to Maurice for repair. Maurice agrees to fix her car, which needs engine repair and body work. Maurice does the engine repair himself, but sends the car down the street to Alain for the body work. When Saroj gets her car back, she finds that the body work was not done properly.

  In this case, vicarious performance is common and acceptable. Saroj needs the work done; presumably she does not care who does it. However, Maurice is responsible for the poorly done body work even though he did not do it himself. Saroj may sue him for breach of contract. Maurice may then in turn sue Alain for breach of contract.

- Glass Hammer Productions Ltd. hires Roberto Forte, a famous opera singer, for a concert. Roberto is feeling poorly on the day of the performance, so he sends his protégé, Bruno Pelizzari, to sing in his stead.

  In this case, the nature of the performance of the contract is personal, and vicarious performance is not acceptable. Glass Hammer Productions is not required to accept a substitute for the performer it hired.

Trusts

A strict rule that only the parties to an agreement can enforce it has the potential to lead to unfair results. If a contract conferred a benefit on a third party, and the parties to the agreement were unwilling to enforce it, the third party would be prohibited from enforcing the agreement. The law of trusts developed to deal with this situation. A **trust** is the result of a contract in which property is transferred from one person to another for the benefit of a third party. The law of trusts allows the person who is to receive the benefit of the contract, the beneficiary, to enforce

trust
a legal entity created by a grantor for a beneficiary whereby the grantor transfers property to a trustee to manage for the benefit of the beneficiary

trustee
a person who holds property in trust for, or to the benefit of, another person

express trust
a trust that arises as a result of an agreement, usually in writing, that is created in express terms

the contract against the person who is to administer the property for her or his benefit, the **trustee**. A trust that is declared in clear and unequivocal terms, usually in writing, is called an **express trust**.

■ EXAMPLE OF AN EXPRESS TRUST

Gwyn wants to create a trust for her son, Sean, in case she dies before he turns 18 years of age. In her will, she directs that all of her estate is to be invested for the benefit of Sean until he is 18 years old, and she names her sister Bethan as the trustee. After Gwyn dies, the property is transferred to Bethan. However, instead of administering the trust for the benefit of Sean, Bethan spends the money on herself.

Sean is not a party to the trust agreement—Gwyn and Bethan are the only parties. However, the law of trusts allows Sean to enforce the agreement because he is the beneficiary of the trust.

In other cases, the parties to a contract may create a benefit for a third party without expressly calling it a trust or without using language in the contract that would allow the third party to enforce the contract. In those cases, the third party must argue that a trust was created by inference or implication. The courts will examine the terms of the contract and the acts of the parties to determine whether the true intent of the contract was to create a trust. This can be a difficult argument to make because the courts are reluctant to impose a trust unless there is clear evidence that the parties intended to create a trust. When the courts find that a trust can be inferred from the contract, it is called a **constructive trust**. The beneficiary of a constructive trust may enforce the terms of the trust.

constructive trust
a trust created by the operation of law, as distinguished from an express trust

■ EXAMPLE OF A CONSTRUCTIVE TRUST

Natasha and Evelyn form a partnership. The partnership agreement states that if either of them should die, then her share of the profits of the partnership should be paid to her husband. Evelyn dies, and Natasha refuses to pay the profits to Evelyn's husband, Luis. Luis is not a party to the partnership agreement. The partnership agreement did not set up an express trust. He would have to argue that it is a constructive trust that had been created in his favour. If successful, Luis would be able to obtain a share of the profits.

**chose in action/
thing in action**
an intangible right of ownership in a tangible thing that carries the right to take legal action on it—for example, debts, insurance policies, negotiable instruments, contract rights, patents, and copyrights

assignor
a party who assigns his or her rights under a contract to a third party

assignee
a party to whom rights under a contract have been assigned by way of an assignment

ASSIGNMENT OF A CONTRACT

In a commercial context, a contract is a thing of value that can be treated as an asset. For instance, a contract for the lease of equipment is common. Such a lease allows a customer to finance the acquisition of new equipment, and it allows the vendor to gain extra income in the way of interest charges over and above the sale price for the equipment. Because income is generated over the term of the lease, the lease is an asset, or a **chose in action** or **thing in action**, that the vendor can sell, or assign, to a third party such as a financing company. The vendor, the **assignor**, assigns his or her rights under the lease to the financing company, the **assignee**. The assignee collects the moneys owing under the lease from the customer, the party to be charged. This **assignment** differs from novation because no new contract is formed, and the consent of the party to be charged is not required.

While assignments are common business transactions now, at one time the courts would not recognize them. The assignee gained no rights under the contract because of the lack of privity of contract, and therefore could not enforce the contract. However, the courts now recognize equitable and statutory assignments. They still do not recognize the assignment of contracts for personal services, which may be neither vicariously performed nor assigned to a third party.

assignment
a transfer by one party of his or her rights under a contract to a third party

Equitable Assignments

To avoid the privity of contract rule in dealing with assignments, the concept of an *equitable assignment* developed. This allows for assigning contractual rights under some circumstances. Equitable assignments have certain characteristics that can make them cumbersome to deal with, but they have some advantages as well. An equitable assignment can be verbal or in writing, and it can be a partial assignment of the assignor's rights or a complete and absolute assignment of all of the assignor's rights.

To allow an assignee to enforce a contract by equitable assignment, the following requirements must be met:

- All the parties must be brought before the court. This means that in any action to enforce the contract the assignor must be a party, even if she or he no longer has any interest in or rights under the contract.

- The court must be satisfied that the intention of all parties (but not the party to be charged) is to assign the contractual rights.

- The party to be charged must have notice of the assignment before the assignee can enforce the contract against her or him.

Statutory Assignments

The widespread practice of assigning contracts and the inconvenience of having to make the assignor a party to any actions to enforce the contract led to the development of the statutory assignment. All the common law provinces have legislation that recognizes the assignment of contractual rights. Statutory assignments have different requirements than equitable assignments. They do not replace equitable assignments, so in deciding how to enforce a contract that has been assigned, it is necessary to determine whether it is a statutory or an equitable assignment.

An assignee to a statutory assignment may enforce a contract without involving the assignor if

- the assignment of rights is absolute and unconditional;

- the assignment is in writing and signed by the assignor; and

- express notice of the assignment, in writing, is given to the party to be charged.

Note that the party to be charged does not have to consent to the assignment—he or she must only be given notice of the assignment. The assignment is effective against the party to be charged as of the date that he or she receives the notice. If the assignor has assigned the same contract to two different assignees, either accidentally or fraudulently, the assignee who first gives notice to the party to be charged is entitled to enforce the contract.

Defences and Assignments

All assignments, either equitable or statutory, are subject to any "equities" that exist between the original parties to the contract up until the time of notice. These equities might include rights that arise because of fraud, duress, or undue influence on the part of the assignor at the time the contract was entered into. For example, if the creditor uses duress to force a debtor to enter into a contract, the debtor can use duress as a defence if the creditor tries to enforce the contract. If the creditor assigns the contract, the debtor can claim duress as a defence to payment under the contract in an action by the assignee. Even though it was not the assignee who used duress, the assignee takes the assignment subject to all the conditions that existed between the original parties up until the time notice of the assignment is given to the party to be charged. The assignee can be in no better a position than was the assignor. Defences such as fraud, duress, and undue influence are discussed in more detail in chapter 4, Contractual Defects.

In addition, if the assignor owes money to the party to be charged under this or another contract, the party to be charged can claim the defence of **setoff** and deduct this debt from the moneys now owed to the assignee under the contract. This creates some risk for the assignee in taking an assignment, and assignees usually require some form of assurance from the assignor that no equities or setoffs exist that would interfere with enforcement of the contract.

setoff
in an action for debt, a defence where the debtor admits that he or she owes a debt to the creditor but also claims that the creditor owes a debt to him or her, and uses this to cancel or reduce the debt owed to the creditor

■ EXAMPLE OF EQUITIES

Pierre is employed with Auto Leasing Corp. As part of the terms of his employment, he is entitled to the use of a car. Pierre leases a car from his employer. He signs an agreement that states that he is not required to make any lease payments while he is employed with Auto Leasing Corp. If his employment with Auto Leasing Corp. ceases for any reason, Pierre must start making the lease payments himself. Auto Leasing Corp. experiences business problems and stops paying its employees. In an effort to raise capital, it assigns all its car leases, including Pierre's lease, to United Financing Ltd. At the time of the assignment, it owes Pierre $8,000 in unpaid wages. Auto Leasing Corp. then goes out of business. Pierre's employment is terminated, and United Financing Ltd. wants Pierre to make the payments under the lease. They give him notice of the assignment and demand payment.

The equities that exist between the original parties, Pierre and Auto Leasing, at the time of the assignment include the wages owed to Pierre. Because United Financing takes the assignment of the lease subject to any equities that exist between the original parties until the time that the notice is given, Pierre can claim a setoff and deduct the $8,000 owed to him by Auto Leasing from the money he owes to United Financing under the lease.

Assignments by Operation of Law

Some assignments occur automatically when certain events occur. These assignments are governed by statutes that set out the duties of the assignor. For example, when a person goes bankrupt, all of his or her contractual rights are assigned to the trustee in bankruptcy. When a person dies, all contractual rights are assigned to the estate trustee with a will (if the person died with a will) or the estate trustee without a will (if the person died without a will). Similar provisions exist for situations where a person becomes incapable of managing her or his affairs due to a mental disability.

SUMMARY

As a general rule, a third party who is not a party to a contract cannot incur any liability or claim any benefit under that contract due to lack of privity of contract. However, some statutes provide an exception to this rule, as in contracts of insurance or contracts that involve partnerships. A third party may gain rights under a contract by novation, where the third party is substituted for one of the parties and a new contract is formed. Contracts that do not require personal services may be vicariously performed by a third party. Parties to a contract may create a trust, which expressly confers a benefit on and may be enforced by a third party. Parties may also enter into a contract that confers a benefit on a third party by implication or inference and that the third party can argue is a constructive trust. Third parties may also acquire rights and liabilities under a contract by way of an equitable assignment or a statutory assignment. Assignments are subject to the equities that existed between the original parties to the contract.

KEY TERMS

assignee	novation
assignment	privity
assignor	setoff
beneficiary	trust
chose in action/thing in action	trustee
constructive trust	vicarious performance
express trust	

REVIEW QUESTIONS

1. Explain the doctrine of privity of contract. What is the rationale for its existence?

2. What are the requirements of novation?

3. Define vicarious performance.

4. Describe the difference between a novation and an assignment of a contract.

5. What are the requirements of an equitable assignment?

6. What are the requirements of a statutory assignment?

7. Under what circumstances do assignments occur as an operation of law?

8. Describe the risks the assignee assumes when taking the assignment of a contract.

9. What is a setoff, and when may it be used?

DISCUSSION QUESTIONS

1. Sturdy Tires Ltd. manufactures tires and sells them to wholesalers. Sturdy Tires has an agreement with all its wholesalers that they will not sell the tires for less than the list price except where they are selling to approved dealers. In that case, the wholesalers may sell at a reduced price as long as they obtain an agreement in writing from the dealers that the dealers will not sell the tires below the list price.

   Sturdy Tires sells tires to Selkirk & Sons Inc., a wholesaler. Selkirk & Sons then sells the tires at a reduced price to Doucet Auto Limited, an approved dealer. Despite the agreement with Selkirk & Sons, Doucet holds a promotion and sells the tires for less than list price. Sturdy Tires then brings an action to prevent Doucet from selling its tires for less than list price. Will Sturdy Tires be successful in its action? Why or why not?

2. Peter is an elderly man who owns a hardware store. Because of his failing health, he can no longer run the business. He wants to sell it to his nephew, Jonathan, who often helps out in the store. Jonathan cannot afford to buy the business outright, so a contract is agreed upon whereby the business will be transferred to Jonathan. In exchange, Peter will be kept on as a consultant for the rest of his life, and Jonathan will pay Peter a monthly sum. The contract also states that when Peter dies, Jonathan will continue to pay the monthly sum to Peter's widow, Lesia.

   Jonathan pays the monthly sum to Peter while he is alive, but after Peter's death he refuses to pay the sum to Lesia. Can Lesia enforce this contract? Why or why not?

3. Dead Poodles is a famous rock band. The lead singer is Wendy Leather. The popularity of the band is based almost solely on the vocals of the lead singer. The band is engaged by Rock Promotions Inc. to give a concert on Canada Day on Parliament Hill in Ottawa to an expected crowd of 100,000. The day before the concert, Rock Promotions receives a fax from Wendy stating that she will not be attending the concert because she is getting married that day. Wendy sends her sister, Candy Leather, to sing in her place. The concert is a big success. Even though the crowd is disappointed not to hear Wendy, they love Candy. Can Rock Promotions sue the Dead Poodles for breach of contract?

4. Dixon & Flagel Ltd. manufactures chemicals. Calder's Chemical Supply Inc. is one of its customers. To finance the purchase of its chemical inventory, Calder's enters into inventory financing agreements with Dixon & Flagel for each order of chemicals. On February 1, Dixon & Flagel delivers an order to Calder's. Under the inventory financing agreement, Calder's is to pay Dixon & Flagel the sum of $14,000 over a period of six months for the chemicals.

   On February 10, Calder's discovers that some of the chemicals are defective and demands a refund in the amount of $6,500. On March 1, Dixon & Flagel assigns the contract to Capital Financing Corp. Capital Financing gives Calder's notice in writing of the assignment on March 5. On March 15, Dixon & Flagel delivers another order of chemicals to Calder's. The cost of the second order is $8,000, to be paid over six months. When delivering the second order, Dixon & Flagel damages Calder's loading dock, which costs Calder's $1,500 to repair. Calder's refuses to pay for any of the chemicals until Dixon & Flagel pays the demanded refund and pays for the damage to the loading dock. What options do the parties in this situation have?

CHAPTER 6

Contract Interpretation

THE GOAL OF INTERPRETATION: MAKING THE CONTRACT WORK

Every contract case that comes to court does so because one party either disagrees with the other about what its provisions mean, or because he or she knows very well what the provisions mean and seeks to escape the consequences of that meaning. In either situation the case will turn on the court's interpretation of the language of the agreement. Over the centuries, the courts have established rules about classifying contract provisions to determine their consequences, resolving ambiguity or uncertainty, and determining the consequences of attempts to use language to limit the negative consequences of a contract for a party.

The primary aim of the court is to interpret contracts so as to find and give effect to the intention of the parties. In doing this the court may pay some attention to commercial realities, but generally will not use the rules of interpretation to remake a bad bargain. Instead, it will try to interpret a contract to salvage it, in whole or in part, and make it work as it thinks the parties intended. Where a provision is found to be so incoherent as to be impossible to interpret in a reasonable way, the court may determine it to be void for vagueness but will try to save the balance of the contract. Only as a last resort will the court declare a whole contract void because its meaning and purpose is uncertain, or because the original purpose is impossible to carry out.

This does not mean a court will never intervene to declare a contract to be void or voidable. It may do so where one or both parties have made a major mistake about an important element of the contract. Mistake and its effects are discussed in chapter 4, Contractual Defects. Where contract performance becomes impossible because of circumstances beyond the control of either party, the court may find that the contract is frustrated, and bring it to an end. The court will also intervene where one side has engaged in fraud, misled the other party, or exercised some kind of undue influence arising from the nature of the relationship or the relative bargaining position of the parties. These issues are discussed in chapter 3, Protecting Weaker Parties, and in chapter 4, Contractual Defects.

Here we will introduce some of the major concepts used by courts to interpret contracts. First we will examine how the court classifies and interprets representations, terms, conditions, and warranties in a contract in terms of the effect those provisions have on the rights and responsibilities of the parties. Next, we will look at the search for certainty and the way in which the court assesses evidence using the parol evidence rule to decide the meaning of an unclear term or provision.

Then we will examine how the courts interpret exclusion and penalty clauses—provisions that seek to enhance or limit liability and damages under a contract when there is a breach. Last, we will examine how courts determine when and how a contract may become frustrated so that it has become impossible to perform due to circumstances beyond the control of either party.

CONTRACT PROVISIONS: REPRESENTATIONS, TERMS, CONDITIONS, AND WARRANTIES

As a contract is being made, the parties may make a number of statements to each other. Some will be statements that are made in the course of negotiations, and some will be statements that are terms agreed to in the contract itself. It is not always clear whether a statement is part of the negotiating process or part of the contract itself. And when we determine that a statement is part of the contract, we have to then determine what the effect of the contract statement means in terms of consequences for the parties, particularly if there is a breach of contract.

We must first consider whether a statement is a **representation** or a term of the contract. If a statement is a representation, it is not a part of the contract that either party has agreed to. Instead it is classed as a statement made by one party during negotiation of the contract. Representations are important in contract law because some misrepresentations may permit the party who is misled to avoid the contract. To have this effect, a representation must be a statement of fact, not opinion, and must be material; that is, a **material representation** is one that induced the other party to enter into the contract. Misrepresentation is discussed in more detail in chapter 4, Contractual Defects.

representation
a statement made to induce someone to enter into a contract

material representation
a statement of fact, not opinion, made by one party, of sufficient weight to induce the other party to enter into the contract

■ EXAMPLE OF REPRESENTATION

Alphonse is looking for a load of Freestone peaches for his jam factory. Freestone peaches have the right texture, and it is crucial that the peaches be of that type. Bertrand has a warehouse full of peaches he wants to sell. Alphonse asks Bertrand, "Are these Freestone peaches?" If Bertrand says "yes," that is a material representation. If Bertrand says, "I think so," that is merely his opinion and not a material representation. If Bertrand says "peaches have lots of vitamins" that is not a material representation because the presence or absence of vitamins is not important to Alphonse in making peach jam. It would not influence him in deciding whether to enter a contract with Bernard.

If a statement related to a contract is not a representation, it may be a **term**. A term is part of the contract itself, an element of what one party or the other has promised. Terms fall into two categories.

term
a provision of a contract; terms are either conditions or warranties

condition
an essential term of a contract, the breach of which denies the innocent party of the benefit of the contract, or defeats the purpose of the contract

warranty
a minor term of a contract, the breach of which does not defeat the purpose of the contract

1. If the term of the contract is essential or goes to the root of a contract, it is called a **condition**.

2. If the term is a minor or subsidiary term of the contract, it is called a **warranty**.

Whether a term is a condition or a warranty determines what the effect will be if it is breached. A breach of condition is considered so serious as to destroy the value of the contract for the victim of the breach so that he or she is deprived of most or all of the value of the contract. If the breach is one of warranty only, it is adjudged less serious, and the remedies may be more restricted than would be the case for breach of condition. Determining whether a term is a condition or a warranty is not always easy. You have to examine the contract as a whole, as well as the context in which the agreement was made, including what representations and statements the parties made during negotiations. What may be a breach of condition in one case may be a breach of warranty in another, depending on the circumstances. The effects of breach of condition and breach of warranty are discussed in more detail in chapter 8, Breach of Contract and Remedies.

■ EXAMPLES OF CONDITIONS AND WARRANTIES

Mai Ling signed an agreement to purchase the latest model of a Zephyr sports car. The model she chose was fast and manoeuvrable, and this was important because she drove from Toronto to Montreal every weekend to visit her boyfriend. She chose green for the exterior colour. The car that was delivered was a different model from what she ordered, although it was green. This would be a breach of condition because the car itself, the subject matter of the contract, was quite different from what she bargained for. Had the right model been delivered but in the wrong colour, the colour would likely have been a breach of warranty, because the colour was not her primary concern.

If Mai Ling had contracted to have her house painted and chose green, and the house was painted purple, the difference in colour would amount to a breach of condition. Here, colour would be a key and essential part of the contract, rather than a subsidiary consideration.

THE SEARCH FOR CERTAINTY: THE PAROL EVIDENCE RULE, ITS EXCEPTIONS, AND RECTIFICATION

Where an oral contract exists, you can imagine how the parties might get into a disagreement about the terms, each party relying on his or her memory as to what was agreed to and remembering the terms of the contract differently. However, when the contract is in writing, it is reasonable to expect that a dispute about its terms can be settled by looking at what is written, and by giving the language used in the contract its plain and ordinary meaning when interpreting the terms. It is also reasonable to say that if the contract is in writing, the parties should not be able to drag in other evidence, oral or written, to contradict the written terms of the agreement.

This is the approach that the common law takes in interpreting written contracts. The approach is expressed in the **parol evidence** rule, which states that if the contract is in writing and the language of the written agreement is clear and unambiguous, then no other oral or written evidence can be used to interpret, vary, or contradict the terms of the written agreement. The court interprets the agreement by looking only at its written terms, and does not consider other evidence because it is not relevant to determining what the contract means.

parol evidence
if a contract is in writing and is clear, no other written or oral evidence is admissible to contradict, vary, or interpret the agreement

When a court applies the parol evidence rule, it has to consider whether there is evidence outside the written agreement that is relevant to interpreting the agreement. As a result of considering this outside evidence, the courts have developed several exceptions to the parol evidence rule where outside evidence may be deemed to be relevant and admissible in interpreting a written contract. These exceptions are as follows.

Ambiguous Contract Language

Where it can be shown that the language of the written agreement is unclear or ambiguous, so that the meaning of a term or provision is not certain, oral evidence or other written evidence may be used to assist in interpreting the agreement.

■ EXAMPLE OF AMBIGUOUS CONTRACT LANGUAGE

A contract for membership in a professional organization has a term that says: "All members who are doctors and lawyers may vote at membership meetings." Fred argues that it is clear that a member must be a doctor *and* a lawyer to vote. Ginger argues that the language is ambiguous and that it could also mean members who are members of either the medical or the legal profession may vote. Ginger, by arguing that the language is ambiguous, may introduce evidence to show that only 2 of 700 organization members are members of both professions and that, in context, Fred's interpretation is nonsensical. Ginger, having argued ambiguity, is entitled to present evidence from outside the contract to resolve the alleged ambiguity. If the court decides that the evidence is relevant to proving that point, the evidence will be admitted to assist in interpreting the meaning of the contract notwithstanding the parol evidence rule.

Essential Collateral Agreement

A collateral agreement is a separate and independent contract with valuable consideration that could be enforced independently of the main contract or that has some impact or effect on the main contract, but is not specifically referred to in it. In this case, the court, by giving effect to the collateral contract, will modify the main contract, despite its written terms.

■ EXAMPLE OF ESSENTIAL COLLATERAL AGREEMENT

Alberto agrees to purchase a boat from Marina's Marina. He decides he wants a fire control system installed in the boat. The contract for the purchase of the boat is in writing and sets out a price for the boat. It also states that a fire control system is to be added, with the price to be added to the purchase price. Alberto and Marina then agree on the fire control system to be installed by Marina. Marina presents an invoice setting out the cost of the equipment plus labour for installation. Alberto says that he is not paying for the labour. He says that the contract for the purchase of the boat included the addition of the cost of the parts for the system, not its installation. Marina argues that the cost is the cost of the parts and includes the cost of installation. If the court finds the original purchase agreement unclear as to what "a fire control system is to be added" means, it may permit Marina to introduce evidence of the collateral agreement to provide and install the fire control system, in order to determine the meaning of the disputed term in the main contract.

Essential Implied Term Exists

If the parties use a form of contract that by custom of a trade or by convention usually contains a term that has been inadvertently left out, a party may be able to use oral and written evidence of the custom or convention to show that an implied term of the agreement has been left out.

■ EXAMPLE OF ESSENTIAL IMPLIED TERM

Kris orders a load of grade A lumber from the building supply company to be delivered to a lot where Kris is building a house. The lumber is loaded on the truck but gets rained on and warps prior to delivery. Kris complains about the quality. The building supply company says, "You ordered grade A lumber, you got grade A lumber. The contract didn't say anything about the state of the goods on delivery." If it is a custom of the building supply business to deliver supplies as ordered in good condition, Kris may be able to use oral or written evidence to show that this is an implied term of the written contract and that the court should "read" the implied term into the written agreement.

Condition Precedent Exists Outside Contract

Parties to a contract may also separately agree that the contract does not have to be performed until after a particular event, called a **condition precedent**, has occurred. If so, a party who claims that he or she is not obliged to honour the written contract because the condition precedent has not occurred may advance oral and written evidence of non-performance of the condition precedent to contradict the terms of the written agreement.

condition precedent
an event (or non-event) that must occur (or not occur) before a contract can be enforced

■ EXAMPLE OF CONDITION PRECEDENT

Ivan and Nan agree by written contract that Ivan will sell his car to Nan for $3,000. Nan tells Ivan before she signs that first she will have to see if she can borrow the money from the bank; if she cannot borrow the money, she says she will not be able to buy the car. Ivan orally agrees and Nan signs. Nan is unable to borrow the money, and Ivan says she is bound by the written contract. Nan may be able to contradict the written terms of the contract by producing written or oral evidence that there was a condition precedent that makes the written sale contract unenforceable.

Rectification

Rectification is an equitable remedy available to alter the terms of a written agreement where a mistake has been made in the document. It is available in circumstances where the common law might not permit altering the written terms.

The right to this remedy arises where the parties to the contract have held long negotiations and have reached an agreement that is reduced to a written document where a mistake was made recording the terms. Consequently, the effect of the contract is quite different from what was intended by the parties. Rectification does not alter the intention of the parties. Rather, it ensures that the wording of the written agreement accurately corresponds to what the parties intended to do. Rectification is a powerful remedy and is used with caution, because the courts watch carefully to ensure that it is not simply a cover for trying to undo a bad bargain. The court's focus is not on interpreting the terms of the contract (as is the case when the parol evidence rule is used) but on whether the terms the parties agreed to, whatever they are or however they are interpreted, are accurately reflected in the written contract.

For a party to successfully invoke the remedy of rectification, the party has to show the following with strong and clear evidence:

- *A mistake in recording the intentions of the parties.* The mistake must be clear and unambiguous. It must also be a mutual mistake—that is, both parties are mistaken, and both are mistaken in the same way. Some cases of unilateral mistake give rise to rectification but only in unusual circumstances, such as where a deed of gift has been used and the promisor unilaterally dictates the terms of the contract.

- *Formation of a common intention.* In Canada and England, even if no prior contract has been concluded to show that a mistake has been made, if there is strong and convincing evidence that the parties achieved a position where they had a common intention, that suffices for rectification where that common intention is not reflected in the final contract document.[1]

- *Clear and cogent evidence of a mistake.* There must be clear and convincing proof of a mistake in expressing the parties' intention. The evidence may be written or oral. The standard of proof required appears to be more than the usual civil standard in contract cases of proof on the balance of probabilities. The standard of proof may be as high as the criminal law standard of proof beyond a reasonable doubt, but there is some difference of opinion among commentators on whether the standard is as strict as that.[2] Clearly, if the case turns on oral evidence, the court is likely to scrutinize this evidence with great care to ensure that a claim for rectification is not an attempt to remake a bad bargain.

Remember that since this is an equitable remedy, it is subject to the usual equitable bars or defences. Delay by the party claiming rectification may be seen as evidence of insincerity. Negative effects on third parties who are not party to the agreement but who rely on it may act as a bar to rectification. Attempts to carry out the agreement may be seen as accepting it as it stands, and rectification may then be refused. Also, if the parties cannot be restored to their original position before making the agreement, rectification may be refused.

---

1   This is the statement of the law on this issue in the English Court of Appeal case *Jocelyne v. Nissen*, [1970] 2 QB 86 (CA). This decision has been followed in Canada.

2   G.H.L. Fridman, *The Law of Contract in Canada*, 3d ed. (Scarborough, ON: Carswell, 1994), 830-32.

■ EXAMPLE OF REQUEST FOR RECTIFICATION

Woodlot Canada Ltd., in Newfoundland, enters into an agreement to ship lumber to Woodhouse Ltd. in England. There have been complex negotiations involving exchanges of faxes and emails, and eventually a formal written agreement is prepared and signed by both parties. The price agreed to is £40,000, as reflected in the negotiation correspondence. When the contract is printed, the price is listed as $40,000. Woodlot immediately applies to have the contract rectified. Woodlot argues both parties intended the price to be in British pounds sterling (£), not dollars, that the recording of the price in the written contract as a dollar amount was a mistake in recording the terms of the contract, and that the evidence, in the form of negotiation correspondence, clearly indicates that the price should have been expressed in pounds sterling.

EXCLUSION AND PENALTY CLAUSES

Exclusion (Exemption) Clauses

Sometimes a party will insist on including in a contract an **exclusion clause**, also called an **exemption clause**, that protects that party from liability for negligence in performing contractual obligations or from failing to carry out contractual obligations. For example, most parking lot contracts include a clause that states that the lot owner is not liable for damage to your car or its contents, or for theft of the car or contents however the damage is caused. In other contracts, the clause limits liability. For example, if you buy a roll of film that includes developing the pictures you take, the contract is likely to include a clause that says if the company loses or damages the film or fails to develop it, it is liable only for the cost of the film, even if you are a professional photographer and your pictures are worth thousands of dollars. Generally, a party to a contract who wishes to limit liability for negligent conduct or for conduct where that party is liable though not at fault may limit liability. It is clear, however, that fraud by the party relying on an exclusion clause will not be excluded no matter what the clause says. An exclusion clause does not exclude liability for a fundamental breach of the terms of the contract, although as we will see later in this section, the law on fundamental breach is changing.

exclusion/exemption clause
a clause in a contract that limits the liability of the parties

NOTICE OF AN EXCLUSION CLAUSE

For an exclusion clause to operate, the party relying on it must be sure to bring the clause to the other party's attention and notice. The act of giving notice must include reasonable steps to draw the clause to the other party's attention. If, for example, the clause is buried in fine print on the back of the contract, even if the other party has accepted the contract and it is otherwise binding on her or him, she or he may be able to show that the placement of the clause does not constitute reasonable steps to bring it to her or his attention. These clauses are often inserted by the party relying on them in printed form contracts or documents that are separate from but part of the contract, such as parking lot, film-processing, and dry-cleaning receipts. In these cases, the courts have required that the party relying on the clause demonstrates that the offeree knew the clause was there or had ample opportunity to know it was there. For example, if a parking lot posts a large, illuminated sign that sets out the liability exclusion in plain language in large print right where you drive into the lot and pay, that may be a reasonable way of giving the necessary notice. So may printing the clause on the contract in plain language and in larger print of a different colour from that of the rest of the contract. Where the exclusion clause is referred to on the contract but posted elsewhere—for example, on a receipt—that may be insufficient to constitute proper notice of the clause.

Generally, the courts will carefully examine how notice was given. They are reluctant to permit a party from contracting out of her or his own negligence, particularly where bargaining power is unequal, as it often is with printed form contracts, where negotiation of the terms at the time you park your car, for instance, is simply impractical.[3] However, where the contracting parties have roughly equal bargaining power, where there is time to consider the terms carefully, and where both parties are independently advised, the courts are more likely to let the clause stand on the ground that, with equality of bargaining power, the exclusion clause is not unilaterally imposed on one party by the other.

The courts have also made it clear that notice must be given before the contract is entered into, not afterwards.[4] However, express notice need not be given in every case, particularly where both parties are relatively sophisticated and are experienced with the type of contract in question, or are knowledgeable about the practices and conventions in a particular trade. For example, in one case an owner of goods sued when the goods were damaged by the shipper. The evidence showed that the plaintiff had worked in the shipping industry and was familiar with the standard form shipping contract, which contained a standard exclusion clause. The court held that while the plaintiff was not given express notice of the clause, he certainly was aware of the existence of the clause and what it meant from his experience in the industry.[5]

STRICT INTERPRETATION

contra proferentem
a rule used in the interpretation of contracts when dealing with ambiguous terms according to which a court will choose the interpretation that favours the party who did not draft the contract

If the court is satisfied that the party relying on the clause gave appropriate notice, the court may interpret the clause narrowly against the person relying on the clause. In particular, the ***contra proferentem*** canon of interpretation may be used so that the party relying on the exclusion clause must show strict compliance with the contract. For example, if a parking lot contract excludes liability for theft or damage to the car by the parking lot company, but damage is done by an employee and not by the company, the clause might not operate to exclude liability. For that to happen, the clause would also have to include a phrase that excluded liability caused by the owner or by the negligent acts of employees. Similarly, if such a clause had been drafted, it would not exclude liability if the damage was intentionally done by the employee, because only negligence is excluded. Here the clauses are construed narrowly against the person who relies on them.

---

3   *Browne v. Core Rentals Ltd.* (1983), 23 BLR 291 (Ont. HC); *Tilden Rent-A-Car v. Glendenning* (1978), 83 DLR (3d) 400 (Ont. CA).

4   *Campbell v. Image*, [1978] 2 WWR 663 (BC Co. Ct.); *Mendelsohn v. Normand Ltd.*, [1970] 1 QB 177.

5   *Captain v. Far Eastern Steamship Co.* (1978), 97 DLR (3d) 250 (BCSC).

When an employee or agent of the contracting party relying on an exclusion clause causes harm, it is clear that there must be explicit language to cover the act if the party relying on the clause is to escape liability. If the clause does not cover employee or agent negligence, then the contracting party who is the principal or employer is liable for the employee's or agent's negligence. What is not so clear is whether the employee is protected by the employer's exclusion clause if the employer's contract covers employee negligence when the employee is not a party to the contract. Normally, strangers do not acquire rights under a contract because they are not parties and because they gave no consideration. Therefore, while the employer may not be liable for an employee's negligence, an employee may have to deal with personal liability issues if his or her acts caused damage to the employer's customer.

The courts, while acknowledging the need for strict construction of exclusion clauses, are uneasy about a result where liability is shifted from the employer to the employee, who is least likely to be able to bear the financial burden of covering the loss. The courts have dealt with employee liability in two ways. First, they have relied on agency law, where the employer is seen as an agent of the employee, contracting on the employee's behalf as well as her or his own, when employee acts are covered by the exclusion clause. This effectively prevents the injured party from pursuing either the employer who prepared the contract or the employee on whose behalf the employer negotiated the exclusion clause.[6] Second, in Canada, the Supreme Court has focused on the special nature of the employer–employee relationship and the way in which that relationship should be affected by the exclusion clause.

In *London Drugs Ltd. v. Kuehne & Nagel International Ltd.*,[7] the corporate defendant stored a transformer for the plaintiff. The defendant's contract excluded liability for any amount over $40 unless the plaintiff paid a surcharge. The plaintiff declined to pay the surcharge. The defendant's employees, in moving the transformer, damaged it. The plaintiff sued the corporate defendant and its employees. The trial court held that the corporate defendant was protected by the exclusion clause and was liable for $40, but, strictly interpreting the clause, the employees were liable for the full amount of the plaintiff's loss on the ground that they were not covered by the clause. In the Supreme Court of Canada, the majority held that the employees were covered by the exclusion clause, allowing for a relaxation of the strict construction rule for third parties who are agents of the contracting party relying on the clause. Iacobucci J, however, focused on the special relationship of employer–employee and the common interest both have in performing the employer's contractual obligations. In the view of Iacobucci J, if the customer knows that the employer's obligations are to be carried out by employees and the contract has a term limiting liability of the employer for work to be done by employees, it is not sensible to uphold the strict privity of contract rules, which will result in employees shouldering the whole liability burden. In these circumstances, the customer has notice of the risks that he or she is running as a result of the exclusion clause. However, before an employee can shelter under the clause, the clause must extend explicitly to employees and the employee must show that he or she was acting in the course of employment and engaged in providing the very

---

6   *New Zealand Shipping Co. v. A.M. Satterthwaite and Co.*, [1974] 1 All ER 1015 (PC).

7   (1992), 97 DLR (4th) 261 (SCC). See in particular the decision of Iacobucci J. For a further discussion of this case see Fridman, supra footnote 2, at 586-88.

services covered by the contract between the employer and the employee. The effect of this decision is to create a narrow protective right for third parties and a limited exception to the normal privity rules.

EXCLUSION CLAUSES AND FUNDAMENTAL BREACH

In England, the courts developed a limitation of the application and operation of exclusion clauses in circumstances where the exempted conduct or act amounted to more than a breach of a minor term, but was a fundamental breach of the contract, where the breach went to the root or heart of the contract. Determining whether a breach was fundamental was not always easy. If you contracted to ship goods and the shipper negligently allowed them to be destroyed, you could argue that the contract was about shipping goods and their destruction was a fundamental breach, since the subject matter of the contract had been lost. Similarly, where the goods were slightly damaged in transit, it would be hard to argue that the breach was more than minor. The problem with fundamental breach is that it is difficult to determine where the line between these two extremes lies where a breach goes from minor—where exclusion clauses apply—to major—where the breach is so enormous that the exclusion clause cannot be relied on.

The courts in Canada and England have gone back and forth on the effect of fundamental breach on an exclusion clause, and the fortunes of fundamental breach have waxed and waned accordingly. The law of fundamental breach and its effect on exclusion clauses is still uncertain. In the Supreme Court of Canada's major review of the issues in *Hunter Engineering Ltd. v. Syncrude Canada Ltd.*,[8] the court was split, taking two different approaches: one approach applied the doctrine of fundamental breach and considered whether the breach undermined the entire contract so as to go to the root of the contract, in which case the exclusion clause did not apply; the other approach found fundamental breach to be an artificial doctrine that creates unnecessary complexities and uncertainty in the law. If unfairness resulted from applying an exclusion clause, it would be better to simply address the matter as an issue of unconscionability.[9] As a result of the court's split in this case, the future of fundamental breach on exclusion clauses must be regarded as unsettled.

■ EXAMPLE OF EXCLUSION CLAUSE

JoAnn parks her car in Wanda's Parking Lot. The following is printed on the back of the parking receipt: "Wanda is not responsible for loss or damage to your car due to the negligence of Wanda or her employees." Linh, one of Wanda's employees, loses her temper and wilfully bashes in the windshield of JoAnn's car. JoAnn sues Wanda for damaging her car. Wanda says she is not liable because she is exempt as a result of the liability clause.

The clause may not operate if JoAnn can show that she had no notice of the clause and that printing it on the back of the ticket did not constitute a reasonable step in bringing the clause to her attention before the contract

---

8   (1989), 57 DLR (4th) 321 (SCC).

9   For a more detailed review of the fortunes of the doctrine of fundamental breach in recent case law, see Fridman, *supra* footnote 2, at 588-600.

was made. JoAnn may also argue that even if she had notice, the clause has to be construed narrowly—it exempts Wanda and her employees from negligence, but Linh's act was wilful and is not covered by the exclusion. JoAnn could also argue that even if Wanda is exempt, Linh is not because she was not a party to the contract and could not benefit from the exclusion. Against this, Linh might argue that if Wanda is covered Linh might also be, since Wanda could have excluded herself and, acting as Linh's agent, could have bargained an exclusion for Linh, as well. Alternatively, Linh could argue on the basis of Iacobucci J's reasons in *London Drugs* that JoAnn had notice that Wanda's employees would carry out Wanda's contractual obligations and that employees such as Linh are specifically covered by the clause. This argument might fall apart, of course, because Linh's wilful conduct was outside the exclusion clause in any event.

Penalty Clauses

Clauses in a contract that determine in advance the manner and amount of compensation to the injured party in the event of a specific type of breach are called **penalty clauses** or compensation clauses. The courts interpret these clauses very carefully, reserving the right to ultimately decide on damages to be awarded.

Penalty clauses are used in a variety of situations and usually take one of three forms.

- A clause that provides a very low amount of compensation for a specific harm done. This may be seen as an exclusion clause rather than one providing a penalty or compensation.

- A clause that prohibits the parties from suing for breach of contract to obtain damages and allows instead substitution of other goods or repairs.

- A clause that provides for the payment of a specific sum or forfeiture of a performance bond or other security, where the sum is expressed as a pre-assessment of the parties' loss from non-performance. This is sometimes referred to as a **liquidated damages clause**, where an amount is agreed to that will presumably cover the actual loss that is likely to occur.

A penalty clause that provides for a clearly inadequate amount for a loss is really an exclusion clause and is subject to controls imposed by the courts discussed in the preceding section. A clause that limits the right to sue for damages and provides alternative remedies is also subject to court scrutiny on the issue of whether the clause provides adequate compensation. If a court finds that the clause provides inadequate remedies, the injured party may be able to sue for damages despite the clause.

The type of penalty clause that has attracted much court attention is one that provides for liquidated damages on breach. Here the issue is whether the amount forfeited really is designed to compensate for damages or whether it is in the nature of a penalty. If the amount is a real pre-estimate of damages made in good faith, the court will allow the clause to stand. However, if the amount claimed is out of proportion to the damages likely to be sustained, the court may perceive it as a penalty. If the court sees it as a penalty, the court is also likely to see it as a threat or form of coercion and is likely to prevent the party benefiting from the clause from

penalty clause
a term in a contract that imposes a penalty for default or breach

liquidated damages clause
a term in a contract that attempts to reasonably estimate the damages that will be suffered if the contract is breached

relying on it. This type of compensation clause often sets out an amount to be paid "as liquidated damages and not as a penalty." The courts are not deflected by this phrase from determining whether the amount really can be construed as damages or whether it constitutes a penalty. If it is determined to be a penalty, the court may provide relief to the party who is required to pay. The question whether a specific amount constitutes damages or a penalty must be determined on the facts of a particular case. Some reference points are as follows:

- If the amount is extravagant and unconscionable with regard to the maximum loss that could possibly follow from the breach, the clause is likely to be seen as a penalty clause.

- If the obligation requires payment of a certain sum and if that sum is not paid, a much greater sum must then be paid, and the clause is likely to be seen as a penalty clause.

- If there is only one event that triggers payment, the sum is likely to be seen as liquidated damages.

- If one sum is payable on any of several events occurring, some serious and others trifling, there is a presumption that the sum is a penalty. However, this may not be the case where it is difficult to prove or project the actual losses for any of the events.[10]

Generally if the court determines that a sum is a penalty, it will not enforce the clause whether the clause withholds a payment or compels one to be made. The burden of proving a penalty lies with the person who alleges that it is a fact. However, where the court finds that the sum is a penalty, it may not interfere if the clause is not unconscionable or if it is protected by statute.[11] Where a clause has been found to require court intervention, the court may substitute a reasonable amount for the sum set out in the clause. It is not clear whether a clause that is found to be a penalty clause is simply void or not, but there are cases where the court has granted relief from forfeiture by relieving a party from having to pay the penalty, particularly where the clause has been found to be unconscionable.

EXAMPLE OF PENALTY CLAUSE

Khan wants to have a marina showroom built by Fly By Night Construction. Khan is anxious to have the showroom completed and open by the Victoria Day weekend, because his most profitable season begins then. Based on past experience, he figures he will average about $10,000 a week in sales. Khan insists that Fly By Night substantially complete the building so that it can be opened by the Friday of the Victoria Day weekend. He also insists on a penalty clause in case the building is not completed on time, with Fly By Night paying $30,000 to Khan for each week after the deadline until the building is substantially completed. Fly By Night is three weeks late and objects to the clause, saying it is a penalty and not liquidated damages. The amount claimed is 200 percent more than the actual estimated damages

---

10 *Dunlop Pneumatic Tyre Co. v. New Garage & Motor Co.*, [1915] AC 79 (HL).

11 *Dimensional Investments Ltd. v. R*, [1968] SCR 93.

and could be seen as a penalty, although Khan could argue that it is reasonable because actual losses are hard to estimate, and there may be other ancillary costs to Khan as well that cannot be anticipated. If Fly By Night is successful, the court could set an appropriate amount for damages, relieving Fly By Night of the obligation to pay a penalty.

FRUSTRATION

A contract may become impossible to perform through no fault of either party. In some situations the court invokes the **doctrine of frustration of contract**, declaring that the contract has been frustrated and that the parties to it should be relieved of their obligations under it. The doctrine of frustration began to develop only in the 19th century. At common law, before this time, parties who made promises were expected to remain bound to carry out the terms of the agreement no matter what. The contractual promise was seen as absolute, and impossibility of performance did not excuse the obligation of performance unless the parties explicitly provided for a termination of the contract because of impossibility. For example, if Mona engaged a famous portraitist, Leon, to paint her portrait, the contract might set out what would happen if Leon died before finishing the painting. In this situation, the parties might decide to terminate the contract, because Mona may not have wished to have a lesser painter do it, and Leon might not want his estate to be bound by an obligation to find someone to complete the work.[12]

However, by the 19th century, in cases where no explicit provision was made to terminate because of impossibility of performance, the courts in some circumstances began to imply terms permitting termination on the grounds of impossibility. This marked the beginning of the development of the doctrine of frustration of contract, in which the courts held that in some circumstances the occurrence of certain events beyond the control of the parties made it impossible to perform the contract.

> **doctrine of frustration of contract**
> a legal doctrine that permits parties to a contract to be relieved of the contractual obligations because of the occurrence of some event beyond their control that makes it impossible for them to perform the contract

Factors Affecting Frustration of Contracts

The following are some of the situations that can lead to a finding that a contract has been frustrated:

- The impossibility arises from an act of some third party.

- The impossibility arises from some natural or external force: fire, flood, earthquake, weather, or other *force majeure*.

- The impossibility cannot be prevented by the parties and is beyond their control.

- The impossibility is not, directly or indirectly, brought about by the party who is arguing that the contract has been frustrated.

- The impossibility is caused by the death or serious physical incapacity of a party where a personal attribute of that party was required to perform the contract—for example, where the party was obliged to compose a piece of music and had been chosen for her or his particular skills.

> ***force majeure***
> a major event that the parties to a contract did not foresee or anticipate that prevents performance of the contract and thus terminates the contract; such an event, for example, a natural disaster or war, is outside the control of the parties and cannot be avoided with due diligence

---

12 *Paradine v. Jane* (1647), 82 ER 897.

- The impossibility is caused by the subject matter of the contract ceasing to exist—for example, where a theatre is leased for a concert, burns down, and is no longer available.

- The impossibility is caused by a change in the law that is not contemplated by the parties.

- The impossibility is caused by serious delay that is not caused by or contemplated by the parties.

Frustration Based on the Implied Term Theory

The courts used two approaches to develop the law of frustration of contract:

- the assumption of an implied term of the contract permitting termination, and

- the construction of the purpose of a contract to decide whether the contract could be terminated because the purpose could not be fulfilled.

In the implied term approach, the term can be seen as a condition precedent to performance of a contract. For example, if A rents a theatre from B for a performance and the theatre burns down so that it is impossible for A and B to carry out their contractual obligations, the court might see the existence of the theatre as an implied condition precedent to performance of the contract by either party, even though the parties made no explicit provision for this possibility.[13] In other cases, other suitable terms have been implied to deal with the frustration of a contract by the occurrence of some event neither party explicitly contemplates, but which clearly makes impossible the performance of the contract the parties agreed to.

The implied term approach rests on the idea that the contract the parties agreed to, by its nature, must have assumed or implied certain things or situations to exist in order for the contract to be performed. If the contract cannot be performed because some intervening event makes it impossible through no fault of the parties, then the contract can be seen to be frustrated because performance is no longer possible. The test for determining whether there is an implied term requiring discharge due to frustration is an objective "reasonable person" test rather than what the parties say they contemplated. If the contract has express terms for termination because of frustration, the courts will not imply a term for a situation not covered by the express term. In this situation, the courts hold that the parties, having directed their minds to include express terms, must have excluded any other basis for finding that the contract has been frustrated.[14]

Frustration Based on Contract Construction Theory

Another approach the courts took in developing the doctrine of frustration was determining that a contract had become frustrated or impossible to perform

---

13 *Taylor v. Caldwell* (1863), 122 ER 309; *Appleby v. Myers* (1867), LR 2 CP 651. These cases were followed in Canada, starting with the Supreme Court of Canada decision in *Kerrigan v. Harrison* (1921), 62 SCR 374.

14 Fridman, supra footnote 2, at 640.

because the very basis or purpose of the contract had ceased to exist; what remained was not the contract the parties had agreed to or contemplated. In these cases, the courts subjectively tried to determine what the parties' "purpose of the adventure" or "common object of the agreement" was. Finding the common purpose of the parties involved a subjective analysis of what the parties actually said the contractual purpose was. If intervening events made fulfilling the contractual purpose impossible so that there was a radical change in the obligations of the parties, then the contract could be deemed to be frustrated, and the parties then would be relieved of their obligations to continue.[15]

The cases indicate that courts in both Canada and England are now more inclined to follow the construction theory. G.H.L. Fridman sets out some sound reasons why this should be so. His comments about the need to be realistic and practical rather than formulaic and overly abstract in interpreting contract problems applies to all areas of contract law, not just to the doctrine of frustration:

> What, then, is the purpose behind replacing the "implied term" theory … by the "construction theory," with its emphasis on a radical change in the obligation? The answer seems to be the desire by courts to escape from … the need for fictions, replacing them by a more realistic approach that provides an explanation of what the courts are truly performing rather than an explanation that employs such facile expressions and notions as "implied terms." To imply a term in order to resolve the issue is obviously legal sleight-of-hand, concealing what is really being done. To inquire into the true nature of the contractual obligation, for the purpose of discovering whether it is in conformity with that obligation that it can validly outlast and survive the change of circumstances that has occurred is more direct, honest, open, and rational. Such an approach is consistent with what has been happening generally in the law of contract, namely, the realization that contracts cannot be understood and interpreted except by reference to the surrounding circumstances.[16]

Distinguishing Between Impossibility and Frustration

In some cases the terms "impossibility" and "frustration" are used interchangeably, but they are not quite the same. "Impossibility" refers to situations where performance is physically or legally impossible. "Frustration" includes situations where performance is physically or legally possible but would be very different from the purpose of the contract that the parties had contemplated. Today, cases that deal with contract frustration have gone beyond the narrower concept of impossibility to include contracts that, while technically possible to perform, are in practical and commercial terms frustrated because the original contract purpose has disappeared.

▓ EXAMPLES OF FRUSTRATED CONTRACTS

- Farah wants to buy a load of eggplants for processing. They must be very ripe and bought late in the season. Timothy agrees to supply them. There is an express provision discharging the contract if the goods are destroyed by

---

15 *Davis Contractors Ltd. v. Fareham Urban District Council*, [1956] AC 696 (HL); *Capital Quality Homes Ltd. v. Colwyn Construction Ltd.* (1975), 61 DLR (3d) 385 (Ont. CA).

16 Fridman, supra footnote 2, at 636-37.

hail or lightning. Before they can be harvested, there is a violent earthquake that creates a fault line that swallows up and destroys all the eggplants. Farah sues for breach of contract, and Timothy's response is that the contract has been frustrated by the destruction of the eggplants. The earthquake is an act of nature not caused by either party and wholly outside their control. While there is an express term contemplating discharge from frustration, it does not contemplate earthquakes, so that it could be said that the parties did not contemplate or foresee the cause of the destruction. Further, it could be said that the parties, knowing that eggplants are fragile, might have contemplated that the contract could not be carried out if the eggplants were destroyed, so an implied term permitting discharge might be found by a court. On the other hand, because the parties did make express provisions for discharge by frustration, by not including earthquakes it could be argued that they did not intend to treat the contract as frustrated. However, if one analyzed the contract to determine what the parties intended, it could be said to be the delivery of eggplants. Where that was no longer possible, performance would be radically different from what was originally contemplated, and the contract therefore could be treated as discharged because doing what the parties intended was no longer possible.

- The Prince of Ptomania is to be crowned king. Lady Hinkle rents rooms from Professor Baloneya along the coronation route at a very high price so that she can watch the coronation procession. Unfortunately, the week before the procession there is a revolution, and Prince Ptomania is overthrown and sent into exile. Baloneya demands payment, saying, "You rented rooms for the day, Hinkle—you have to pay." Hinkle's answer is that Baloneya knew the purpose of the rental, which was why the rent was so exorbitant. Since the purpose of the contract has ceased to exist, Hinkle says she should not have to pay; the contract has been frustrated and cannot be enforced.

Common Law Remedies for Frustration

At common law, when a contract was terminated because performance was frustrated, the position of the parties was crystallized or frozen. The cases left the loss where it fell at the time of crystallization. If one party had paid a deposit, it could not be recovered. If the other party had done some work, the cost could not be recovered. In this situation there might be a setoff, where a party could apply the deposit in his or her hands to compensate for the work he or she had done. But what of an executory contract? If a party had paid a contract price and the other party had done nothing, a windfall situation would be created for the party who was paid, while the other party was out of pocket with nothing to show for the payment. Furthermore, if money was due in advance and a frustrating event occurred, the money might still have to be paid if the due date occurred before the frustrating event.[17] The unfairness of this situation was addressed by the House of Lords in the case of *Fibrosa Spolka Akcyjna v. Fairbairn Lawson Combe Barbour Ltd.*[18] The court held

---

17 *Chandler v. Webster*, [1904] 1 KB 493.

18 [1943] AC 32 (HL).

that where there was a total failure of consideration due to frustration of the contract, parties were entitled to recover moneys paid before the crystallizing event, although the court did not allow the party who made the expenditures to carry out her or his obligations to recover money for those expenditures. While some later cases seem to be more flexible, allowing recovery on the basis of what is just and reasonable whether there was total failure of consideration or not,[19] the case law does not create much order or certainty. It has been left to the legislature to do what is necessary to create clear rules for compensation when a contract is frustrated.

■ EXAMPLE OF APPORTIONING LOSSES FOR FRUSTRATION AT COMMON LAW

Zora wants to build a house along a clifftop for the scenic view. She hires Tariq Contractors Ltd. to design and build the house. Tariq has completed the design and bought some custom building supplies when Zora is notified by the municipality that the zoning for the property is being changed to prevent her from building any structure on the land. She has paid Tariq a deposit of about 15 percent of the value of the work done and the materials supplied by Tariq.

At common law, once the contract is frustrated, the parties' position is crystallized, and the losses lie where they fall. Tariq could keep the deposit but has to absorb losses for the work done and the materials supplied. Zora loses her deposit and is left with the vacant land.

Legislation Governing Frustration of Contracts

An act to deal with frustrated contracts was passed in England in 1943 and became the model statute for frustrated contracts legislation in all provinces except British Columbia, Nova Scotia, and Saskatchewan. Ontario's *Frustrated Contracts Act* is typical of this kind of legislation.[20] British Columbia has a modified form of the statute that is used in the other provinces.[21] Nova Scotia and Saskatchewan still rely on the common law. Where the contract concerns the sale of **specific goods**, except in British Columbia, the subject matter may be covered by the provincial *Sale of Goods Act* rather than by the common law or the provincial *Frustrated Contracts Act*.

specific goods
specific, identifiable chattels that have been singled out for contract purposes

FRUSTRATED CONTRACTS ACT

The Act covers most but not all contracts. Among the exclusions are

- contracts governed by a specific statute that has frustration provisions, on the basis that a specific statute overrides the provisions in a general statute, such as the *Frustrated Contracts Act*;

- contracts where the parties have created express terms to deal with frustration;

---

19 *Cahan v. Fraser* (1951), 4 DLR 112 (BCCA).

20 RSO 1990, c. F.34.

21 RSBC 1979, c. 144. Discussion in the text is based on the legislation in other provinces.

- certain contracts for the carriage of goods by sea;

- insurance contracts;

- contracts for the sale of goods when the goods cease to exist before the contract is entered into without fault by either party and before risk passes to the buyer (this is likely to be a case of mistake, rather than frustration); and

- contracts where the goods cease to exist after the contract is entered into without fault by either party and before risk passes to the buyer.

The operation of the legislation is triggered when a contract that is governed by the law of the province where the *Frustrated Contracts Act* is in operation has become impossible to perform or has been frustrated, and the parties have been discharged from the further performance of the contract because of frustration or impossibility. The Act does not create rules for deciding when a contract is frustrated—that is still left to the case law. What the statute does is to regulate post-contract collapse recovery:

- Money that is paid before discharge is recoverable.

- Debts accrued but not yet paid are not to be paid.

- Total failure of consideration is not required. Even if some value was obtained, the contract can be terminated for frustration and parties may receive compensation.

- Where a party has incurred expenses to carry out the contract, the party may be allowed to keep part or all of a deposit paid by the other party, or to recover some or all of the expenses.

- The court is given a reserve power to apportion losses and benefits so that if one party receives some benefit, where failure of consideration is not total, she or he will have to pay the other side a reasonable amount for that benefit.

SALE OF GOODS ACT

Where there is a contract for the sale of specific goods and the goods are destroyed after the contract was made but before risk passes to the buyer, either party may back out of the agreement. If the goods are not specific goods, are not destroyed, or are subject to express terms, or the risk has passed to the buyer, the parties have to look to the *Frustrated Contracts Act* or to common law for relief.

SUMMARY

The role of the court is to try to find and give effect to the intention of the parties to a contract when there is a dispute about its meaning or its consequences. The initial step is to classify contract statements. Representations, if factual and if they induce a party to enter into an agreement, may allow the injured party to avoid a contract if the representation is incorrect. Where there is a dispute about a term, if the term is a condition, it is deemed to be a serious provision affecting the principal purpose of the contract. If it is a warranty, it is deemed to be a subsidiary or minor provision for which the consequences for breach are less serious.

Where a contract is in writing, the courts normally interpret the words of the agreement and will not look at oral evidence of what the parties intended. However, where the language of the agreement is ambiguous, the court may use the parol evidence rule to hear oral or written evidence about what the parties intended. Where the terms of the written agreement are clear, but the result of a mistake, the court may invoke the equitable remedy of rectification to correct the mistake.

Where parties have attempted to exclude liability, the court may intervene to relieve a party from the effects of an exclusion clause where one party has exempted himself or herself from liability or imposed a clause requiring one party to pay damages to the other for failure to meet contract terms. The courts interpret exclusion clauses strictly and limit their application. Damage or penalty clauses are also closely examined to see whether the fixed damage amount bears some resemblance to the actual damage done, and is not a penalty.

Sometimes a contract becomes impossible to perform through the happening of an event that is no fault of either party. In this kind of situation, the courts may hold that the contract is frustrated, relieving both parties of the obligation to continue performance from the time of the frustrating event, although both sides may have to bear their own losses and benefits under the contract from the time of frustration.

KEY TERMS

condition	material representation
condition precedent	parol evidence
contra proferentem	penalty clause
doctrine of frustration contract	representation
exclusion/exemption clause	specific goods
force majeure	term
liquidated damages clause	warranty

REVIEW QUESTIONS

1. Why is distinguishing between representations, conditions, and warranties important?

2. What is the parol evidence rule, and what is its purpose?

3. In what circumstances can oral and other written evidence be used to interpret a written contract?

4. What is the effect of rectification on an agreement?

5. How is the parol evidence rule different from rectification?

6. In what circumstances can a party to a contract successfully obtain the remedy of rectification?

7. What are penalty clauses? What forms do penalty clauses take?

8. When might a court intervene with respect to the application of a penalty clause?

9. Why was it necessary for the courts to depart from the strict rules of contract to create a doctrine of frustrated contracts?

10. What sort of events give rise to a frustrated contract? What sort of events will not give rise to a frustrated contract?

11. If Dante owes Beatrice money but he dies before he can pay it, is the contract ended by frustration because Dante died? Why or why not?

12. Describe the theory of implied term and the theory of construction of a contract as they are used in frustration of contract cases. Which approach are courts likely to use now, and why?

13. What is the difference, if any, in the meaning of "impossibility" and "frustration" as those terms are used in frustration cases?

14. What were the shortcomings of the common law in granting remedies in frustration cases?

15. To what extent were the problems with common law remedies overcome by

    a. the *Fibrosa* case,

    b. the *Frustrated Contracts Act*, and

    c. the *Sale of Goods Act*?

DISCUSSION QUESTIONS

1. Leah owns a motorboat specially equipped for fishing. In addition to the outboard engine, it has special seats, trolling rigs, and an electronic fishfinder. She offers to sell the boat with the motor to Tranh for $20,000. They also agree that the special seats, trolling rigs, and electronic fishfinder will be included for $2,000. The written agreement refers to the sale of a boat and motor with "fishing equipment" for $22,000, with a deposit of $2,000. Before the sale is completed Leah decides she would like to keep the fishfinder. When Tranh objects, Leah tells him they agreed to sell only what was specifically in the written agreement, and that the fishfinder is not included. Assess Tranh's chances of obtaining the fishfinder, and discuss his alternative remedies.

2. Employees of a contracting party need and deserve protection when damage occurs and an exclusion clause is invoked. Explain why employees might need protection and how the courts have approached this issue. (You may want to read *London Drugs Ltd. v. Kuehne & Nagel International Ltd.* (1992), 97 DLR (4th) 261 (SCC).)

3. Dimitri is a fashion photographer. He is off to a "shoot" and realizes that he needs to buy some film. He drops into a retail film store in a mall that does not ordinarily deal with professional photographers. Dimitri notes that the film is close to its expiry date. He asks the clerk whether the film will be OK and tells the clerk a lot of money is riding on this, because he is using the film for a fashion shoot. The clerk says the film will be fine and that Dimitri should not worry about a thing. There is an exclusion clause on the side of the film box that says "WARNING" in large print "The manufacturer will not be liable for loss of the film, or negligence in manufacture or processing, however it may arise" in small print. The clerk says nothing about the exclusion clause. Dimitri is in a hurry; he takes the film, uses it, has it processed, and discovers a lot of poor exposures. Discuss the basis of liability to Dimitri of the seller and the manufacturer of the film, and the remedies Dimitri may be entitled to if he is successful.

4. Cleopatra wants to buy a load of grapes to make into wine. Antony agrees to supply what is required. Cleopatra inspects one of several of Antony's vineyards in Italy and likes what she sees. She specifies that the grapes should be selected from "those located on Antony's property" and that risk will pass to the buyer on delivery to Cleopatra at her processing plant in Alexandria. Antony accepts these terms. There is express provision discharging the contract if the grapes are destroyed by hail or go down in a sinking ship. Before they can be harvested, a severe heat wave ripens them too early. The grapes are good for nothing but vinegar. Cleopatra sues for breach of contract and Antony claims the contract is ended due to frustration. Set out arguments for and against each party's position.

5. Gangrene Ltd., located in Lower Slobovia, manufactures custom agricultural machinery. Typhus and Co. orders some custom-designed equipment from Gangrene for delivery to them in Ptomaine. Before the equipment can be delivered, war breaks out between Slobovia and Ptomaine, and all commercial contracts between the two countries become illegal in both countries. Gangrene has spent a considerable amount of money developing and producing this custom machinery, for which there is no other market. Typhus and Co. paid a deposit worth about 10 percent of the costs incurred by Gangrene.

    Advise Gangrene on its legal position with respect to contract remedies at common law and under statute. Assume that Slobovia's law is the same as the law of every province except British Columbia, Nova Scotia, and Saskatchewan.

6. "The doctrine of frustration is really just another version of the law of mistake." In discussing this statement, explain how the law of mistake is both similar to and different from the doctrine of frustration.

CHAPTER 7

Discharge of Contract

DISCHARGE GENERALLY

Once a contract has been **discharged**, the obligations under that contract are cancelled, and the contract itself is **null and void**.

Contracts may be discharged:

- by performance,
- by agreement,
- as of right,
- by operation of law,
- by frustration, or
- by breach.

Frustration was discussed in chapter 6, Contract Interpretation, and breach is discussed in chapter 8, Breach of Contract and Remedies.

discharged
released, extinguished; a discharge of a contract occurs when the parties have complied with their obligations or other events have occurred that release one or both parties from performing their obligations

null and void
of no force, validity, or effect

DISCHARGE BY PERFORMANCE

The most common way to discharge a contract is by performing the obligations under the contract. Performance may consist of performing services, paying money, delivering goods, and so on. Offering to perform the obligations under a contract is called **tender of performance**. For the contract to be discharged, both parties must tender performance. However, if one party tenders performance and the other party does not accept it, the refusing party is in breach of contract unless he or she has a valid and lawful reason. At that point, the party who tendered performance need not attempt to tender performance again and may sue the other party for breach of contract. In addition, one party must not interfere with, hinder, or prevent the other party from tendering performance. Any hindrance can be treated by the tendering party as refusal and breach of contract.

tender of performance
offering to perform that which the contracted party is obligated to perform under a contract

▨ EXAMPLE OF TENDER OF PERFORMANCE AND REFUSAL

Susan and Tanya have a contract whereby Tanya has agreed to buy Susan's crop of tomatoes for an agreed-upon price. However, when the crop is ready, the price of tomatoes has dropped and Tanya no longer wants to buy Susan's tomatoes. She now wants to buy her tomatoes at a lower price from another farmer. Susan delivers the tomatoes to Tanya, but Tanya refuses to accept them. Susan has tendered performance, but Tanya has refused to accept it. Tanya is in breach of contract.

Note that tender of performance must be within the exact terms of the contract. If the performance tendered does not comply with the terms of the contract in any way, the other party need not accept it. Performance must be exactly as specified in the contract and must occur on the right date, at the right time, and in the right place.

■ EXAMPLE OF NON-COMPLYING PERFORMANCE

Willem and Thomas have a contract whereby Thomas has agreed to buy 1200 litres of molasses from Willem. The contract states that the molasses must be delivered in 80 15-litre containers. Willem delivers the molasses in 100 12-litre containers. Because the tender of performance does not comply with the terms of the contract, Thomas is not obligated to accept it. Even though the total amount of molasses delivered (1200 litres) is correct, Willem did not perform his obligations and is in breach of contract.

legal tender
notes (bills) issued by the Bank of Canada and coins issued by the Royal Canadian Mint, subject to certain restrictions

Where the performance required of a party is the payment of money, this is called *tender of payment*. The precision required for the tender of performance also extends to the tender of payment. To comply with the terms of the contract, payment must be tendered either in **legal tender** or in the method specified in the contract, if any. If the contract states that payment must be made by way of certified cheque, delivery of an uncertified cheque will not constitute performance, and the receiving party need not accept it. If the contract does not specify a form of payment, legal tender must be used. The *Currency Act*[1] states that legal tender consists of notes (also called bank notes or bills) issued by the Bank of Canada and all coins issued by the Royal Canadian Mint. However, tender of payment using coins is subject to some restrictions. Section 8(2) of the *Currency Act* states:

> A payment in coins … is a legal tender for no more than the following amounts for the following denominations of coins:
>   a) forty dollars if the denomination is two dollars or greater but does not exceed ten dollars;
>   b) twenty-five dollars if the denomination is one dollar;
>   c) ten dollars if the denomination is ten cents or greater but less than one dollar;
>   d) five dollars if the denomination is five cents; and
>   e) twenty-five cents if the denomination is one cent.

Section 8(2.1) goes on to state:

> In the case of coins of a denomination greater than ten dollars, a payment … may consist of not more than one coin, and the payment is a legal tender for no more than the value of a single coin of that denomination.

---

1   RSC 1985, c. C-52.

Therefore, paying a debt with a truckload of pennies is not performance and need not be accepted by the creditor. However, unless the contract states otherwise, payment in Canadian notes is always legal tender. The amount tendered must also be the exact amount, as a party is not obligated to make change. Therefore, offering a $1,000 bill to pay a $10 debt (especially when the party knows that the other will not be able to make change) is not proper tender of payment.

In the business world, large sums of money are rarely paid in cash. Cheques and electronic transfers of funds are the preferred forms of payment. Using cash is inconvenient and creates potential security problems. Despite the common practice of using forms of payment other than legal tender, it is important to remember that unless the contract states otherwise, a party to a contract is not obligated to accept any form of payment except legal tender. This fact can be used by unscrupulous parties to get out of a contract to which they would otherwise be bound. This can be avoided by specifying in the contract how tender of payment is to be made or by using cash.

◼ EXAMPLE OF TENDER OF PAYMENT

Paolo agrees to sell his kayak to Allison for $2,500. They agree that Allison will pick up the kayak the following day. Later the same day, Paolo gets an offer of $2,900 from Renée. Paolo wants to sell the kayak to Renée instead. Allison hears about this and shows up at Paolo's the next day with payment in cash. Paolo cannot refuse the tender of payment. However, if Allison had arrived with a cheque, even a certified one, Paolo would be able to refuse payment because a cheque is not legal tender.

If a debtor tenders payment in the correct form, on the right date, and at the right time and place but the creditor refuses it, the debtor still has the obligation to pay the creditor. However, the debtor is not obligated to try to make another attempt at payment. In addition, even though the money remains outstanding, the creditor might be prohibited from charging interest on the debt after the date of tender. If the creditor tries to sue the debtor for payment after the date it was originally tendered, a court could use its discretion to punish the creditor by awarding the costs of the litigation to the debtor.

Of course, it would be foolish for a party to refuse a reasonable form of payment for the sole reason that the form was wrong, apart from any other lawful reason for refusing the tender of payment. If a debtor tries to make payment in the form of a certified cheque and the creditor refuses it because it is not legal tender, the creditor is within his or her rights, and the debtor still has the obligation to pay the creditor. However, the creditor might still be prohibited from charging interest on the debt after the date of tender; if the creditor tried to sue the debtor for payment, he or she might face the same cost consequences.

DISCHARGE BY AGREEMENT

The parties to a contract may agree between themselves not to proceed with the contract before the terms of the contract are fully performed. This is a **waiver**, and it discharges the contract. By agreeing to a waiver, neither party can insist on the performance of the other party's obligations. If neither party to the contract has

waiver
a voluntary agreement to relinquish a right, such as a right under a contract

performed any of the terms of the contract, then there is a mutual release of the parties from their obligations. As such, there is consideration for the waiver, and it is enforceable. If one of the parties has performed her or his obligations but the other has not, then the waiver lacks consideration. To be enforceable, other consideration should be present, or the waiver should be in writing and under seal. A waiver must be voluntary and cannot be imposed by one party on another.

■ EXAMPLE OF WAIVER

Margit agrees to build a garage for Ramesh for $5,000. Before Margit begins construction, Ramesh tells her that he has changed his mind and he does not want a new garage after all. At this point, if both Margit and Ramesh agree, they can each waive the other's obligations under the contract and the contract is discharged. Margit is under no obligation to agree but may do so voluntarily if she wishes. The consideration for the waiver is the mutual release of their obligations: Margit from her obligation to build the garage, and Ramesh from his obligation to pay $5,000. Such a waiver would be enforceable. If Margit has already built the garage and Ramesh then states that he no longer wants it, then any agreement by Margit to forgo payment would be without consideration and unenforceable.

material alteration

a change in a contract that changes its legal meaning and effect; a change that goes to the heart or purpose of the contract

The parties to a contract may voluntarily decide to alter or amend the terms of the contract. If they change only minor terms, the contract itself remains intact. However, if the changes amount to a **material alteration** of the terms of the contract, the original contract is discharged and a new contract (the altered contract) is substituted. It is often difficult to determine whether the terms that have been altered are only minor or are material or substantial terms. To make this decision it requires examining the effect of the alterations. If the alterations change the effect, meaning, or purpose of the contract, they may be material alterations. The alterations must go to the heart or root of the contract. If so, the original contract is discharged, and a new contract has been substituted for the original.

■ EXAMPLE OF MATERIAL ALTERATION

In November, Ibrahim orders a camper from Bayshore RV Ltd. The camper is to be of a certain size, have a custom layout, and have various custom luxury fittings for the interior. The contract states that the camper will be ready no later than the following May. Over the next few months, Ibrahim keeps changing his mind about what he wants. He changes the fittings, the size of the camper, and the layout. When Bayshore finally has the camper ready, it is nearly July, two months after it was supposed to be ready. Ibrahim refuses to take delivery, claiming that Bayshore is in breach of contract.

Bayshore argues that the changes made to the original contract were not just cosmetic: Ibrahim ordered a different-sized camper with a different layout. Therefore, the alterations were material, the original contract had been discharged, and a new contract had been substituted. The new contract makes no mention of a delivery date, so Bayshore is not in breach of contract.

The parties to a contract may also agree that a new contract will be substituted for an existing contract. If the new contract is between the existing parties, it is a *substituted agreement.* If the new contract involves the substitution of a new party, it is *novation.* In either case, the original contract is discharged.

In some cases, a party to a contract may find that she or he is unwilling or unable to fulfill her or his obligations under the contract and wants to terminate the contract. The other party may be willing to allow the contract to be terminated upon the payment of a sum of money or some other compensation. For example, if a supplier of goods finds that it cannot deliver the goods requested by a buyer, it may offer to substitute other goods. If a party who had agreed to supply services finds that he or she cannot complete the job, the other party may be willing to accept payment of money as compensation for the delay and expense of finding someone else to complete the work. This form of compromise is called **accord and satisfaction**. There is a distinction between accord and satisfaction and the material alteration of terms or a substituted agreement, which is found in the intent of the parties. With accord and satisfaction, the primary intent of the parties is to discharge the existing contract. In the case of a material alteration of terms or a substituted agreement, the primary intent of the parties is to form a new contract.

In the case of *British Russian Gazette & Trade Outlook Ltd. v. Associated Newspapers Ltd.*,[2] the court stated:

> Accord and satisfaction is the purchase of a release from an obligation arising under contract … by means of any valuable consideration, not being the actual performance of the obligation itself. The accord is the agreement by which the obligation is discharged. The satisfaction is the consideration which makes the agreement operative.

Parties may also discharge a contract by **merger**. If the parties enter into a verbal agreement that they later commit to writing, they have actually formed two contracts. The first is the verbal contract, and the second is the written contract. If the terms of the contract are identical, the first contract is merged with or absorbed into the second contract. The first contract is thereby discharged. If the terms of the contracts are not identical, then either novation or the material substitution of terms has occurred.

DISCHARGE AS OF RIGHT

The terms of a contract can allow one or both parties to discharge or terminate the contract. This is an **option to terminate**. This is also a form of discharge by agreement, as the option is included in the contract by the agreement of the parties. Ordinarily, the option must be exercised before the complete performance of the contract, and exercising the option is usually subject to certain terms. For example, a contract of employment may be terminated by the employer upon reasonable notice to the employee. A mortgage may be terminated by the mortgagor upon payment of the outstanding principal, plus an interest penalty, to the mortgagee. The exercise of the option to terminate does not depend on any event—the party with such a right may exercise it at will.

A contract may provide that one or both parties have the right to terminate the contract if some event in the future does or does not occur. This is called a

accord and satisfaction
a means of discharging a contract whereby the parties agree to accept some form of compromise or settlement instead of performance of the original terms of the contract

merger
the discharge of one contract by its replacement with, or absorption into, an identical contract

option to terminate
a term in a contract that allows one or both parties to discharge or terminate the contract before performance has been fully completed

---

2   [1933] 2 KB 616, at 644 (CA).

condition precedent
an event (or non-event) that must occur (or not occur) before a contract can be enforced

condition precedent. For example, someone buying a house may make the agreement to purchase conditional upon obtaining financing. If the financing is not obtained, he or she is not required to purchase the house. Someone buying a business may make the purchase conditional upon receiving a favourable audit of the financial statements of the business. If the auditor's report is negative, the purchase need not be completed. If a certain area of land is currently being considered for rezoning, a land developer may wish to purchase the property only if the rezoning application is *not* approved. If the rezoning application is approved, the developer has no obligation to purchase the property. These are all conditions precedent that may be included in the terms of the contract. The contract does not come into existence before the fulfillment of the condition precedent. The parties cannot withdraw their offer and acceptance, but they incur no obligation to perform the contract until the condition is fulfilled. The obligation to perform is, in effect, postponed. However, if one of the parties decides to terminate the contract before the fulfillment of the condition, she or he is in breach of contract.

condition subsequent
an event that, if it occurs, will terminate an existing contract

A condition precedent must be distinguished from a **condition subsequent**, which is a future event that, if it occurs, terminates or discharges an existing contract. In the case of the condition precedent, the contract does not come into existence until the event occurs. With a condition subsequent, the contract exists and performance is required, but the contract may be discharged if the event occurs. For example, a contract to attend an outdoor concert may contain a term that states that the ticket price is refundable if the concert is cancelled due to weather conditions. In a contract to construct a building, the building plans may be subject to approval by the owner at various stages through the ongoing construction. Failure to obtain approval from the owner, or the owner withholding approval, will terminate the contract.

A contract may also provide that in the event of a natural disaster or an "act of God," strike or lockout, war, or insurrection, the contract is terminated. This kind of a condition subsequent, when written into a contract, is often referred to as a *force majeure* clause and is commonly found in contracts for the transport of goods and for construction. To rely on a *force majeure* clause, the events in question must be beyond the control of the parties to the contract and not able to be avoided through the exercise of **due diligence**.

due diligence
the attention and care that a reasonable person would exercise with respect to his or her concerns; the obligation to make every reasonable effort to meet one's obligations

DISCHARGE BY OPERATION OF LAW

The *Bankruptcy and Insolvency Act*[3] provides that upon being released or discharged from bankruptcy, all of the contracts under which the bankrupt had any obligations are discharged. There are some exceptions to this, which include obligations to pay child support and to repay student loans.

All of the provinces have statutes of limitations that limit the time period within which actions to enforce contractual rights may be commenced. The Ontario *Limitations Act, 2002*,[4] for example, states that a proceeding shall not be commenced in respect of a claim after two years from the date the claim was

---

3 RSC 1985, c. B-3.

4 SO 2002, c. 24, s. 4.

discovered. The time limits imposed by these statutes are inflexible—it is impossible to enforce a contract if the action is brought outside these time limits.

This does not actually discharge the contract, which remains valid and binding. However, the obligations under the contract can no longer be enforced, so that the effect is the same as if the contract had been discharged.

The time limits imposed by the various limitations statutes are a statute codification of the common law **doctrine of laches**, which is based on the premise that failure to bring an action for the enforcement of contractual rights within a reasonable time may result in prejudice to the other party. If this is the case, the action will be barred and the courts will refuse to hear the action or enforce the contract. The *Limitations Act* does not replace the doctrine of laches. The difference between the two is that the limitations statutes impose specific time limits, while the doctrine of laches relies on the concept of a "reasonable" time limit. Therefore, it is theoretically possible to bring an action within the time limits imposed by the limitations statutes but still be barred by the doctrine of laches if the court thinks that a reasonable time limit is shorter than that specified in the statute.

The doctrine of laches simply bars the enforcement of the contract; it does not discharge it. However, the effect is the same as with the limitations statutes. If the contract is unenforceable, it is the same as if it had been discharged.

doctrine of laches
a common law doctrine that states that the neglect or failure to institute an action or lawsuit within a reasonable time period, together with prejudice suffered by the other party as a result of the delay, will result in the barring of the action

SUMMARY

Once a contract is discharged, it is null and void. Contracts are most commonly discharged through performance of the obligations under the contract. Performance usually takes one of two forms: performing an action (for example, delivering goods or performing services) or paying money. The act of offering to perform the obligations under a contract is called tender of performance or tender of payment. The performance must comply exactly with the terms of the contract, or the tender need not be accepted by the other party. Once all obligations are performed, the contract is discharged.

Parties to a contract may also agree to discharge it. If this occurs before performance of the contract, this is called a waiver, and the contract is discharged. If the parties agree to materially alter the terms of the contract, a new contract is formed and the original contract is discharged. If the parties agree that the terms of the contract will not be fulfilled and a compromise or settlement is reached instead, this is called accord and satisfaction, and the original contract is discharged. If the parties enter into a verbal contract that is later put in writing, the original verbal contract merges with the written contract and is thereby discharged.

The terms of a contract may also provide that one or both parties have the option to terminate or discharge the contract, usually upon terms such as notice or the payment of money. The terms of a contract may also include a condition precedent, the occurrence of which is necessary before the contract becomes enforceable. If the condition precedent is not fulfilled, the contract is discharged. Another term of a contract may be a condition subsequent, the occurrence of which will discharge the contract.

A contract may be discharged by the operation of law, such as through the operation of the *Bankruptcy and Insolvency Act*, or be in effect discharged, such as through the operation of the *Limitations Act* or the doctrine of laches.

KEY TERMS

accord and satisfaction   material alteration

condition precedent   merger

condition subsequent   null and void

discharged   option to terminate

doctrine of laches   tender of performance

due diligence   waiver

legal tender

REVIEW QUESTIONS

1. In what ways can a contract be discharged? What is the effect of discharging a contract?

2. For what reasons might a party legitimately refuse to accept tender of performance?

3. Define "legal tender." When is legal tender required for the tender of payment?

4. If a creditor refuses to accept tender of payment, is the debtor freed from the obligation to pay? Explain. What might be the effect of a creditor refusing tender of payment?

5. Define a "waiver." What is the consideration for a waiver? What should you do in a case where there is no consideration for a waiver?

6. What is the material alteration of the terms of a contract? What is its effect on the contract?

7. Explain the difference between novation and a substituted agreement.

8. Describe the difference between accord and satisfaction and material alteration of the terms of a contract.

9. Describe when merger of a contract might occur. What is the difference between merger and a substituted agreement?

10. Describe an option to terminate.

11. Define "condition precedent." Does a contract that is subject to a condition precedent exist before the fulfillment of the condition precedent? Why or why not?

12. Define "condition subsequent."

13. What is a *force majeure* clause? When can a party rely on such a clause?

14. Under what circumstances can a contract be discharged by the operation of law?

DISCUSSION QUESTIONS

1. Nils and his wife Wanda enter into a contract with Robert whereby Robert agrees to invest $50,000 in their custom furniture manufacturing business in exchange for a share of the business and its profits. Shortly after entering into this contract, Nils dies and the business has to be shut down. Wanda is left with no source of income, enormous debts, and five children. Out of the goodness of his heart, Robert offers to accept the sum of $10,000 instead of the anticipated profits, even though shutting down the business constitutes a breach of the terms of the contract. How would you characterize Robert's action? What danger does Wanda face in accepting this generous arrangement? What can Wanda do to protect herself?

2. Creative Designers Ltd. agrees to redecorate Carmen's home for the sum of $20,000. The services are to include completely redecorating the living room, den, and dining room. The work is to start on May 1 and be completed no later than August 1. After work begins, Carmen changes her mind about the colour of the paint she wants in the den and the type of carpet she wants in the living room. She also wants Creative Designers to redecorate the hall and the foyer. Creative Designers agrees to make all the changes. However, the work is not complete on August 1. Carmen claims that Creative Designers is in breach of contract. What arguments may Creative Designers make?

3. Northern Sawmills Inc. contracts to supply The Building Depot Ltd. with a shipment of its first-quality hardwood. The Building Depot wants Northern Sawmills' lumber because it has access to the best-quality hardwood in the area. To obtain the same quality lumber from any other source would be much more expensive. However, Northern Sawmills finds that it cannot deliver the hardwood as promised. It is out of first-quality hardwood but has lots of second-best-quality hardwood. What options are available to the parties in this case?

4. Adam has a rare Picasso painting for sale. He enters into an agreement with Wendy whereby she agrees to purchase the painting for the sum of $50,000. The terms of payment of the contract specify that Wendy will make a series of payments of $10,000 each to Adam by certified cheque or cash over a period of five months. At the fifth month, Adam will take the painting to Wendy's home and exchange it for the final payment. Wendy is consistently late in making the initial four payments. However, by the end of the fourth month she has caught up with the payments. On the date that Adam is supposed to bring the painting to her home and collect the final payment, Wendy telephones him and states that she has not had time to get to the bank and get either the cash or a certified cheque. She says she can give him either an uncertified cheque or get the money to him tomorrow. She offers to delay the exchange for one day if Adam insists on a certified cheque or cash. Adam states that he will not be coming to her home at all and that he no longer wants to sell her the painting. Discuss the arguments that would be raised by the parties in this fact situation.

CHAPTER 8

Breach of Contract and Remedies

INTRODUCTION

This chapter discusses the actions and non-actions that constitute **breach of contract** and the remedies that are available to the injured party.

When one party to a contract fails or refuses to fulfill his or her obligations under the contract without legal excuse, this is considered a breach of contract. However, different types of breaches have different consequences. The method of the breach must first be established, and then the nature or seriousness of the breach must be examined. Then, the remedies available to the injured party can be determined. The injured party may be able to claim compensation for damages suffered as a result of the breach; declare that the contract has been discharged, thereby releasing the injured party from her or his obligations; compel the party in breach to perform the obligations; or a combination of all three.

breach of contract
failure, without legal excuse, to perform any promise that forms part of a contract

METHOD OF BREACH

A party to a contract may **repudiate** the contract, thereby breaching the contract. The most common form of repudiation is failing or refusing to perform the obligations of the contract when they become due. This form of repudiation is known as **express repudiation** or **express breach**. The repudiation must be clear, unambiguous, and explicit. It may take the form of an actual declaration of refusal, or simply a failure to perform.

repudiate
to renounce or reject an obligation

express repudiation/ express breach
the failure or refusal to perform the obligations of a contract when they become due

■ EXAMPLE OF EXPRESS REPUDIATION OR BREACH

Samuel promises to deliver a load of gravel to Northwest Contracting Limited on a certain day. On that day he fails to deliver the gravel as promised. In the alternative, on the day of delivery, he telephones Northwest Contracting and states that he cannot deliver the gravel as promised.

If the repudiation occurs before the date of performance, it is an **anticipatory breach**. Again, the repudiation must be clear, unambiguous, and explicit.

anticipatory breach
an express repudiation that occurs before the time of performance of a contract

EXAMPLE OF ANTICIPATORY BREACH

Samuel promises to deliver a load of gravel to Northwest Contracting Limited on a certain day. Before that day, he discovers that the company that supplies his gravel has increased its price, with the result that if Samuel delivers gravel to Northwest at the agreed-upon price, he will lose money. Samuel calls Northwest before the day of delivery to say that he will not be delivering the gravel.

More difficult is the situation where one party repudiates the contract by implication. **Implied repudiation** is a form of anticipatory breach, since it occurs before the performance date. The innocent party must ascertain, from the actions or statements of the other party, that he or she does not intend to perform the obligations under the contract when the time for performance arrives. The innocent party is in a difficult position. The party who appears to be repudiating by implication may still perform the contract as specified when the time comes. However, if he or she does not, the innocent party may suffer increased damages as a result of the delay in waiting to address the situation. Further, if the innocent party assumes that the other party intends to breach when that is not the case, the innocent party may take steps that result in a breach on his or her part. Because the very nature of implied repudiation relies on speculation and inference, misunderstandings may occur.

implied repudiation
repudiation that is not express and must be implied or deduced from the circumstances

EXAMPLE OF IMPLIED REPUDIATION

Dawn enters into a contract with Emil to paint his house. Two weeks before the day she is supposed to start work, Emil finds out that she has sold all of her painting equipment to one of her competitors. Clearly, without her painting equipment, Dawn will be unable to perform her obligations under the contract. Emil might want to treat this as an implied repudiation of the contract. However, if Dawn buys new equipment before the day she is supposed to start painting, she could still perform her obligations. On the other hand, if Emil waits to find out what Dawn will do, he may not be able to find a replacement for her in time to have his house painted.

However, in some cases the nature of the implied repudiation is such that there can be no misinterpretation. This includes situations where the implied repudiation makes performing the contractual obligations impossible.

EXAMPLE OF IMPLIED REPUDIATION THAT IS CERTAIN

Lindsey and Scott enter into a contract whereby Lindsey agrees to sell Scott her stereo. Before the date that Lindsey is supposed to deliver the stereo to Scott, he finds out that she has sold it to someone else. While this is still a case of implied repudiation, because of the certainty that Lindsey will be unable to deliver the stereo to Scott on the agreed-upon date, Scott may treat this as a breach of contract.

NATURE OF BREACH

Once it has been established that a contract has been breached, the nature or effect of the breach must be examined. The nature of the breach is determined primarily on the basis of its seriousness. A term of a contract that is essential or goes to the root of the contract is called a condition. A minor or subsidiary term is called a warranty. It is important to examine the contract as a whole and in context to determine whether any given term is a condition or a warranty. For instance, in a contract to buy a car, the make and model of the car would be a condition, while the colour of the car might be a warranty. The delivery of a car of the correct make and model, but the incorrect colour, would be breach of a warranty but not breach of a condition. However, in a contract to paint a house, the colour of the paint might be a condition. In such a case, painting the house the wrong colour would be breach of a condition. A breach of a condition must wholly deprive the innocent party of the benefit he or she expected to receive under the contract. The distinction between a breach of warranty and a breach of condition is important in determining what remedies are available for the breach.

Fundamental breach is another category of breach. Fundamental breach is difficult to distinguish from breach of a condition. Both are breaches of a major term of the contract, a term that goes to the root of the contract. However, a fundamental breach is often seen as more serious than the breach of a condition. A fundamental breach undermines or destroys the whole contract. The difference between fundamental breach and breach of a condition is important where the effect of an exclusion clause is being considered. *Exclusion clauses* in a contract limit the liability of one of the parties and are discussed in more detail later in the chapter. The law in this area is still developing, and recent developments seem to indicate that "the concept of fundamental breach is considerably more important and relevant to the determination of the rights of the parties after breach than the categorization of the term that has been breached."[1] While there is still some ambiguity in this area, it seems that the concept of fundamental breach goes deeper than the idea of breach of a condition. The court must investigate the underlying purpose and nature of the contract, the benefits that the parties intended to obtain, and the consequences of the breach to determine whether fundamental breach occurred. This can be done only by examining each individual contract and interpreting it in all the surrounding circumstances.

fundamental breach
the failure to perform a primary obligation under a contract, which has the effect of depriving the other party of substantially the whole benefit of the contract

REMEDIES

The remedies available in the event of breach of contract include

- damages,
- specific performance,
- injunctions,
- rescission,

---

1   G.H.L. Fridman, *The Law of Contract in Canada*, 3d ed. (Scarborough, ON: Carswell, 1994), 564.

- discharge,

- *quantum meruit*, and

- substantial performance.

Damages

The most common remedy for breach of contract is the award of damages. Damages are a sum of money to compensate the injured party. The intent of the court in making such an award is, as far as possible, to put the injured party back into the position that she or he would have been in had the contract been fully performed. This is a popular remedy because with most contracts it is easy to translate the non-performance into monetary loss. Unless there is some compelling reason to award some other form of relief, the court will only award damages.

▇ EXAMPLE OF MONETARY LOSS FROM NON-PERFORMANCE

Catherine agrees to sell her lawnmower to Suzanne for $100. Suzanne takes the lawnmower and gives Catherine a cheque. However, the cheque is returned NSF. The contract has clearly been breached. The loss suffered by Catherine is the sum of $100, and an award of damages in the amount of $100 (plus, perhaps, interest on that sum) would fully compensate her.

It is important to distinguish between **liquidated damages** and **unliquidated damages**. Liquidated damages are easily ascertainable, usually by examining the terms of the contract and applying some form of mathematical calculation. If, for example, the contract specified payment of the sum of $4,000 but only $1,500 was paid, applying the mathematical formula $4,000 - $1,500 = $2,500 calculates the liquidated damages. However, sometimes the damages are not so easy to calculate because the breach of a contract can have far-reaching consequences. **Consequential damages** do not flow directly from a breach of contract but from the consequences of the breach. These damages are, in a sense, one step removed from the breach itself. Consequential damages include those based on a loss of expected profits, often referred to as **expectancy damages**, and damages based on a longer-term loss of business, often referred to as **lost opportunity damages**.

Consequential damages are often unliquidated. Unliquidated damages cannot be easily calculated with a mathematical formula and usually require information that is outside the contract itself. For example, in calculating damages for loss of profit, it might be necessary to look at evidence from other, similar contracts or at the particular industry as a whole to determine the actual loss suffered. In other cases, it may be necessary to hire an appraiser, an accountant, or some other expert to assist in calculating the damages.

If the consequences of the breach were reasonably foreseeable by the parties at the time that the contract was performed, the party in breach may be liable for all the losses that flow from the breach, including consequential damages. The injured party must prove that the damages were reasonably foreseeable at the time that the contract was made. The party in breach wants to argue that the damages claimed by the injured party are too "remote" and could not have been reasonably foreseen.

liquidated damages
damages that are easily determined from a fixed or measurable standard, or can be assessed by calculating the amount owing from a mathematical formula or from circumstances where no subjective assessment has to be made

unliquidated damages
damages that cannot be fixed by a mathematical or measured calculation but require information from a source outside the contract

consequential damages
secondary damages that do not flow from the breach of contract but from the consequences of the breach, such as loss of future profits

expectancy damages
damages that are based on a loss of expected profits

lost opportunity damages
damages that are based on a longer-term loss of business

■ EXAMPLE OF REASONABLY FORESEEABLE DAMAGES

Tents R Us Ltd. contracts to buy a load of grommets from Trusty Parts Inc. for the sum of $7,500. Trusty Parts fails to deliver the grommets, and Tents R Us is forced to buy them from another manufacturer for $8,500. Clearly, the damages immediately suffered amount to $1,000. However, Tents R Us needed the grommets to finish making a shipment of tents due to Backpacker's World Limited, for which Tents R Us expected to earn $15,000 in profits. Because of the breach by Trusty Parts, Tents R Us cannot deliver the tents on time and so loses its anticipated profits.

The consequential damages suffered include the lost profits of $15,000. In addition, the failure to deliver the tents on time to Backpacker's World, a long-time customer of Tents R Us, has damaged the relationship between the two companies. Backpackers World will no longer do business with Tents R Us, so the long-term losses include the future loss of business from Backpacker's World. The damages might then include loss of anticipated profit over the next few years, amounting to many thousands of dollars. To claim all of these damages, Tents R Us must prove that Trusty Parts knew or ought to have known that these consequences would reasonably flow from its failure to perform its obligations under the contract. The damages claim for loss of profit over the next few years is clearly unliquidated and requires some form of external evidence to support it.

It is often difficult to accurately calculate the losses suffered by the injured party as a result of a breach. To address this problem, some parties include a clause in the contract that sets out the damages to be paid in the event of a breach. If this clause is a genuine attempt to calculate in advance the loss that might be suffered, it is referred to as a liquidated damages clause. Such a clause provides incentive to the parties to comply with the terms of the contract. The courts usually uphold such a clause, even if the actual damages suffered are greater or less than the clause provides for. However, this clause must be distinguished from a penalty clause, which provides for a payment of damages far in excess of the actual damages that could be suffered or that makes no genuine attempt to correlate the damages payable with the damages suffered. The courts often ignore penalty clauses and instead calculate the damages award based on the actual loss. Whether a clause is a liquidated damages clause or a penalty clause is often difficult to determine and is decided on the facts of each case.

DUTY TO MITIGATE

The injured party has a duty to **mitigate** her or his losses. She or he is not entitled to remain inactive in the face of the other party's breach of contract, but must take positive steps to minimize the loss suffered as a result of the breach, though not extraordinary steps. Failing to mitigate losses may result in a court not awarding compensation for the full loss suffered. Compensation will be limited to those damages that could not have reasonably been avoided.

mitigate
to take steps to minimize or reduce the damages one will suffer as a result of another's breach of contract

■ EXAMPLE OF MITIGATION AND LOSSES

André contracts to sell his computer to Teresinha. She breaches the contract by refusing to complete the transaction. André can claim against Teresinha the full purchase price of the computer as the damages he suffered as a result of her breach. However, if he takes no steps to mitigate his loss by trying to sell his computer to someone else, he may be denied recovery of the full amount of his loss. If he is forced to sell the computer at a lower price than the one Teresinha contracted to pay, he will be able to claim as his damages the difference between the price he would have received from Teresinha and the price he did receive. However, if he is lucky enough to sell the computer for more than the price Teresinha had contracted to buy, André will not be able to recover any damages against her because he suffered no loss. Even though she is clearly in breach, she would suffer no consequences.

Specific Performance

equitable remedies
remedies developed by the court of equity that are based on fairness instead of the strict application of common law

specific performance
a remedy requiring the party who is in breach of a contract to perform his or her obligations under the contract

In some cases, damages cannot adequately compensate the injured party. In those cases, **equitable remedies** may be available. An example of an equitable remedy is **specific performance**, which requires the party who is in breach to perform his or her obligations under the contract. If this party refuses to comply and perform, he or she will be in contempt of court and could be subject to quasi-criminal penalties such as fines or imprisonment. Specific performance is usually available only when the contract is for the sale of unique goods or real property.

Real property is ordinarily considered unique because no two parcels of land are identical. If a buyer expects to buy land and the vendor breaches the contract by failing to complete the transaction, it is not possible for the buyer to take an award of monetary damages and replace the land that is lost. If the buyer can prove that she or he was ready, willing, and able to complete the transaction and fulfill all her or his obligations under the contract, the court can compel the vendor to complete the transaction through an order for specific performance.

If the contract is for the sale of unique goods, specific performance may be an available remedy. However, this is less common than with real property. The goods must be so rare and unique that the disappointed buyer cannot readily find the same or similar goods from another source; examples include antiques, works of art, and rare coins or stamps.

Specific performance is not available for contracts that involve personal services performed by an individual, such as in an employment contract. In such a case, the courts are unlikely to force an individual to provide personal services, as this would amount to a form of servitude. Monetary damages are considered adequate compensation.

Because specific performance is an equitable remedy, certain restrictions are placed on the party asking for the remedy. Equity requires that this party come to court with "clean hands"—that is, free of any unethical behaviour. If a party does not have clean hands, he or she will be denied the equitable remedy and will be awarded monetary damages. Equitable remedies can also be denied if the injured party was partly at fault or contributed to the breach of contract in some way, or if he or she delayed for an unreasonable length of time in pursuing a remedy for the breach. These restrictions apply to all equitable remedies.

■ **EXAMPLE OF UNCLEAN HANDS**

Hisham, Kamal, and Salwa were business partners. Hisham leaves the partnership and then sues Kamal and Salwa. He claims that as part of the mutual agreement to dissolve the partnership, he should be allowed to take certain client contracts with him. Kamal and Salwa claim in their defence that Hisham has tried to steal customers from the partnership by spreading untrue stories about the remaining partners' business practices. If the defence allegations are true, Hisham would likely be unable to claim specific performance, because his actions in defaming his former partners leaves him with unclean hands. However, he might still be able to claim legal remedies such as damages (subject to any counterclaims by his former partners).

Injunctions

An **injunction** is another form of equitable remedy. Injunctions govern the behaviour of a party, either to prohibit certain actions or to compel certain actions. A **prohibitory injunction** directs a person not to do a certain thing. A **mandatory injunction** commands a person to do a certain thing. The most important considerations for the court in determining whether to grant an injunction are whether the injured party could be adequately compensated by damages instead of an injunction, and whether it is fair and just to grant the request for the injunction. The court will not grant an injunction if the injured party could be adequately compensated by an award of damages, or if it would be unfair to, or cause irreparable harm to, the party in breach.

The courts most often grant a prohibitory injunction when the contract contains an express provision that is a promise by one party that it will not do a certain thing. This is also known as a **negative covenant**. If the party then commits the prohibited act, the injured party could then apply to the court for an injunction to stop it.

injunction
a court order that prohibits someone from doing some act or compels someone to do some act

prohibitory injunction
an injunction that directs a person not to do a certain thing

mandatory injunction
an injunction that commands a person to do a certain thing

negative covenant
a promise in a contract to refrain from doing a certain thing

■ **EXAMPLE OF NEGATIVE COVENANT**

Chem-Products Ltd. rents land from Pristine Properties Inc. The rental agreement contains a negative covenant that Chem-Products will not use the land to store certain chemicals. If Chem-Products then uses the land to store these chemicals, one of the options available to Pristine Properties is to ask the court for an injunction prohibiting Chem-Products from doing so.

While it is helpful to have a negative covenant in the contract, it is not necessary to have such a covenant before the court will grant a prohibitory injunction. A contract may include an implied promise that could be used as the basis for a prohibitory injunction.

◼ EXAMPLE OF IMPLIED PROMISE

Assume that in the above example, Pristine Properties carries on business on the property adjacent to Chem-Products. Chem-Products dumps garbage on the property and emits loud sounds from the property at all hours of the night and day, which adversely affect the business next door. Pristine Properties can make a request for a prohibitory injunction. Although there may not be a specific negative covenant in the contract prohibiting garbage dumping and noise, the court may recognize an implied promise not to interfere with Pristine Properties' business. This would be true even if there was no statutory remedy available to Pristine Properties (for example, municipal noise bylaws).

A mandatory injunction, while it is not the same as specific performance, can often have the same effect. Courts are less willing to grant mandatory injunctions in circumstances where they would not grant specific performance, as in contracts involving personal services performed by an individual. However, the courts have granted mandatory injunctions in cases "to prevent the breach of an agreement under which the plaintiff obtained from the defendant exclusive rights to the manufacture and distribution in two provinces of certain patent and proprietary remedies, [and] to prevent the improper termination of an automobile franchise agreement."[2]

Injunctions can be a very powerful remedy but, because the litigation process can be long and time-consuming, a lawsuit in which a party is seeking an injunction may take years to come to trial. By then, the behaviour that the injured party sought to prohibit may have done irreparable damage. In such a case, a party may seek an **interlocutory injunction**, also called an **interim injunction** or temporary injunction. This allows the injured party to prevent ongoing damage from occurring while awaiting the trial and final determination of the matters in dispute. At trial, the injured party will usually ask for the injunction to be made permanent.

Rescission

Rescission is both a common law remedy and an equitable remedy, although the term is used most commonly to refer to the equitable remedy. The purpose of rescission is to put the parties in the position they would have been had the contract never been made. This is in contrast to the purpose of damages, which is to put the parties in the position they would have been in if the contractual obligations had been performed.

Common law rescission may be available to a party if the contract is **void** or **voidable** at her or his option. This would be an option with a void contract, such as a contract in which one party is a minor, or with a voidable contract, where the terms of the contract allow one party to avoid it as of right or upon the occurrence of some event. In these cases, that party has the right to rescind the contract without having to resort to the court for a remedy. The right to rescind a contract is different from the right to terminate or discharge a contract. A contract that is discharged is terminated or ended. A contract that is rescinded never existed.

---

interlocutory/interim injunction
a temporary injunction granted by a court before the final determination of a lawsuit for the purpose of preventing irreparable injury

rescission
the cancellation, nullification, or revocation of a contract; the "unmaking" of a contract

void contract
a contract that does not exist at law because one or more essential elements of the contract are lacking; an unenforceable contract

voidable contract
a contract that may be avoided or declared void at the option of one party to the contract; once it is declared invalid no further rights can be obtained under it, but benefits obtained before the declaration are not forfeit

---

2   Ibid., at 798.

Equitable rescission can be granted by a court only as a remedy for a breach of contract by the other party. The intent is to restore the parties to their original positions. There is some similarity between common law and equitable rescission, but equitable rescission is broader and is available in more circumstances. However, those circumstances must be exceptional. Again, the courts will not award an equitable remedy, including the remedy of rescission, where damages would adequately compensate the injured party. In restoring the parties to their original positions, the courts will order that moneys and property that had been exchanged be returned and that both parties be relieved of their obligations under the contract.

Rescission is awarded most often in cases that involve fraud, misrepresentation, or duress. Rescission can also be granted in cases that involve mistake, which is discussed in more detail in chapter 4, Contractual Defects.

■ EXAMPLE OF RESCISSION

Lina buys a refrigerator from Arnold's Appliances for $750. When the refrigerator is delivered and installed, Lina discovers that the freezer section of the refrigerator does not work. She wants to return the refrigerator and get her $750 back. She is asking for rescission. Arnold's Appliances offers to refund half the purchase price to compensate her for the non-functioning freezer. Arnold's Appliances is offering damages. In such a case, the court would likely award the remedy of rescission, since a refrigerator with a non-functional freezer section is of little value to Lina, and she could not be adequately compensated by an award of damages.

There are some restrictions on granting rescission in addition to the usual restrictions on equitable remedies. First, rescission cannot apply to part of a contract. If rescission is granted, the whole contract is rescinded. Second, it must be possible to restore the parties to their original positions (for example, the property that was the subject matter of the contract has not been destroyed or has not diminished substantially in value due to use). Third, the rescission cannot prejudice any innocent third party (for example, a third party who has purchased the property that is the subject matter of the contract).

Restitution

Restitution is an equitable remedy, the purpose of which is to restore the parties, as much as possible, to the position in which they would have been had no contract ever been made. Often, restitution can be accomplished by the remedy of rescission, discussed above. In some cases, however, simply rescinding the contract might not restore the parties to their pre-contract positions, because it could allow the party in breach to retain the benefits obtained under the contract, such as earned profits. In such cases, some form of compensation or recovery is necessary. Restitutionary recovery is based on the idea that the party in breach must disgorge to the injured party any benefits he or she gained under the contract before its rescission, where it would be unjust for him or her to retain such benefits. This must be distinguished from damages. The measure of damages is the amount of the loss of the injured party. The measure of restitutionary recovery is the amount by which the party in breach was unjustly enriched under the contract. Under the

restitution
a remedy in which one seeks to rescind a contract; if granted, restitution restores the party, as far as possible, to a pre-contract position

unjust enrichment doctrine
principle that a person should not be permitted to inequitably gain a profit or benefit at the expense of another

unjust enrichment doctrine, a party who breaches a contract at the expense of another should not be permitted to benefit from his or her wrongdoing. Therefore, a person who has been unjustly enriched at the expense of another can be required to make restitution in the form of payment of money.

Discharge

discharged
released, extinguished; a discharge of a contract occurs when the parties have complied with their obligations or other events have occurred that release one or both parties from performing their obligations

In some circumstances, an injured party may choose to treat a contract as having been **discharged** as a result of breach by the other party. This is most common in cases where the injured party has not yet completed performance of his or her obligations under the contract. If this common law remedy is available, the injured party no longer has any obligations under the contract and may treat the contract as being at an end. The injured party may then claim damages for breach of contract. The party in breach cannot compel the injured party to perform his or her obligations under the contract and cannot claim damages for non-performance by the injured party. However, an injured party who chooses to treat a contract as having been discharged may not claim remedies that are incompatible with this remedy, such as specific performance or rescission. In addition, an injured party who continues to accept the benefits of a contract after becoming aware of the breach may later be prohibited from claiming that the contract has been discharged by the breach and may be restricted to claiming damages only.

Quantum Meruit

quantum meruit
an equitable doctrine that states that no one should unjustly benefit from the labour and materials of another; under those circumstances, the law implies a promise to pay a reasonable amount, even in the absence of a contractual term for price; loosely translated as "as much as is deserved"

The doctrine of *quantum meruit* is most commonly relied on in two situations: first, where the contract is silent as to the consideration for the goods or services and, second, where the contract has been partially performed and the value of the performance must be determined.

If one party requests goods or services from another whose occupation it is to provide such goods or services, payment is understood and expected. That person may deliver such goods or services without a price being discussed. Nevertheless, this is not a situation of a gratuitous promise; payment is expected by both parties, and only the amount of the consideration has not been specified.

Even though the consideration is not specifically mentioned in the request, an agreement of this type will not fail for lack of consideration. The law will imply a promise to pay in a request for goods or services.

Where there is no mention of price, the implied promise is for payment of what the services are reasonably worth, or payment for *quantum meruit*. However, parties who have negotiated a contract that contains a term as to the price to be paid for the goods or services cannot later rely on the doctrine of *quantum meruit* to get a better price. *Quantum meruit* can be relied on only where the contract is silent as to the amount (*quantum*) of the consideration.

In determining what goods or services are reasonably worth, the courts look to the prices charged by similar suppliers and fix the contract price accordingly.

The remedy of *quantum meruit* is also available when the injured party has partly performed his or her obligations under the contract at the time of the repudiation by the other party. *Quantum meruit* is considered a quasi-contractual remedy. The injured party is entitled to compensation for the work performed even if it was not completed. The terms of a contract usually do not include a valuation of partially completed work. The doctrine of *quantum meruit* allows the injured party to obtain a valuation of, and compensation for, the work performed. The injured party must show that it was in fact the other party who repudiated the contract or made the completion of the contract impossible. This remedy is not available when the injured party has completed his or her obligations under the contract, in which case the appropriate remedy is damages.

■ EXAMPLE OF QUANTUM MERUIT

Cameron hires Deborah to renovate his kitchen for the sum of $5,000. Deborah has completed approximately 75 percent of the job when Cameron decides that he no longer wants the renovations and refuses to pay her or to let her finish. Deborah must prove that Cameron repudiated the contract, and because she did not complete the contract, she must claim the remedy of *quantum meruit* for compensation for the work done. Since she completed 75 percent of the contract, she is entitled to claim 75 percent of the contract price, or $3,750.

Substantial Performance

Quantum meruit is normally not available to the party who repudiates a contract. However, the doctrine of **substantial performance** may be available. This doctrine recognizes that performing contractual obligations that do not entirely meet the terms of the contract but nevertheless confer a benefit on a party is of value and must be taken into consideration in determining the damages recoverable by the party claiming injury for non-performance and by the party claiming compensation for the partial performance.

substantial performance
performance of contractual obligations that does not entirely meet the terms of the contract but nevertheless confers a benefit on a party

■ EXAMPLE OF SUBSTANTIAL PERFORMANCE

Tony agrees to build a cottage for Marijke for $40,000. Tony builds the cottage but fails to complete the porch according to Marijke's design. Marijke claims that Tony has breached the contract and refuses to pay him the $40,000. Tony can argue the doctrine of substantial performance because he has substantially complied with the terms of the contract. A court would likely award Marijke damages to compensate her for the porch and deduct these damages from the amount of money it would order Marijke to pay Tony. If, for instance, it would cost Marijke $4,000 to have someone else complete the porch according to her design, she would be ordered to pay Tony the remaining $36,000.

Exclusion Clauses

Many modern contracts include an exclusion clause, also known as an *exculpatory, exemption,* or *limitation* clause. The purpose of such a clause is to limit, exempt, or exclude the liability of one party for breaching the contract. In a standard form contract, a contract that is preprinted and whose terms are non-negotiable, the exclusion clause favours the party who drafted the contract. Such a contract is also known as an **adhesion contract**.

adhesion contract
a standardized contract for goods or services offered to consumers on a non-negotiable or "take it or leave it" basis, without offering consumers the opportunity to bargain over the terms of the contract

■ EXAMPLE OF EXCLUSION CLAUSE

A standard form contract to lease equipment might include an exclusion clause as follows (the customer is the lessee and the leasing company is the lessor):

> The lessee acknowledges that the lessor has made no representation or warranty with respect to the equipment, its condition, or fitness for purpose. The lessee shall unconditionally and without setoff pay the rent stipulated even if the equipment does not operate as intended by the lessee, or at all, or totally fails to operate or function. The lessor shall not be liable to the lessee for any loss, cost, expense, or damage caused directly or indirectly by the equipment or for any loss of business or other damages whatsoever.

Exclusion clauses are widely used by vendors because they allow a vendor to protect itself against liability and transfer any risk to its buyers. This is common where the vendor is not the manufacturer of the product but just the distributor, or in cases where the vendor is financing only the purchase of goods or equipment, such as with a financing or leasing company. If the product is faulty, the buyer then has the option of pursuing the manufacturer for a remedy. However, the exclusion clause prevents the buyer from seeking remedies against the vendor. In most cases this will mean that the buyer must still pay the vendor for the faulty product, although it may make a claim against the manufacturer for compensation.

The problem with exclusion clauses is that they are usually found in contracts where there is unequal bargaining power between the parties. The buyer is often unaware of the existence of the clause in the contract before signing it. Even if the buyer is aware of the clause, she or he may not understand its implications. In many cases, the buyer, even if objecting to the clause, has no choice but to sign the contract as is if she or he wants to buy the goods, since the vendor is unwilling to change the terms of its contract. An ordinary consumer simply does not have the bargaining power to negotiate the terms of such a contract. However, the courts have traditionally been wary of such onerous clauses, especially in contracts in which one party has little or no bargaining power. As a result, the courts have developed an approach that prevents many exclusion clauses from being used in circumstances that are unfair to the weaker party.

One requirement developed by the courts is that of **adequate notice**. In most cases, the courts assume that a party who signs a contract intends to be bound by the terms of the contract, even if he or she did not read the contract before signing it. However, if the contract contains a clause that is unexpected and unfair and that could not reasonably be expected to be found in a contract of that nature, the party who wishes to rely on the clause must bring the clause to the other party's attention and explain its legal implications before the contract is signed. If there is no notice of the existence of the clause, the court will not uphold the clause. The onus is therefore on the party relying on the clause to prove that the other party had adequate notice of it.

adequate notice
the requirement for a party who wants to rely on an exclusion clause in a contract to bring the clause to the other party's attention and explain its legal implications before the contract is signed

Another requirement developed by the courts is that the clause must be strictly interpreted. Exclusion clauses are usually drafted in very broad terms in an attempt to apply to the maximum number of possible situations. The courts have attempted to balance the notion that parties should have the freedom to contract (even if that means entering into contracts that are foolish) with the notion that allowing parties to evade responsibility under a contract is unfair. As a result, the courts apply the *contra proferentem* rule, which requires that a term of a contract, such as an exclusion clause, be interpreted strictly. In the event of any ambiguity, or where there may be more than one interpretation of the term, the court must favour the interpretation of the term that favours that party who did *not* draft the clause. This rule is applied to all areas of contract interpretation but is of great importance in interpreting exclusion clauses. Over the years, the courts have refused to uphold exclusion clauses for a variety of reasons. For example, the courts have stated that a clause that exempts a party from liability under the contract does not exempt the party from liability in tort. In other cases, if the party did not perform the terms of the contract exactly as agreed upon, the courts have stated that the exclusion clause does not apply as a different contract has been performed than that originally agreed upon. The result has been that exclusion clauses have become longer, broader, and more detailed in an attempt to prevent the ambiguity that might lead to applying the *contra proferentem* rule.

If the breach is a breach of a condition or a breach of a warranty and (1) adequate notice was given of the clause, and (2) the clause is carefully drafted and the *contra proferentem* rule does not prevent the application of the clause, the courts will uphold the application of the exclusion clause and relieve the party in breach from liability. However, if it is a fundamental breach, the courts are less likely to uphold the application of the clause. The problem arises in trying to categorize the breach. Is it a breach of a condition, or is it a fundamental breach? The party who committed the breach and wants to rely on an exclusion clause for relief from liability is likely to argue that the breach was a breach of a condition and that the exclusion clause ought to be upheld. The injured party is likely to argue that the breach was a fundamental breach and therefore the exclusion clause ought not to be upheld. The determination will depend on the interpretation of the contract as a whole and on the facts of each case. It is apparent that the line between breach of a condition and fundamental breach is very fine, but ultimately the court must decide.

CHOICE OF REMEDIES

The remedies available to an injured party depend in part on the method of breach and the nature of the breach. In the case of *anticipatory breach*, the injured party has the option of waiting for the date on which the performance is due. If the other party fails to perform on that date, the anticipatory breach becomes an *express breach* or *express repudiation*, and the injured party may proceed according to the nature of the breach. However, the injured party also has the option of claiming a remedy as soon as he or she learns of the anticipatory breach.

If the nature of the breach is the breach of a *warranty*, or a minor term of the contract, the injured party may not choose to treat the contract as having been discharged or to rescind the contract. If the term breached is a warranty, the court will usually award damages to compensate the injured party. This means that the injured party must still comply with her or his obligations under the contract. However, if the breach is a breach of a *condition*, or a major term of the contract, the injured party may choose to treat the contract as having been discharged or may rescind the contract. The injured party also has the choice of treating a breach of a condition as a breach of a warranty and accepting the lesser remedy of damages. However, the injured party does not have the option of treating a breach of a warranty as a breach of a condition.

If the contract contains an exclusion clause, the injured party may have no remedies available for breach of a warranty or breach of a condition. However, if the breach is a *fundamental breach*, the injured party may be able to argue that the exclusion clause should not apply. If successful, the injured party would be able to claim damages, discharge, rescission, or other equitable remedies where appropriate.

The availability of equitable remedies to the injured party depends on the facts of each case. While the courts will look at the nature of the breach in determining whether to grant an equitable remedy, the primary considerations are still whether common law remedies will adequately compensate the injured party and whether the injured party has come to court with "clean hands."

SUMMARY

A party may breach a contract through an express or implied repudiation by failing to perform the contract obligations. A party may also commit an anticipatory breach by communicating his or her intention to repudiate the contract before the time or date set for performance. A party may commit a breach of a condition, which is a breach of a term that goes to the root of the contract, or a breach of a warranty, which is a breach of a minor term of the contract. A party may also commit a fundamental breach, which is a breach of the foundation upon which the contract is based. Fundamental breach is usually considered in contracts where there is an exclusion clause that purports to relieve one party of liability in the event of a breach. Exclusion clauses are often found in adhesion contracts, which are preprinted contracts, the terms of which are usually non-negotiable. Such a clause must be brought to the attention of the weaker party and will be strictly interpreted by the courts. Even so, exclusion clauses may not be upheld in cases of fundamental breach.

In the event of a breach of contract, the injured party is most commonly entitled to an award of damages to compensate for the loss flowing from and consequential to the breach. Damages are intended to put the injured party in the position that she or he would have been in had the contract not been breached. An injured party may also claim the equitable remedies of specific performance, injunction, rescission, or the quasi-contractual remedy of *quantum meruit*. In the event of a breach of a condition, the injured party is ordinarily entitled to claim rescission, discharge, or damages. However, in the event of a breach of a warranty, the injured party is usually restricted to an award of damages.

KEY TERMS

adequate notice

adhesion contract

anticipatory breach

breach of contract

consequential damages

discharged

equitable remedies

expectancy damages

express repudiation/express breach

fundamental breach

implied repudiation

injunction

interlocutory/interim injunction

liquidated damages

lost opportunity damages

mandatory injunction

mitigate

negative covenant

prohibitory injunction

quantum meruit

repudiate

rescission

restitution

specific performance

substantial performance

unjust enrichment doctrine

unliquidated damages

void contract

voidable contract

REVIEW QUESTIONS

1. What is the most common form of repudiation of a contract?

2. What options are available to the innocent party in the event of anticipatory breach?

3. Explain the difference between breach of a condition and breach of a warranty.

4. Explain the difference between breach of a condition and fundamental breach.

5. What is the purpose of damages?

6. Compare a clause that provides for liquidated damages and one that is a penalty clause. How do they differ?

7. Define "consequential damages."

8. What is the test for determining the remoteness of consequential damages?

9. When is an injunction available? What are the different types of injunctions?

10. Describe the duty to mitigate. What is the result of a failure to properly mitigate damages?

11. What is the purpose of rescission?

12. With what conditions must a party comply to claim an equitable remedy?

13. Under what circumstances is the remedy of specific performance available? When will specific performance not be awarded?

14. When does breach of contract give rise to the right of rescission? When does it give rise to the right to treat the contract as having been discharged?

15. What conditions must be present for the courts to enforce a claim for *quantum meruit*?

16. Explain the purpose of an exclusion clause. What must be proven by the party seeking to uphold an exclusion clause?

17. When a party has abandoned a contract, can he or she claim recovery for the work performed? If so, how?

18. If a party has been prevented from performing some of the obligations under a contract, can she or he claim recovery for the work performed? If so, how?

DISCUSSION QUESTIONS

1. Cheryl contracts to sell her moped to Jean for $900. However, a few days before Jean is supposed to pick up the moped, Cheryl phones to tell her that she has changed her mind and no longer wants to sell it. Jean is concerned, because to buy the same or similar moped elsewhere would cost at least $1,200. How would you characterize the breach committed by Cheryl? What remedies are available to Jean? If she claims damages, how would she calculate such damages? Would such damages be liquidated or unliquidated?

2. Sylvie, a scientist, enters into a contract with Central Hospital to perform research for them exclusively for a period of two years. However, during that time, Central Hospital discovers that Sylvie is also working on a research project for another hospital. What remedies are available to Central Hospital? What factors would the court take into consideration in determining what remedies to grant to Central Hospital?

3. Nicholas, a carpenter, contracts with Alexandra to build an addition to her house for $15,000. When he has completed all the work except the installation of two windows, he refuses to complete the contract. Can Alexandra discharge the contract? Can she rescind the contract? Is Nicholas entitled to be paid anything for his work? Why or why not? What remedies are available to Alexandra?

4. Gilbert bought a vacuum cleaner from Sullivan Cleaning Machines one month ago. During that time, the vacuum cleaner has broken down eight times, and Gilbert has been able to use it only once. Gilbert wants to return the vacuum cleaner and get his money back. Sullivan Cleaning

Machines says that the vacuum cleaner can be repaired and has offered to repair it at no cost. However, Gilbert says that he has returned the vacuum cleaner twice for repairs but the problem has not been solved. The contract also states that Sullivan Cleaning Machines is not liable for any defects in the vacuum cleaner and that it makes no warranties as to the condition or fitness for purpose of the vacuum cleaner. The company further states that the customer shall be entirely responsible for the cost of any repairs. What remedies are available to Gilbert? What remedy would he prefer? What arguments would Sullivan Cleaning Machines make? What remedy would a court be likely to award?

5. Elite Manufacturers Ltd. has prepared a contract bid for a lucrative contract with Bijou Theatres Inc. to construct its new multiplex theatre. Elite Manufacturers Ltd. is told by an inside source at Bijou Theatres that it has a very good chance of getting the contract because none of the other bidders has much experience in building theatres. The bid must be submitted by noon on January 15. Elite Manufacturers contracts with Express Courier Co. to deliver the bid package. Express Courier advises that it can deliver the package by 10:00 a.m. on January 15. The courier slip, which is filled out and signed by an employee of Elite Manufacturers, states in very fine print on the back, "Carrier's liability for loss, damage, destruction, or injury to a shipment shall not exceed the lesser of $1.50 per pound or $50." Unfortunately for Elite Manufacturers, the bid is not delivered on time and the company does not win the contract. Discuss the issues that arise in this case with respect to breach of contract, and render a decision.

CHAPTER 9

Consumer Protection

INTRODUCTION

As a rule, the courts have been reluctant to interfere with contracts that parties have entered into, apart from ensuring that these agreements contain all the necessary elements of a valid contract and are not illegal. However, consumers have long been considered to require the protection of special laws. A **consumer** is an individual who purchases goods or services, generally for his or her own use. A consumer is distinguished from someone who buys goods for the purpose of resale, such as a wholesaler, retailer, or distributor, or to use in producing other goods, such as a manufacturer. A consumer is not someone who purchases goods or services required to carry on a business. **Consumer goods** are intended only for personal, household, or family use.

Ancient laws protected consumers from unscrupulous merchants and money lenders, or from harsh treatment from creditors. These laws included inspecting and measuring goods to ensure uniformity. Other laws were designed to protect consumers from unfair interest rates. These limited laws were generally sufficient since the marketplace was small. If the buyer of a product was unhappy with it, she or he could address the issue directly with the manufacturer of the product. In a small marketplace, the manufacturer had to address legitimate consumer complaints in order to stay in business. However, in recent times, the nature of the sale of goods has changed dramatically. Changes in manufacturing processes, technology, marketing practices, and distribution methods have made manufacturing and selling increasingly complex. Most goods are no longer purchased from those who made them, and consumers cannot easily check the quality of the goods they are purchasing. The average consumer no longer has the bargaining power that he or she once had. Exemption clauses in contracts for the sale of goods have become commonplace and they further reduce consumers' bargaining power. In addition, issues of the safety of goods sold, advertising methods, and unethical business practices have become common concerns for consumers. Another change in the marketplace is the widespread use of credit to purchase goods, and from this has arisen concerns about unfair interest rates and the failure of lenders to disclose the true cost of borrowing to the consumer.

To address the changing nature of the marketplace, consumer protection legislation has been passed in all provinces in Canada. Unfortunately, for the most part, the legislation has been piecemeal and often addresses only a particular concern in a particular industry in response to particular consumer complaints. To further complicate matters, some areas of consumer protection fall within federal

consumer
an individual who purchases goods or services, generally for his or her own use

consumer goods
goods purchased by a consumer that are intended only for personal, household, or family use

jurisdiction and some within provincial jurisdiction. It is therefore necessary to examine many different statutes to determine the rights and remedies available to consumers.

Approaches to addressing these problems vary greatly from province to province, although the issues generally fall into the following categories:

- standards of safety,

- standards of quality,

- prohibition of unethical business practices, and

- requirements of disclosure in credit transactions.

This chapter reviews the provisions of only the most common statutes that provide protection to consumers. In addition, some of these statutes apply not only to consumers but to all users of the goods in question, while others are restricted to consumers only. In applying these statutes, legislators have tried to balance the concept of contractual freedom (the right of parties to enter into any contract they choose) with the necessity to address the issues of consumer protection that arise in a marketplace where the parties do not have equal bargaining power. In most cases, the provisions of the applicable statute will override any contractual provision that conflicts with the statute.

ISSUES OF SAFETY

Consumers have remedies in both tort and contract law if they suffer injury as a result of defective or hazardous goods, but such remedies are usually available only after the injury has occurred. To address issues of safety before injuries arise, various statutes impose obligations on the manufacture of goods to ensure that the goods are safe to use, or to ensure that the consumer understands the risks involved in using them. For example, some statutes impose a duty on the manufacturers of hazardous goods to warn consumers of the dangers associated with these products. Other statutes impose safety standards for the manufacture of goods that are used in consumer products, such as motor vehicles. Still other statutes ensure that manufacturers label and package goods to disclose to consumers important information about the products, such as the ingredients or materials used. All of these statutes contain provisions for appointing inspectors, who are granted broad powers of investigation to determine whether the provisions of a particular act are being complied with, including the right to enter premises and seize goods. The acts also contain quasi-criminal sanctions for non-compliance, such as fines or terms of imprisonment for individuals or, in some cases, the directors of an offending corporation.

ISSUES OF QUALITY

For the most part, the courts see little reason why the law should protect the careless consumer, and they adhere to the philosophy of *caveat emptor*, or "let the buyer beware," meaning that it is the responsibility of the buyer to inspect, test, and judge goods before buying them. However, this philosophy works well only in a marketplace in which all parties have equal bargaining power. Sometimes the buyer does not have the knowledge to judge accurately the quality of goods and must rely on the seller's knowledge. In addition, if goods are purchased by description (for example, from looking at a picture or description in a catalogue) or by sample (for example, by choosing broadloom carpeting or tile from a small sample square), the buyer may not even have the opportunity to examine the goods before purchase to ensure that they are of good quality.

UNETHICAL BUSINESS PRACTICES

Legislation that is designed to prevent unethical business practices is intended both to protect consumers from unfair and questionable practices and to protect honest sellers from unfair competition. In this category are statutes of general application as well as statutes aimed at specific areas of business. In addition to the statutes discussed below, there are statutes that subject certain business activities to licensing and registration requirements in an attempt to protect the public interest. For example, people who sell real estate, securities, or motor vehicles must have a licence to engage in business, and those who engage in unethical practices may have their licences revoked.

ISSUES OF CREDIT

The use of credit to purchase consumer goods is relatively recent. Credit became popular only after World War II, and complaints about lending practices followed soon after. Many complaints arose because the lenders did not make adequate attempts to disclose to the borrowers the cost of borrowing. Because the documentation used was confusing and difficult to understand for the average consumer, the true cost of borrowing—including the interest rate, special financing charges, penalties and late charges, and service charges—was hidden. As a result, legislation was enacted across Canada requiring lenders to clearly disclose the cost of borrowing to the borrowers, including service charges, penalties, and the annual interest rate.

With the increased use of credit came the increased use of and need for credit reporting. Credit reporting agencies supply credit reports on potential borrowers to lenders. Concerns over this use of information and its accuracy led to legislation to license and regulate credit reporting agencies.

Finally, legislation also protects consumers from criminal rates of interest and provides relief from transactions in which the cost of a loan is excessively high.

MAJOR CONSUMER PROTECTION STATUTES

Consumer Packaging and Labelling Act

The federal *Consumer Packaging and Labelling Act*[1] governs the packaging, labelling, selling, importing, and advertising of certain products. The Act applies to *any* product sold in Canada (note that "product" does not include land), except those

---

1 RSC 1985, c. C-38.

products that are dealt with under the *Food and Drugs Act* (described below). The Act is designed to protect the public from false or misleading product packaging or labelling. For example, it prohibits selling, advertising, or importing any prepackaged product that does not have a label stating the number of items in the package or the weight, volume, or other unit of measurement of the package. The Act specifically prohibits false or misleading labelling that might deceive a consumer as to the quantity or weight of the product. Failure to comply with the Act is punishable by a fine of up to $10,000 and a term of imprisonment of up to one year, or in the case of an offence relating to the packaging of food, of up to $250,000 and imprisonment for up to two years.

Food and Drugs Act

The federal *Food and Drugs Act*[2] regulates many aspects of the manufacturing, selling, labelling, and advertising of food, drugs, cosmetics, and devices. Its purpose is to protect the public from products that could be harmful if improperly used or ingested, and to ensure the purity of food products and drugs sold to the public. In addition, the selling and advertising of drugs are controlled in an effort to ensure their proper application.

For example, the Act prohibits the advertising or labelling of any food, drug, cosmetic, or device as a treatment, preventive, or cure for certain diseases and disorders, such as alcoholism, arthritis, epilepsy, cancer, obesity, or sexual impotence. Generally, the Act prohibits advertising and selling food, drugs, cosmetics, and devices that are harmful, unfit for human consumption or use, adulterated, exposed to unsanitary conditions, or misleadingly or deceptively labelled. Contravening the provisions of the Act can result in a fine of up to $5,000 and a term of imprisonment of up to three years, or in the case of an offence relating to food, a fine of up to $25,000 and imprisonment of up to three years.

Hazardous Products Act

The federal *Hazardous Products Act*[3] deals with the importing, selling, and advertising of certain hazardous products. It is not restricted to consumers or consumer products. Hazardous products are those described in the statute as prohibited, restricted, or controlled. Prohibited products include such things as articles intended for use by children that have been painted with lead or other toxic paint; products that contain certain hazardous chemicals or substances, such as asbestos or urea formaldehyde; mechanisms that are intended to be used as bombs; and sports equipment that does not meet minimum safety standards as set by the Canadian Standards Association. Restricted products include chlorine bleach, antifreeze, pressurized containers, certain types of children's toys, kettles, paints, and sleeping bags. Controlled products include compressed gas and flammable, poisonous, or corrosive materials. The government has broad powers to add items to the list of prohibited, restricted, or controlled products if it deems them a hazard to the public. However, this Act does not apply to all hazardous materials—for

---

2 RSC 1985, c. F-27.

3 RSC 1985, c. H-3.

example, it does not apply to items that come within the jurisdiction of the *Explosives Act*, the *Food and Drugs Act*, the *Pest Control Products Act*, the *Atomic Energy Control Act*, or the *Tobacco Act*.

The *Hazardous Products Act* bans outright the selling, advertising, or importing of prohibited products, and specifies the conditions under which restricted and controlled products may be sold, advertised, or imported. For example, labels on controlled products must disclose necessary information about the product (such as an ingredients list) and display the proper hazard symbols (the familiar "exploding" warning labels found on aerosol cans, for example). Failing to comply with the provisions of the Act can lead to fines of up to $1 million and a term of imprisonment of up to two years.

Motor Vehicle Safety Act

The federal *Motor Vehicle Safety Act*[4] sets national standards of safety for motor vehicles and vehicle parts manufactured in Canada or imported. It also requires the manufacturers of vehicles to give notice of any defects in their vehicles or parts to the purchasers of the vehicles and to the government. The purpose of the Act is to reduce the risk of death, injury, and damage caused by defective motor vehicles. One way this is achieved is through using "national safety marks," which are prescribed by the government and constitute proof that the vehicle and its parts comply with the Canada Motor Vehicle Safety Standards, which include emission standards. The Act also provides that the manufacturer, seller, or importer of motor vehicles or equipment, upon becoming aware of a defect in the design or functioning of the motor vehicle or equipment, must notify the government and every person who has obtained or purchased the vehicle or equipment of the defect and provide directions for correcting it. Contravening the Act carries a maximum fine of $1 million and a term of imprisonment of up to two years.

Motor Vehicle Repair Act

The most common consumer complaints relate to the sale and repair of motor vehicles. Consumers are especially vulnerable in transactions that involve repairs to motor vehicles. As vehicles become increasingly technologically complex, fewer and fewer consumers have the skill and knowledge to be able to judge the necessity and quality of repairs. The Ontario *Motor Vehicle Repair Act*[5] imposes obligations on repairers with respect to estimates and repairs to vehicles. This Act applies to all individuals who contract for vehicle repairs, not just to consumers.

A consumer may request a written estimate for repairs, and the repairer cannot charge for any work until this estimate is given to the consumer. The estimate must include, among other things, a description of the work to be done to the vehicle, the parts to be installed, the price of the parts, the hours of labour, the hourly rate for labour, and the total to be charged for labour. Once the estimate has been given to the consumer, the amount charged for the work cannot exceed the estimate by more than 10 percent.

---

4 SC 1993, c. 16 (unofficially, RSC 1985, c. M-10.01).

5 RSO 1990, c. M.43, as amended.

No charge can be made for repairs unless the consumer authorizes the repairs, although this authorization may be given by telephone. In addition, if requested, the repairer must return any parts that were removed from the consumer's vehicle. Once the work has been completed, the repairer must provide the consumer with an invoice, which must include, among other things, the odometer reading of the vehicle at the time of return; a description of the work done; the parts installed and whether they are new, used, or reconditioned; the price of the parts; the hours of labour; the hourly rate for labour; the total charged for labour; the total billed; and the terms of the warranty provided. Every repairer must provide a warranty on all new and reconditioned parts and labour for a minimum of 90 days or 5000 kilometres, whichever comes first. The Act specifically prohibits the practice of charging more for repairs when they are to be charged to an insurance company.

The Act provides for remedies to a wronged consumer. If the repairs done or the parts supplied are defective, the consumer has the right to recover the cost of the work and repairs plus any towing charges incurred as a result of the defective work. If the repairer attempts to charge a consumer for any work that contravenes the Act, the consumer has no obligation to pay such charges. If the consumer has already paid such charges and the repairer refuses to refund the moneys paid, the consumer has the right to obtain a court order for repayment.

The Act also provides for penalties that can be imposed on a repairer for contravening the Act. The maximum penalty is a fine of $25,000 and imprisonment for one year.

Textile Labelling Act

The federal *Textile Labelling Act*[6] governs the labelling, selling, importing, and advertising of consumer textile articles, including textile fibres or fabrics and items made in whole or in part from textile fibres or fabrics for consumer use. This Act requires all items of clothing to bear a label that identifies the fabric used in the clothing. The Act also encourages manufacturers to label clothing with cleaning and care instructions. The Act prohibits selling, advertising, or importing consumer textile articles that are not labelled or are falsely or misleadingly labelled. Contravening the Act carries a fine of up to $10,000 and a term of imprisonment of up to one year.

Sale of Goods Act

The *Sale of Goods Act*[7] is an Ontario statute that, among other things, provides for minimum standards of quality by imposing warranties and conditions on the goods sold.

chattels
items of personal property

The Act applies to all contracts for the sale of goods, including **chattels**, or items of personal property, but does not apply to contracts for the sale of land.

The Act makes a distinction between conditions and warranties. A breach of a condition gives the wronged party the right to treat the contract as having been

---

6   RSC 1985, c. T-10.

7   RSO 1990, c. S.1, as amended.

repudiated, while a breach of a condition gives rise to the right to claim damages. The Act further states that the wronged party may elect to treat the breach of a condition as the breach of a warranty. In this way, the Act codifies the common law in this area.

The Act imposes the following implied conditions and warranties:

1. It is a condition that the seller has the right to sell the goods.

2. It is a condition of goods sold by description (such as from a catalogue) that the goods will correspond with the description.

3. It is a condition that goods sold by sample will correspond with the sample, that the buyer will have a reasonable opportunity to compare the goods with the sample, and that the goods will have no hidden defects.

4. It is a warranty that the buyer will have **quiet possession** of the goods.

   quiet possession
   the right to possess and use goods without interference or disturbance from other parties

5. It is a warranty that the goods will be free of any charge or encumbrance (such as a lien or chattel mortgage) in favour of any third party.

6. It is a warranty that the goods will be reasonably fit for the purpose required and of merchantable quality *only* under the following circumstances:

   a. where the goods are those that the seller supplies in the course of his or her business, and the buyer makes known to the seller the purpose for which the goods are required and relies on the seller's judgment and skill in choosing the goods; or

   b. where the goods are those that the seller supplies in the course of her or his business, and where the goods are bought by description; or

   c. where it can be implied by usage of trade—that is, by the widely held and understood standards of the industry in question.

Consumer Protection Act

The Ontario *Consumer Protection Act*,[8] addresses a number of issues arising from consumer contracts. The Act describes a consumer sale as

> a contract for the sale of goods made in the ordinary course of business to a purchaser for the purchaser's consumption or use, but does not include a sale to a purchaser for resale … [or] whose purchase is in the course of carrying on business, [or] to … a partnership or a corporation.

The Act specifically states that the implied conditions and warranties of the *Sale of Goods Act* apply to consumer sales and that any part of a contract that purports to vary or exclude these implied conditions and warranties is void. This means that a contract for the sale of consumer goods cannot waive or exclude the minimum standards set by the *Sale of Goods Act*, even if the parties agree to do so. If a contract purports to exclude the application of the *Sale of Goods Act*, the courts will, if possible, sever the offending portion of the contract and enforce the remainder.

---

8 RSO 1990, c. C.31, as amended.

executory contract
a contract between a buyer and a seller in which full payment is not made at the time of the contract; a contract to buy on credit

Part II of the Act deals with **executory contracts**, which are contracts for the sale of goods or services in which the buyer does not pay for the goods or services in full at the time of making the contract. In other words, the purchase is made, at least in part, on credit. Where the purchase price exceeds $50, the contract must contain

- the name and address of the seller and the buyer;

- a description of the goods or services;

- itemized prices of the goods or services and a detailed statement of the terms of payment;

- a statement of any security for payment under the contract, including the particulars of any **negotiable instrument**, **conditional sale contract**, or **chattel mortgage**;

- a statement as to the cost of borrowing (as described below);

- any warranty or guarantee applying to the goods or services; and

- the signature of both parties.

negotiable instrument
a promise in writing and signed to pay a specific sum of money to the bearer—for example, a cheque or promissory note

conditional sale contract
a contract for the sale and purchase of goods in which title to the goods does not pass to the buyer unless conditions are fulfilled

chattel mortgage
a contract that grants one party a security interest in goods or personal property to secure payment of money, often the purchase price of the goods

Each party must be given a duplicate original of the contract. In addition, if the contract is entered into at any place other than at the seller's permanent place of business (for example, in the buyer's home, as with a door-to-door salesperson), the buyer has the right to rescind the contract within two days of receiving the duplicate original of the contract. To exercise this right, the buyer must give notice to the seller and immediately return any goods received to the seller at the seller's expense. The buyer is then entitled to recover any moneys paid to the seller.

The Act also restricts the right of the seller to repossess the goods sold due to non-payment. Security agreements, such as chattel mortgages, conditional sales contracts, and leases, are often used to finance the purchase of consumer goods. These contracts usually provide that if the buyer defaults in making payments under the contract, the seller may repossess and sell the goods. However, the Act states that if the buyer has paid two-thirds or more of the purchase price, the goods cannot be repossessed despite any provision in the contract to the contrary. The only remedy available to the seller is to bring an action for payment of the remaining purchase price.

Part III of the Act deals with disclosing the cost of borrowing. These requirements apply both to transactions for the purchase of goods or services on credit and to transactions for lending money. Before giving credit, every lender must give the borrower a statement in writing that includes the following:

- the sum received by the borrower;

- the cash price of the goods or services, if applicable;

- the amount of any downpayment, if applicable;

- the total cost of borrowing;

- the interest rate, expressed as an annual rate;

- any amount charged for insurance;

- any amount charged for fees; and

- any amount to be charged in the event of default by the borrower.

The Act also deals with the problem of unsolicited goods—goods that are sent to a consumer that have not been requested or accepted by the consumer. The seller hopes that the recipient will assume that simply by receiving the goods he or she has an obligation to keep and pay for them. However, the recipient is not obligated to pay for such goods and has no obligation to keep or preserve them. The seller cannot force the recipient to pay or hold the recipient responsible for any use, misuse, loss, or damage to the goods.

The Act also allows the director of the Ministry of Consumer and Business Services to prevent false advertising. If she or he believes, on reasonable and probable grounds, that a seller or lender is making false, misleading, or deceptive statements in any advertisement or other material, she or he may order an immediate end to the use of the advertisement.

The maximum penalty for contravening this Act is a fine of $100,000 and imprisonment for three years.

Business Practices Act

The Ontario *Business Practices Act*[9] is designed to protect consumers from parties who attempt to induce them to enter into contracts based on misleading or false representations or by taking advantage of them. Note that the remedies set out in the Act are in addition to the remedies the consumer has under general contract law with respect to issues such as misrepresentation and undue influence. However, the rights and remedies provided by the Act are broader than those provided by common law.

The Act sets out a list of prohibited practices that it deems unfair. Some of these include

1. making false or misleading representations, including

   a. claiming that a product contains ingredients or has uses or benefits that it does not have;

   b. claiming that a product has sponsorship or approval that it does not have;

   c. claiming that a product is new or unused when it is not, or misrepresenting the extent to which a product has been used;

   d. claiming that a product needs servicing, parts, or repairs when it does not;

   e. claiming that the product has a price advantage when it does not; and

   f. making a claim using exaggeration, innuendo, ambiguity, or omission with the intent to deceive;

---

9 RSO 1990, c. B.18, as amended.

2. entering into any unconscionable transaction, especially when the seller knew or ought to have known that

   a. the consumer is unable to protect his or her interests because of physical infirmity, ignorance, illiteracy, or inability to understand the language;

   b. the price for the goods grossly exceeds the price at which similar goods or services are available elsewhere;

   c. the consumer is unable to receive a substantial benefit from the transaction;

   d. the terms of the transaction are so unfair to the consumer as to be inequitable; and

   e. misleading statements or undue pressure were used to induce the consumer to enter into the transaction.

If a consumer is induced to enter into a contract because of an unfair practice, she or he may rescind the contract and may also make a claim for damages. If rescission is no longer possible, the consumer may make a claim for the difference between the fair value of the goods and the amount actually paid. In addition, in cases where the practices of the offending party are especially egregious, a court may award the consumer **exemplary or punitive damages**.

exemplary or punitive damages
damages awarded to an injured party over and above compensation for actual loss to punish the wrongdoer or to act as a deterrent to other wrongdoers

However, note that the consumer must give written notice to the other party within six months of entering into the contract if he or she wishes to exercise the rights granted by this Act.

In addition to the rights granted to the wronged consumer, the Act grants the director of the Ministry of Consumer and Business Services the power to investigate suspected unfair practices or to order a person to stop engaging in an unfair practice. Engaging in unfair practices, failing to comply with an order prohibiting an unfair practice, or any actions that are intended to obstruct an investigation under the Act are offences under the Act and carry penalties of fines of up to a maximum of $100,000 and imprisonment of up to one year. The director may also revoke an offender's business licence.

Collection Agencies Act

Collection agencies are hired to collect debts on behalf of creditors. Because of complaints received by the government about the methods employed by collection agencies and their collectors, the Ontario *Collection Agencies Act*[10] was enacted. The Act regulates collection agencies and the methods they use to collect debts, with the purpose of protecting the public from harassment, threats, or intimidation. However, the Act does not apply to persons who collect debts in the course of their ordinary business, such as lawyers, insurance agents or brokers, trustees in bankruptcy, real estate agents or brokers, banks, or credit unions, or to a person who is assisting a creditor in collecting a debt in an isolated incident.

---

10 RSO 1990, c. C.14, as amended.

A collection agency must be registered with the Registrar of Collection Agencies in order to carry on business, and a creditor may not use an unregistered collection agency to assist in collecting a debt. Registration can be denied, revoked, or suspended if the past conduct of the agency leads the registrar to believe that the agency will not act with integrity and honesty.

The practices prohibited by the Act include

- attempting to collect more than the debt owing (for example, trying to collect service charges or penalties that are not provided for in the original agreement), and

- making collect telephone calls or sending collect telegrams to the debtor to demand payment.

Additional practices are prohibited by the regulations to the Act:[11]

- attempting to collect payment from a debtor or commencing a legal action against the debtor without first attempting to notify the debtor in writing;

- threatening to commence a legal action without being authorized by the creditor to commence such an action;

- making demand for payment without revealing the name of the creditor;

- contacting the debtor on a Sunday or a statutory holiday, or on any day other than between the hours of 7:00 a.m. and 9:00 p.m.;

- releasing to anyone information that is false or misleading and that may be detrimental to the debtor or her or his family;

- contacting the debtor's spouse, relatives, neighbours, or friends, except for the purpose of obtaining the debtor's address or telephone number; and

- contacting the debtor's employer for the purpose of obtaining the debtor's address or telephone number, obtaining verification of employment, or to garnishee (seize) wages.

Penalties for violating the Act or Regulations include a maximum fine of $100,000 and imprisonment for one year.

Competition Act

The *Competition Act*,[12] a federal statute that was discussed earlier in the context of business practices that are restraints on competition, also deals with other types of trade practices. This Act applies to consumer and non-consumer transactions.

The Act prohibits persons from making misleading representations to the public with respect to the use or supply of a product, including representations about the performance or efficacy of a product, the warranty or guarantee of a product, and the price at which a product will be sold or is being sold by other suppliers. It also prohibits the use of telemarketing to sell products or services

---

11 RRO 1990, reg. 74, as amended.

12 RSC 1985, c. C-34.

unless the telemarketers comply with the obligations of the Act, which include disclosing, in a timely fashion, the identity of the party on behalf of whom the sales pitch is being made and the price of the goods or services. The Act prohibits **pyramid selling schemes** and imposes disclosure obligations on **multilevel marketing schemes**.

Contravening the provisions of the Act carries a maximum penalty of a fine of $200,000 and one year of imprisonment.

Criminal Code and Unconscionable Transactions Relief Act

Section 347 of the *Criminal Code*[13] makes it an offence to charge interest in excess of 60 percent per annum. This offence is punishable by a maximum fine of $25,000 or imprisonment for up to five years.

While the cutoff rate of 60 percent may seem unreasonably high, the *Unconscionable Transactions Relief Act*,[14] an Ontario statute, can also provide relief to a debtor from interest rates that are high but do not exceed the criminal rate of interest. A court will examine the loan, the risk involved, and all other relevant circumstances. If the court decides that the cost of the loan is excessive and the transaction is harsh and unconscionable, it may reopen the agreement and change its terms, order that the creditor repay moneys to the debtor, and/or relieve the debtor of further payment.

Consumer Reporting Act

The *Consumer Reporting Act*,[15] an Ontario statute, regulates the activities of consumer reporting agencies. Consumer reporting agencies must be registered with the Ministry of Consumer and Business Services to carry on business, and must act with integrity and honesty to maintain and renew their registration. Consumer reporting agencies are also called credit reporting agencies or credit bureaus. These agencies maintain files that contain information about consumers, such as current address and employment, credit history, judgments, pending lawsuits, bankruptcies, payment history, and criminal convictions. Since this information is personal and potentially damaging, the agencies are restricted in how they use and release this information.

A consumer reporting agency cannot release the information in its files except

- in response to a court order;

- in response to written instructions from the consumer;

- to a party it believes will use the information in connection with extending credit to the consumer or entering into or renewing a tenancy agreement with the consumer, or for insurance or employment purposes;

pyramid selling scheme
a multilevel marketing plan whereby a participant in the plan pays for the right to receive compensation for recruiting into the plan another participant who pays for the same right

multilevel marketing scheme
a plan for the supply of a product whereby a participant in the plan receives compensation for the supply of the product to another participant in the plan who, in turn, receives compensation for the supply of the product to other participants in the plan

---

13 RSC 1985, c. C-46.

14 RSO 1990, c. U.2.

15 RSO 1990, c. C.33, as amended.

- to a limited degree, to the government of Ontario or Canada; or

- to another registered agency.

In most contracts that involve credit, such as chattel mortgages, leases, or conditional sales contracts, a term of the agreement states that the buyer agrees that the seller may obtain credit information about the buyer at any time. This constitutes written instructions as required by the Act. Many consumers are unaware that the contracts they have signed contain such a provision.

The contents of the consumer file must be accurate, and there are restrictions on the information that may be kept in the file. The following information may *not* be included in the file:

- credit information that is unreliable;

- personal information that is unreliable;

- information as to judgments, lawsuits, bankruptcies, crimes, and so on that are more than seven years old;

- information regarding crimes for which a pardon has been granted or for charges that were dismissed or withdrawn; and

- information with respect to race, creed, colour, sex, ancestry, ethnic origin, or political affiliation.

The agency must supply a copy of the information in its files to the consumer free of charge upon written request of the consumer. If the consumer advises the agency that information in the file is inaccurate, the agency must try to determine whether the information is complete and must correct, supplement, or delete its information to ensure that it is accurate.

The maximum penalty for contravening the Act is a fine of $100,000 and imprisonment for one year.

Consumer Protection Bureau Act

The *Consumer Protection Bureau Act*[16] is a very short Ontario statute that sets up a branch of the Ministry of Consumer and Business Services known as the Consumer Protection Bureau. The purpose of the bureau is to disseminate information to educate and advise consumers about consumer protection and lending and borrowing practices, to receive and investigate complaints in contravention of the various consumer protection statutes, and to enforce such legislation.

AMENDMENTS

It should be noted that *An Act to enact, amend or revise various Acts related to consumer protection*[17] was passed in 2002 but has not yet been proclaimed. When proclaimed, this act will consolidate many of the existing consumer protection provisions found in the statutes described in this chapter.

---

16 RSO 1990, c. C.32.

17 SO 2002, c. 30.

The new legislation will be called the *Consumer Protection Act, 2002* and will repeal or replace the former *Consumer Protection Act*, the *Business Practices Act*, the *Consumer Protection Bureau Act*, the *Loan Brokers Act, 1994*, the *Motor Vehicle Repair Act*, the *Prepaid Services Act*, and parts of the *Consumer Reporting Act*. This new Act will apply to consumer rights and warranties, unfair business practices, the rights and obligations respecting consumer agreements, advance fees, repairs to motor vehicles and other goods, credit agreements, consumer leasing of goods, consumer remedies, and investigations and enforcement.

This Act will also revise and replace the *Motor Vehicle Dealers Act*, the *Real Estate and Business Brokers Act*, and the *Travel Industry Act*.

Also, amendments will be made to the *Collection Agencies Act*, the *Consumer Reporting Act*, the *Discriminatory Business Practices Act*, the *Licence Appeal Tribunal Act, 1999*, the *Mortgage Brokers Act*, the *Registered Insurance Brokers Act*, the *Safety and Consumer Statutes Administration Act, 1996*, the *Toronto Islands Residential Community Stewardship Act, 1993*, and the *Ministry of Consumer and Business Services Act*.

At the time of writing, this legislation had not yet been proclaimed.

SUMMARY

Consumer protection legislation exists at the provincial and federal levels in all jurisdictions in Canada. The issues addressed by this legislation fall into the general categories of standards of safety, standards of quality, prohibition of unethical business practices, and requirements of credit disclosure. In most cases, the statute will override any contractual term that conflicts with the statute. The main statutes that apply to contracts made in Ontario are the *Sale of Goods Act*, the *Consumer Protection Act*, and the *Business Practices Act*. Other statutes deal with specific marketplace and industry concerns and issues, such as the *Food and Drugs Act*, the *Consumer Packaging and Labelling Act*, and the *Motor Vehicle Safety Act*.

KEY TERMS

chattel mortgage

chattels

conditional sale contract

consumer

consumer goods

executory contract

exemplary or punitive damages

multilevel marketing scheme

negotiable instrument

pyramid selling scheme

quiet possession

REVIEW QUESTIONS

1. What changes in the marketplace have made it necessary to enact consumer protection legislation?

2. Describe some of the differences between the remedies available to consumers under consumer protection legislation and under common law.

3. Explain some of the abuses consumer protection legislation attempts to address.

4. What obligations do lenders have in consumer transactions?

5. Describe restrictions on using credit information obtained by consumer reporting agencies.

6. Which provides better protection to the consumer: remedies available directly to the consumer, such as the right to rescind a contract, or penalties imposed by the government on parties who contravene consumer protection legislation? Explain.

7. Has consumer protection legislation changed the balance of power in the marketplace? Why or why not?

8. What purpose is served by refusing to allow advertising of drugs that claim to be treatments or cures for various diseases?

9. How can compliance with the requirement to label hazardous goods benefit the manufacturer?

10. What are the possible shortcomings of the legislative provisions that require notification of safety defects in motor vehicles?

11. What abuses in the motor vehicle repair industry does the *Motor Vehicle Repair Act* seek to address?

12. What issues of consumer safety does the requirement for textile labelling seek to address?

13. Describe the possible strengths and weaknesses of the legislation for classifying and restricting unfair business practices.

14. What abuses in the debt collection industry does the *Collection Agencies Act* seek to address?

CHAPTER 10

Contract Preparation and Drafting

INTRODUCTION

In the preceding chapters you have learned how to interpret contracts and how contracts can be used to achieve a variety of purposes. In this chapter you will learn how to organize client information to prepare a contract and how to draft a simple contract. If you are working as a law clerk, be sure to have the supervising lawyer review the material you prepare. If you are working independently—for example, as a contract administrator or a paralegal—be careful not to exceed your reach. If you are entering an unfamiliar area or dealing with a difficult drafting problem, ask for help and advice. Even when you are sure of yourself, let a colleague review and critique your work.

PREPARING TO DRAFT A CONTRACT

You should take a number of steps before you begin drafting a contract, including obtaining facts, directions, and instructions, and organizing information. Once that is done, a draft is prepared, reviewed, and revised before it is presented to the other party. It will then be further revised as the parties reform and refine their positions during negotiations. Follow the step-by-step procedure described below to prepare a contract draft, but don't be too rigid about it—occasionally, circumstances will require you to modify your procedures.

1. Obtain Instructions

Get all of the necessary facts, including relevant documents, such as collateral contracts or floor plans for a lease of commercial space. If there is an existing file on the matter, read it, particularly the correspondence, which may identify and highlight many of the important issues. Be sure you understand both the client's and the other party's goals. For example, your client may want to lease commercial retail space for 5 years with a right to renew for a further 10 years at a predetermined rent. Obviously, a standard commercial lease won't be enough to achieve these goals, and you will have to give thought to how to craft provisions that will do what the client requires.

2. Use a Checklist To Review Facts

Often a contract that was previously drafted to deal with a similar situation (called a *precedent*) or a checklist from a text can help you ensure that you have obtained all of the relevant facts and identified all of the legal issues. Many firms maintain files of previously used contracts that can be used as precedents or models for the work you are doing. There are also texts, such as *O'Brien's Encyclopedia of Forms*, published by Canada Law Book, that provide commercial legal documents and contract precedents. Take care with precedents, though, because a precedent will rarely fit your case exactly; as well, a precedent should not be used as a substitute for hard, critical thought about the facts and issues in your case. The cautious use of precedents in connection with drafting the contract is discussed later in this chapter.

3. Identify and Research Legal Issues

Once you have identified legal issues, you may need to do some research to see how the case law has dealt with fact situations similar to yours. For example, if you are trying to provide for a right to renew a lease at a predetermined rent, you may need to look at law that deals with this kind of provision to see how the other side may seek to escape or limit the right of renewal so that you can block those escape routes with appropriate contract language.

4. Continue To Obtain Further Instructions and Clarification from Client

As you research the facts and the law, you may discover problems that the client and the supervising lawyer did not anticipate. Do not hesitate to flag problems and obtain further directions and instructions.

5. Prepare a Pre-drafting Outline

This document should set out client goals, list all relevant facts, identify obligations of the client and the other party, and identify qualifiers of those obligations: conditions precedent, exclusions, warranties, guaranties, dispute settlement mechanisms, and so on.

6. Identify Terms To Be Defined

As you review the facts and legal issues, identify those terms that need to be specifically defined in the contract. Remember that you do not need to define words where the ordinary dictionary meaning is used or where the words are used in their ordinary context. "Time," for example, does not usually require a definition. But if the contract contemplates events across several time zones, it may be necessary to define "time" in terms of an applicable time zone.

7. Create Contract Categories, Headings, and Subheadings

Do not try to immediately draft provisions of the contract without first preparing an outline. Identify legal issues and create contract categories to organize the facts and legal issues. From these categories, create headings to be used in the contract.

8. Create a Logical Sequence of Headings and Subheadings

Sequence the headings and subheadings in a logical way. In doing this you are creating an outline that can also form the basis for a table of contents for the contract. Try to do this without referring to a precedent, and use the precedent later to see if you have missed anything. You may want to write out the categories and headings on index cards, shuffle them at random, and start to lay them out, organizing and reorganizing them into a sequence that seems logical and coherent. The sequence should use a logical approach, but most commonly, important matters come first: price and primary obligations of the parties followed by representations, conditions precedent, contract administrative matters, definitions, schedules, and appendixes. If there appear to be too many headings, determine whether some can be logically grouped as subheadings of a main heading.

You are now ready to prepare a first draft of the contract.

DRAFTING A CONTRACT

Preparing the First Draft of a Contract

Here are some suggestions to help you prepare the first draft.

BE PREPARED TO WRITE THE FIRST DRAFT IN ONE SITTING

Writing the first draft in one sitting gives you some assurance of consistency and that you have included all of the necessary information.

REVIEW PRECEDENTS CAREFULLY

If you have a precedent, review it carefully and critically for appropriate language. Check to see whether the language used has been judicially interpreted. For whom was the precedent used: a client in the same position as your client or someone in the same position as the other party? Look at the precedent as though it came from the other party and examine it critically in that context, being prepared to reject or modify unsuitable provisions and to add suitable ones.

Remember that there are benefits to using precedents: they provide you with checklists, you may be able to use wording someone else has crafted that has withstood judicial challenge, and you may be alerted to legal issues or problems you had not anticipated. But you must be careful—you may spend hours looking for a precedent that "fits" your facts. This is unlikely to happen, and you may end up with a precedent that is too general. You may be lulled into following a precedent that seems to be close to what you want, but read it carefully and do not simply leap at it without thinking critically about it. Beware of including words, terms, or phrases that you do not understand—remember to research before you look at and adopt a precedent. Use the precedent to check your draft to see that important provisions have not been omitted and that appropriate language has been used—that is, that unnecessary jargon and ambiguity have been avoided.

DRAFT THE PROVISIONS OF THE AGREEMENT

Using the headings and subheadings from your outline in an appropriate sequence, draft the necessary provisions, including all necessary facts and covering all necessary issues. If you seem to have too many headings and subheadings, be prepared to reduce the number of headings and create more subheadings. If there are too many long, cumbersome clauses under a heading, consider creating more headings and subheadings.

REVISE THE DRAFT

If you mark the draft, use a red pencil so you can easily spot corrections. Where possible, use a word processor so that you can enter the corrections from the hard copy of each draft after each revision. This will ensure that you always have a clean copy of the latest revision. Drafts should be given to the supervising lawyer and discussed with the client. Do not delete or throw out earlier drafts. Instead, number and date them. As revising continues through the period of negotiations with the other party, the content of a revision may become important if there is a disagreement as to what was decided, or, if after the contract is completed, there is a dispute about the meaning of a term. Previous revisions may show how a particular term was drafted and what it was meant to do. The drafts may even become evidence in interpreting the contract under exceptions to the parol evidence rule.

CHECK FOR INTERNAL CONSISTENCY

Check to see that terms and expressions are used as they are defined and are internally consistent throughout the document.

CHECK CROSS-REFERENCES

Ensure that any cross-references are accurate as to content and paragraph and subparagraph numbers. If, in your first draft, paragraph 3 makes a reference to a term in paragraph 7, make sure that the referenced paragraph is still paragraph 7 in your fourth or fifth draft.

CHECK AGAINST THE CLIENT'S INSTRUCTIONS

Has the client changed or modified his or her instructions? Does the draft reflect the client's instructions?

PROOFREAD THE DRAFT

Proofread for style, punctuation, and grammar. Eliminate unnecessary legal jargon and replace it with simple, clear language. Edit for brevity and simplicity of language. First drafts are often wordier than they need to be and can often be edited down, becoming clearer in the process. Check for ambiguous language and inconsistent or contradictory language or provisions.

HAVE OTHERS REVIEW THE DRAFT

Give each draft to the supervising lawyer and also to the client to ensure that the document reflects the client's goals and instructions.

Common Language and Drafting Problems

When you draft a contract, whether you have a precedent or not, exercise great care with the language. While plain-language drafting makes the job easier than it used to be, you should be aware of a number of common writing problems. While some of the more common problems are identified below, be familiar with and be prepared to use standard texts on interpretation and drafting to help you. Several are listed at the end of the chapter.

STRUCTURE AND PURPOSE OF A LEGAL SENTENCE

All sentences consist of a *subject*, consisting of a noun or pronoun, and a *predicate*, consisting of a verb and an object. Other words may modify the subject and the predicate. Legal sentences have the same structure and observe the same rules of English grammar as other sentences.

Legal sentences, however, follow certain conventions that are different from those used in other writing because legal sentences have a specific purpose—they create rights and obligations. These conventions are as follows:

- The subject consists of an identifiable legal person, *the legal actor*, who will be taking legal action.

- The predicate consists of a verb, object, and other modifying words, *the legal action*, which describes the legal action to be taken by the legal actor, creating rights, grants of power or authority, obligations, duties, and liabilities.

USING ACTIVE VOICE

Generally, the legal actor who is performing the legal action must be identified so that everyone reading the document knows who is to act. This is done by using the active voice so that the reader knows who is to receive a benefit or perform an obligation. Since contracts are about who is to perform obligations and receive benefits, identifying the actors is very important. There are times, however, when you may not be able to identify the actor or you want to maintain uncertainty. For example, the phrase "the premises may be entered" may be used if you do not wish to be too specific as to who may enter. In these situations, using the passive voice is appropriate. The passive voice is also appropriate in **recitals**, definition clauses, and other sentences in contracts where rights and obligations are not being created.

recital
a part of a contract, at the beginning, that recites facts that establish the background and purpose of the parties in entering into the contract

▪ EXAMPLES OF USING PASSIVE AND ACTIVE VOICE

- *Appropriate use of passive voice* "In this agreement, 'support' means support for the children of the marriage." Since no rights or obligations are created, this is an appropriate use of the passive voice.

- *Inappropriate use of passive voice* "Rubbish shall be removed from the work site at the end of each working day." Because an obligation is created here, who is to remove the rubbish is important, but we are not told who has this responsibility.

- *Appropriate use of active voice* "The building contractor shall remove rubbish from the work site at the end of each working day." Here, the person who is to perform the obligation is identified.

USING PRESENT TENSE

Generally, unless there is a specific reason to do otherwise, a legal sentence is in the present tense. The contract is presumed to be speaking from and after the time it is written, in which case the present tense makes this clear. As well, the present tense is appropriate to the state of events at the time the contract is operating.

There are times when other tenses should be used. A form of the past tense should be used to describe actions that precede in time the current action; this makes clear that conditions precedent, for example, must be performed before the current obligation is undertaken or the right is conferred. Where an obligation is to be performed in the future, use a form of the future tense.

■ EXAMPLES OF USING PRESENT AND FUTURE TENSE

- *Using present tense for a constant present obligation* "The contractor *is* to keep the site clear of rubbish at all times."

- *Using form of past tense (present perfect) for condition precedent to a current obligation* "If the contractor *has not cleared* the site of rubbish at the end of the working day, the contractor is to pay the site owner for the cost of removing the rubbish."

- *Using future tense for an obligation to be performed in the future* "On the anniversary of the signing of this agreement, the husband *will pay* to the wife the sum of $10,000."

FACT SITUATION OR CONTEXT

The subject of a legal sentence tells you who is to act, and the predicate says what he or she is to do. The fact situation, or context,[1] tells you in what circumstances the action in the predicate will take place. At times the context is implicit and clear, but at other times specifying the context can simplify meaning. If there are a number of obligations to be performed in a specific situation, stating that situation, and following it with a list of obligations in subparagraphs can simplify and shorten the document, since the context need not be repeated for each of the obligations. The fact situation can be quite complex, containing conditions precedent and other terms that may affect verb tense.

---

1   The English legal writer Coode, in his original and complex analysis, divided sentences into four parts: subject, predicate, case, and condition. The Canadian authority on drafting, Elmer A. Driedger, reduces these to the "fact situation" in which an obligation operates. The authors of this book, great believers in simplicity, prefer the Driedger approach.

■ EXAMPLE OF FACT SITUATION WITH LIST OF OBLIGATIONS

Once the contractor has begun work on the site, in order to ensure the site is a safe workplace, the contractor shall

    a. remove all rubbish from the site at the end of the working day,

    b. erect safety barriers to keep trespassers off the site, and

    c. erect and maintain a lighting system to illuminate the site during hours of darkness.

PROVISOS

In traditional drafting, the writer who is dealing with an obligation or right that is to be limited in some circumstances will often use phrases like "provided that" or "provided always that." Most commentators today believe that these kinds of phrases should be avoided. Usually, "provided that" can be replaced by "if," "except that," "except if," or a new sentence. The result is likely to be a clearer sentence. Provisos often lead to ambiguity, and the phrases used to create provisos are part of an archaic writing style that makes little, if any, grammatical sense.

■ EXAMPLES OF PROVISOS

- *Old style* "The contractor is responsible for maintaining a safe work site, *provided always that* the building owner is not in breach of his obligations."

- *New style* "The contractor is responsible for maintaining a safe work site *except if* the building owner is in breach of his obligations." This version is clearer and simpler.

MISUSING "AND" AND "OR"

"And" and "or" have different meanings in different contexts, which can cause confusion for drafters. "And" can have the following meanings:

- *Joint* "Betty *and* Carlos"—both together, but neither alone.

- *Several-inclusive* "Betty *and* Carlos"—either of them or both together. This version can also use an "or": "Betty *or* Carlos or both of them."

- *Several-exclusive* "Betty *and* Carlos"—either Betty or Carlos, but not both together.

Context can sometimes make the meaning clear. For example, "The contractor shall pay cleaning and disposal expenses" would be given a several-inclusive meaning, since the contractor could pay cleaning expenses, if incurred, and disposal expenses, if incurred, or both sets of expenses, if both are incurred. It is wise to include enough sentence modifiers in the predicate to eliminate any ambiguity and make the meaning clear.

The phrase "and/or" is sometimes used to prevent the reader from assuming that "and" means a joint option and "or" means exclusively one option. This can lead to uncertainty and difficulty in interpretation. For example, consider the following provision: "If the owner has to clean the site, he is entitled to sell and/or lease the contractor's bulldozer on the site to defray the cleanup costs incurred." On its face, this permits the contractor to sell and lease the bulldozer, which is not possible. Because the intention is to give the owner the opportunity to do one thing or the other, but not both, it would be best to make this clear by using "or" in place of "and/or."

■ EXAMPLES OF USING "AND" AND "OR"[2]

1. "contractor's tools that are intended to be used for excavation *and* cleaning"

This could mean

- "contractor's tools that are intended for excavation and tools that are intended for cleaning," creating two separate and exclusive categories of tools. If this meaning is intended, this version should be used.
- "contractor's tools that are intended for doing *both* excavation and cleaning," creating one class of tools to perform both functions. If this meaning is intended, the original phrase 1 can be used, although it could be made even clearer by using this version.

2. "contractor's tools that are intended to be used for excavation *or* cleaning"

This could mean

- "contractor's tools that are intended to be used either for excavation or for cleaning *but not both*." If this meaning is intended, then this phrase should be used.
- "contractor's tools that are intended to be used for excavation or cleaning *or both*." If this meaning is intended, the original phrase 2 can be used, although for greater clarity this version could be used.

3. "contractor's tools that are intended to be used for excavation, *and* contractor's tools that are intended to be used for cleaning"

This could mean

- "*both* contractor's tools that are intended to be used for excavation and tools that are intended to be used for cleaning" in a joint sense—that is, both together and not either one separately, if the sentence containing the phrase is mandatory or in command form. If this is the case, this version should be used.
- "contractor's tools that are intended to be used for excavation, *or* contractor's tools that are intended to be used for cleaning, *or both*," in the sense that either could be used, or both could be used, if the sentence containing the phrase is permissive and grants options. If this is the case, this version should be used.

---

2 This set of examples is based on the approach used in F.R. Dickerson, *The Fundamentals of Legal Drafting* (Boston: Little Brown, 1965).

4. "contractor's tools that are intended to be used for excavation *or* contractor's tools that are intended to be used for cleaning"

This could mean

- "contractor's tools that are intended to be used for excavation or contractor's tools that are intended to be used for cleaning, *but not both*." If this is the intended meaning, this version should be used.
- If the intention is to be permissive and permit either or both to be used, then the original phrase 4 is appropriate.

EXPRESSING TIME

Your biggest problem in expressing periods of time in contracts is being precise about when a time period begins and ends. Here are some helpful drafting conventions.

"From" a Given Date

There is no clear answer from the cases whether the date from which a time period runs is included or not, so very clear language should be used.

■ EXAMPLES OF USING/NOT USING "FROM"

- *Ambiguous* "from the 16th of July to ... ." It is not clear whether July 16 is included in the time period or not.

- *Unambiguous* "for a period of 10 days after July 16th." This version clearly indicates that the period begins on July 17.

"On" a Given Date

If the word "on" is used to mark the beginning of a period of time, the date is included. "On and after" or "on and from" do not add to or clarify the meaning and should not be used.

■ EXAMPLE OF USING "ON"

"Interest on the principal amount begins to run, calculated daily, on May 1" means that interest will be calculated daily beginning with interest for May 1 and for all the following days of the interest period.

"Within" a Period of Time

When an event is to occur within a particular time period, the last day of the period is usually excluded from the time period. This is exactly opposite to what is required under the *Ontario Rules of Civil Procedure of the Superior Court*,[3] where the first day of a period for doing something is excluded and the last day is included. To avoid difficulties, use language that clearly states what you intend.

---

3 Rule 3.01(1)(a), RRO 1990, reg. 194.

■ EXAMPLE OF USING "WITHIN"

"The contractor shall be responsible for cleaning the work site within a period of two days, commencing on the day after the last work is done on the site by the contractor."

"Between" Identifying the Start and End of a Period

Do not use the word "between" because it creates ambiguity. Many cases have excluded both the first date and the last when "between" was used, but the rulings are not consistent. To avoid difficulties, use very clear language to indicate whether the first or the last dates are included or excluded.

■ EXAMPLES OF USING/NOT USING "BETWEEN"

- *Ambiguous* "Between July 16, 2005 and August 1, 2005, the debtor may prepay the amount owing without payment of interest." It is not clear whether the period includes July 16 or August 1.

- *Unambiguous* "After July 16, 2005 and before August 1, 2005, the debtor may prepay the amount owing without payment of interest." The period is clearly defined as starting and including July 17, and ending on July 31.

"Until," "By," or "From/To" a Date

Using these expressions to establish the beginning or end of a period often leads to questions about whether the beginning and end dates are included or excluded. For example, the phrase "by July 31" is usually interpreted to mean the performance of the event *before* that date. To avoid ambiguity, if something may be done until a specific date, it is best expressed by writing "until and including" the date or "until but excluding" the date, depending on your purpose. It is advisable to avoid "from July 1 to July 10," since it is not clear whether July 1 and 10 are included or excluded. Instead, your intention can be expressed clearly by writing "commencing on day 1 and ending on day 10, both days included" (or excluded, if that is what you intend).

Day, Month, Year

A day is presumed to be 24 hours, running from midnight to 11:59:59 p.m. If you wish to have a day start or end at a fixed hour, set out the time: "on July 31, before 4:00 p.m." If you wish a whole day to be included, you can define it as a "clear day" or simply a "day." If you use the word "time" rather than "day," the interpretation is that the event is to occur at a specific time during the day. A "month" usually refers to a lunar month of four weeks. The term "calendar month" is often used, but its meaning is unclear: in some cases it has been deemed to refer to a period between a day in one month to the same day in the next month—for example, from July 6 to August 6—in other cases it has been held to mean that the month ends on the same day as it began, which can lead to a conclusion that July 1 and August 1 are in the same month. The best way to avoid these problems is either to define precisely what you mean by "month" in the definition section of the contract or to use a more precise measure of time, such as a day. A "year" means 12 calendar months, calculated from January 1 or some other chosen date. It includes 365 days, or 366 in a leap year. Fractions of days are not taken into account except by astronomers.

Expressions of Age

Defining a time period by the age of a person leads to ambiguities about whether the age that starts and ends the period is included or excluded. It is also not clear when the event of being a particular age actually occurs. Precision of language is required here.

■ EXAMPLE OF USING AGE TO DEFINE A TIME PERIOD

- *"More than 60 years old"* Is a person more than 60 on the day after her 60th birthday or on the day of her 61st birthday? Either is plausible. This can be clarified by writing "The employee has passed the day of her 60th birthday" or "has passed the day of her 61st birthday," depending on what you intend.

MISUSING "SHALL" AND "MAY"

"Shall" is often used improperly to convey a sense of what is to happen in the future, to address inanimate objects, to give directions, and to declare a legal result. It is properly used to convey a command to do something or to abstain from doing something. To convey a sense of the future, use "will." If you want to create an option or permit something rather than require it, use "may."

■ EXAMPLES OF USING "SHALL"

- *Inappropriate use of "shall": conveying a sense of future* "The contractor shall complete the work by 4 p.m. July 31, or he *shall* forfeit his performance bond." This should be written as "The contractor shall complete the work by 4 p.m. July 31, or he *will* forfeit his performance bond." Note that the first part of the sentence is a command to do something, while the second part indicates what is to happen in the future.

- *Inappropriate use of "shall": addressing inanimate objects* Do not write "The performance bond *shall* contain provisions that … ," since this sounds like a command to a thing that cannot act. Instead, "The performance bond *must* contain provisions that … ."

- *Inappropriate use of "shall": giving directions* Do not use "The contractor shall complete form A" if this is a direction that occurs when an event occurs. Instead, use "The contractor must complete form A," or "The contractor is to complete form A."

- *Inappropriate use of "shall": declaring a legal result* Do not use "excavate *shall* mean …" where the phrase is a declaration of a legal result — in this case, a definition. Instead, use the present indicative "excavate means … ."

- *Appropriate use of "shall"* "The contractor *shall* clean the work site." This phrase uses "shall" appropriately, since it contains a command to the contractor to do something.

- *Appropriate use of "may"* "The contract *may* use a subcontractor to clean the work site." This provision is permissive, giving the contractor an option.

Rules of Construction and Interpretation

If there is a dispute about what the contract language actually means, judges resort to a number of rules of construction to interpret the disputed language.

LISTS

ejusdem generis
a rule of contract construction that requires that general words following specific words take their meaning from the specific words and are confined to the same category as the specific words

expressio unius est exclusio alterius
"to express one thing and exclude another"; a rule of contract construction that requires that the use of one word implies the exclusion of another

Take care when drafting lists as part of a contract, since two contradictory rules may cause mayhem. The **ejusdem generis** rule may result in words in the list being defined as being confined to the category or thing described by the first word in the list. The rule of **expressio unius est exclusio alterius** has a different effect, requiring an interpretation that the things included imply that other things not specifically mentioned in the list are excluded. Neither rule may reflect what you intended.

Ejusdem Generis

This rule provides that general words following specific words are confined to the class or category of the specific words. You can avoid the problems caused by this rule by using appropriate wording. For example, if you have given a list of tools but do not wish to restrict the general meaning of "tools," use a phrase at the end of the list such as this one: "or any other tool, *whether of the same kind of tool previously listed or not.*"

Expressio Unius Est Exclusio Alterius

This rule means that the inclusion of one thing implies the exclusion of those things not listed. If you want to avoid the application of this rule to a list, use a phrase like "construction equipment, *including but not limited to* bulldozers, back hoes, graders … ." Do not use "for greater certainty but not so as to restrict the generality of the foregoing." This phrase, besides being wordy, is used in s. 91 of the *Constitution Act, 1867*,[4] where it has been given a variety of interpretations, some of them contradictory.

RECITALS

Recitals can set out the history and context of an agreement, the principles that guide the parties, or the reasons why they are agreeing to do certain things. Recitals can be important and useful in interpreting ambiguities or uncertainties in the contract. Be sure that descriptions of consideration and other important terms are in the main body of the contract and not in a recital, and avoid using phrases in a recital that describe nominal consideration, such as "for two dollars, and other valuable consideration." These only confuse the interpretation of the contract. If there is a conflict between the contents of the recitals and the main body of the contract, the latter generally prevails.

---

4   30 & 31 Vict., c. 3 (UK).

HEADINGS

Be careful with the language you use in headings in the body of the contract. In some cases, headings have been used to help interpret the terms of the contract.

MATHEMATICAL CONCEPTS

Occasionally you will have a formula in a contract, often to calculate something such as sales commissions, bonuses, or increases in payment that are tied to inflation. Mathematical concepts are not always easy to express in language. Where you have described a formula or method of calculation, include written formulas or describe the calculation method step by step. Give examples in an appendix of how the formula works. If necessary you can include the formula as an appendix too, but reference the appendix in the relevant contract provision so that it becomes a part of the contract.

Inappropriate Use of "Legalese"

In drafting contracts you may feel that you need to use legal jargon to make effective legal documents. Some people maintain that clients expect to see legalese, that legalese is more accurate than ordinary language, that jargon employs necessary technical terms or **terms of art** that are essential to a contract, and that your employers expect you to use legal jargon.

Is legalese necessary, and should you be using it? The short answer is that since the 1980s in Canada and other parts of the common law world there has been a substantial movement away from the use of legalese and toward **plain language drafting** for contracts and other legal writing. Law schools, law societies, bar associations, leading law firms, and judges have all endorsed a movement to clearer language. For example, since 1990 the Law Society of Upper Canada has taught the plain language approach to bar admission students in legal writing courses, as well as in continuing education courses for practising lawyers. Large banks and corporations have also shifted over to plain language documents, particularly for consumer contracts.[5] Legislative bodies have required certain contracts to be drafted in plain language to be enforceable. For example, British Columbia requires plain language to be used in consumer motor vehicle leases. New York State has long required insurance contracts to be in plain language.

Still, there are concerns about plain language drafting, often from older lawyers. Some argue that if a document is in plain language, clients may think they can do the work themselves. However, clients pay for expertise and for results, and surveys indicate that the public thinks that legal drafting in the old style results in hard-to-read documents that are meant to confuse a layperson.[6]

terms of art
words, phrases, or technical terms that have a fairly precise, specific legal meaning, often as a result of being interpreted and defined in previous court decisions

plain language drafting
the modern style of drafting legal documents that employs plain, ordinary language and emphasizes clarity, precision, and brevity

---

5   The plain language approach is sometimes referred to as the "Chase Manhattan" style after the Chase Manhattan Bank in New York pioneered the use of plain language documents.

6   In a Plain Language Institute (Vancouver) survey, 57 percent of the public responded that legal documents are poorly written and hard to read. Quoted in the Law Society of Upper Canada, *Legal Writing: 42nd Bar Admission Course, Phase 1*, Summer 1999, *Instructors Manual*, 12-21.

Another concern expressed about plain language is that it is not as precise or accurate as the older style of legal writing. Again, the evidence does not support this assertion. There have been a number of studies of statutes and contracts that have been redrafted with no loss of precision or specificity of meaning. In many cases, redrafted documents are shorter, clearer, more precise, easier to understand, and less time-consuming to master.[7] In fact, there have been judicial comments that many traditionally drafted documents are anything but clear—their writers use so much jargon that it is impossible to determine what the documents mean. In one case, a judge commenting on notice of a liability exclusion clause relied on by a courier company said: "Notice cannot be said to be reasonable, in my view, when the clause is neither legible nor capable of comprehension."[8]

Another criticism of plain language is that it ignores necessary technical legal terminology and terms of art. Technical terms and terms of art that have been judicially defined in previous case decisions do need to be used, but legal terms of art and technical terms take up very little space in most documents. The rest can be written in plain language.

You may also hear that employers require documents to be drafted in the traditional style. In some cases this may be true, and if you are directed by a superior to use a particular format you must follow the directions given. But you are likely to encounter this situation infrequently. Even older lawyers who do not feel they can change their ways often appreciate plain language, as a number of surveys have shown.[9]

LEGALESE THAT CAN CAUSE PROBLEMS

The following are some of the more troublesome forms of legalese that you are likely to encounter and should avoid.

"Said" and "Aforesaid"

Using these terms rarely results in a better-written or clearer legal sentence. The two terms are often used to refer to someone in a document who has already been identified. If, for example, you refer to "the building contractor" for the first time in a document, you do not add clarity or precision by referring to "the said building contractor" or "the aforesaid building contractor" in later paragraphs. Simply writing "the building contractor" is clearer and uses fewer words. If there is more than one contractor, "said building contractor" can create real confusion, because it does not indicate which person you are referring to.

---

7   Ibid., at 12-22. The Law Reform Commission of Victoria (Australia) reported that in a redraft of one piece of legislation, the length was cut by half with no loss in accuracy or precision. Further, the amount of time taken by lawyers and students to comprehend the material when they were tested was cut by one-third.

8   Ibid., referring to *Aurora TV and Radio Ltd. v. Gelco Express Ltd.* (May 10, 1990) (Man. QB (Small Claims), Oliphant J) [unreported].

9   Ibid., at 12-23, referring to S. Harrington and J. Kimble, "Survey: Plain Language Wins Every Which Way" (1987), 66 *Michigan Bar Journal* 1024.

"Such"

You will often see a phrase like this one: "to divide the residue of my estate into equal shares for *such* children of mine who survive me." Some drafters use "such" like "said," to identify a person previously identified or described. The solution here is the same as it is for "said": "to divide the residue of my estate into equal shares for *the* children of mine who survive me."

"Same"

Using "same" just sounds pompous in sentences like "The contractor shall clear rubbish from the work site, and sweep *same.*" A better solution is "The contractor shall clear rubbish from the work site, and sweep *it.*"

"Any," "Each," "Every," and "All"

Usually, using the definite article "the" or the indefinite article "a" will suffice. "Any piece of cleaning equipment" can be written as "a piece of cleaning equipment." However, there are times when these words are needed, for example,

- *when an obligation is imposed on a group of individuals* "Each contractor's site manager shall ... ," and

- *when a right or power is granted* "Any member may move an adjournment."

Couplets and Triplets

In trying to be precise, traditional writers have often used strings of words rather than simply choosing the right word: "I *give, devise, and bequeath,* the *rest, residue, and remainder* of my estate to my children" can easily be clarified and simplified by "I *give* the *remainder* of my estate to my children." When you are tempted to use a couplet or triplet, usually because you have seen one in a precedent, use the word in the group that best and most clearly reflects your meaning.

Legal Gobbledygook

Most commentators consider the following terms to be legal gobbledygook or nonsense that should not be used:

abovementioned	therewith
afore-granted	to wit
aforementioned	whatsoever
before-mentioned	whereas
henceforth	wheresoever
hereinafter	whereof
thenceforth	within named
thereunto	witnesseth

STRUCTURE OF A CONTRACT

Most contracts include certain basic components, although there may be variations depending on the type of contract you are drafting and how complex it is. The basic components include

- identification of the parties,

- recitals,

- terms,

- testimonium and attestation, and

- schedules and appendixes.[10]

Identification of the Parties

The parties to the contract, the promisee and the promisor, are identified as legal entities showing the capacity in which they contract. The identification of a party may also show the authority the party has to contract—for example, "Jorg Anderson, Litigation Guardian of Sven Anderson."

If the parties are individuals, they should be identified and described by their names as those names appear on official documents such as birth certificates—for example, "Laurence Michael Olivo." If an individual uses variations of his or her name, those need not be referred to in most cases. However, where an individual is contracting with respect to a sole proprietorship, it is a good idea to link the individual and the name of the sole proprietorship—for example, "Laurence Michael Olivo, carrying on business as 'Olivo Legal Training and Services.'"

Where a contracting party is a partnership, the partners should be named individually along with the name of the partnership—for example, "Laurence Michael Olivo and Jean Fitzgerald carrying on business as a partnership under the name 'Fly-by-Night Legal Drafting.'" All partners should sign the contract to be sure that each is personally bound to the contract.

Where the contracting party is an artificial person, such as a corporation, government entity, or other artificial body, take care to use the exact name of the entity. The name of the corporation should be *exactly* as it appears in the Articles of Incorporation or in other records of the Corporations branch of the federal or provincial government, depending on which level of government issued the Articles of Incorporation. If the corporation carries on business under a trade name, then that may be included as part of the contracting party's name, but make sure the correct corporate name is used as well—for example, "123456 Ontario Ltd. carrying on business as 'Drafting to the Max.'"

If a government, a government agency or department, a municipality, or an artificial entity created by statute, such as a university, is a contracting party, you need to check the relevant legislation to see what that body is called legally. The official name may bear no relationship to the name it is usually known by. For

---

10 The structure of a contract used here is adapted with modifications from "Contract Architecture," part of the Law Society of Upper Canada, *Legal Writing: 42nd Bar Admission Course, Phase 1,* Summer 1999.

example, the Ministry of X may be legally described as "The Ministry of X by Her Majesty the Queen in Right of Ontario."

Once you have identified the contracting parties and properly named them, you may also wish to include a short description of the party's capacity, purpose, role, or function—for example, "Laurence Michael Olivo, Author." Avoid phrases like "hereinafter referred to as the Author," because this is pompous and wordy. You may see parties described in some contracts as "party of the first part" or "party of the second part." Do not use these terms—they are uninformative and unhelpful. You may want to include the address of each party after the description of the party's capacity, although this is not mandatory. You can also include a title for the agreement. If the contract is for the sale of your bicycle, for example, you can call it a "bicycle sale contract."

■ EXAMPLE OF IDENTIFICATION OF PARTIES

EMPLOYMENT AGREEMENT

BETWEEN:

HAPHAZARD MANUFACTURING LIMITED, Employer

and

GUNTER GRASSE, Employee

Recitals

Recitals follow the names of the parties and set out background facts and the nature and purpose of the agreement, including references to collateral contracts and other dealings between the parties, events that give rise to the contract, expectations of the parties, and other matters that may be relevant. They should not contain essential terms of the contract, such as consideration, statements of obligations, undertakings, or promises. In older agreements the recitals are preceded by the word "Whereas," although this is no longer considered good drafting practice. Instead, they can be headed by the word "Recitals" or "Preamble" (a "preamble" usually describes the recitals that preface a statute, but the term can be used to preface a contract as well). Each recital can then be numbered (1., 2., 3., etc.) or lettered (A., B., C., etc.).

■ EXAMPLE OF RECITALS

PREAMBLE:

1. The Employer wishes to retain the services of the Employee.

2. The Employee wishes to become an employee of the Employer.

3. The Employee therefore agrees to accept the Employer's offer of employment in the position described in Appendix "A" to this Agreement, on the terms described in this Agreement.

Consideration

You need to distinguish between two types of consideration clauses. The first type is a holdover from older contracts drafted in legalese. It is usually found on the first page, after the recitals or preamble. It uses archaic language such as "Now Therefore Witnesseth that for Two (2) dollars of lawful money of Canada and other consideration … ." Leave this consideration clause out altogether, because it adds nothing to the contract except confusion. The second type of consideration clause is the one your contract should include. It appears as a numbered paragraph as one of the terms of the contract dealing with the parties' obligations to each other. This type of clause and how to draft it is discussed below under Obligations. If you want to avoid having a consideration clause, even as a term of the contract, you may want to have the agreement made under seal, because consideration is then not required. This will affect the form of the attestation clause, which will refer to the contract as being "signed and sealed" and not just "signed." Remember that if you use a seal, the contract may not be subject to the remedy of specific performance.

Terms

This is the body of the contract, sometimes also called the covenants. Set out here the contract provisions, including obligations undertaken by the parties and other substantive matters that are essential to the contract. In setting out the terms or covenants, the most important should go first. The following are generally included.

OBLIGATIONS

These are promises to do something or to refrain from doing something, and it is here that consideration is usually identified and expressed. Because these clauses are expressed as commands, the use of "shall" or "must" is recommended (save "will" to convey something that is to take place in the future). Keep these clauses short and use simple sentences. If a paragraph turns out to be dense and long, consider using more headings and subheadings, in a logical way, to break up the clause.

■ EXAMPLE OF AN OBLIGATION

Compensation:

1. As full compensation for the services provided by the Employee, the Employer shall pay the Employee an annual salary of $60,000.00, to be paid in regular installments in accordance with the Employer's usual payment practices. The employer shall make the payments not less frequently than once a month.

REPRESENTATIONS

As you will recall from chapter 4, Contractual Defects, a representation may be made in the course of negotiating a contract and may induce someone to enter into the agreement. But the representation may also be incorporated into the contract as a term that is a promise about the quality of something or about the existence of a particular state of affairs. Often during negotiations one party tries to keep the representations out of the contract, while the other party tries to include them. If the representations are in the contract, the party relying on them has more options for remedies if a representation turns out to be a misrepresentation, even an innocent one. A representation often begins with the phrase "The seller represents that … ." Consider whether the representation should be open-ended or confined, depending on your position: one side or the other may want to tie a representation to a date and include all parties who may be liable for making the representation; a party may also wish to qualify a representation to certain conditions, as the examples below demonstrate.

▪ EXAMPLES OF REPRESENTATIONS

- The seller represents that to the best of her knowledge, no urea formaldehyde foam insulation was used in construction of the premises.

- The seller and the guarantor represent that at the time of sale, the seller had clear title to the goods.

- The seller represents that at the time of sale, to the best of his knowledge, the vehicle complied with Canadian and US automobile safety legislation.

CONDITIONS PRECEDENT

A condition precedent is a state of affairs that must exist before a contract can be completed. The contract is suspended until the condition is fulfilled. If it is not fulfilled, then the contract can be made void at the request of one or both of the parties. A condition precedent clause can be identified by phrases like "A condition precedent to …" or "Subject to … ." Commonly, a condition precedent clause is used when a person purchasing a house makes the purchase conditional on being able to finance the purchase by obtaining a mortgage loan. The purchaser tries to make the condition as broad and general as possible, and the seller tries to limit and confine it as much as possible. A well-drafted clause (from the vendor's viewpoint) is one that spells out the limits of the condition with precision and specificity, with time limits by which the condition must be met. It also states for whose benefit the clause is created, what happens if the condition is unsatisfied, and whether and how the condition can be waived.

▪ EXAMPLE OF CONDITION PRECEDENT CLAUSE

A. Performance of the purchaser's obligations is subject to the purchaser being able to obtain a mortgage until and including October 3, 20XX for a principal amount of $60,000 at an interest rate of 5 percent per annum for a term of 5 years, with an amortization period of 25 years, permitting prepayment of principal without penalty or bonus.

B. This condition precedent is for the benefit of the purchaser, who may waive the condition. If the purchaser is not successful in obtaining a mortgage on the terms described in paragraph A, the agreement is terminated.

STATEMENTS

In a contract, a statement is something written about the contract itself. It differs from a representation, which is something written about the subject matter of the contract. A statement can be about how the contract is to be interpreted, which law or jurisdiction shall be the place to litigate disputes, or other contract administration matters. There is no magic wording, but each statement should have a separate heading, and the statements should come at the end of the contract, before the testimonium. Some examples of typical statements are set out below.

■ EXAMPLES OF STATEMENTS

43. Severability:

The parties agree that if any provision or term of the Agreement is deemed void, voidable, or unenforceable, the remaining terms shall remain in full force and effect.

44. Cancellation of Prior Agreements:

The parties agree that all prior agreements, written or verbal, express or implied, between the parties relating in any way to the employment of the Employee with the Employer are declared null and void and are superseded by the terms of this Agreement.

DEFINITIONS

Include a definition section after the contract statements if you need one. You may also place the definitions, in alphabetical order, right after the recitals at the beginning of the contract so the reader is alerted to them from the start. Define only terms that are being used in a technical way, or where the definition differs from the usual definition of the word or phrase. Do not use illogical definitions—for example, defining "fast" as "slow." If a word is used in more than one way, define both ways, and make a clear reference to where in the contract each definition is being used. In drafting definitions, keep in mind the maxims *ejusdem generis* and *expressio unius est exclusio alterius*. If you want to restrict a definition, use the word "means." If you want to expand the definition, try using "includes." If you want to exclude certain meanings, use "does not include."

■ EXAMPLES OF DEFINITIONS

45. Definitions:

"paid holiday" includes all statutory holidays, as defined in the Ontario *Interpretation Act*, RSO 1990, as amended, but does not include Easter Monday or Professor Fitzgerald's birthday.

"remuneration" means "net pay after taxes and standard deductions in paragraphs 7a, 11, 32 and 36, and means "gross pay including bonuses" in paragraphs 7b and 23.

Testimonium and Attestation

The testimonium clause comes at the end of the contract and contains a declaration by the party or parties signing the agreement that the agreement has been signed and, if under seal, sealed, and that a duplicate original has been handed over to the other party. The attestation clause is a declaration that the signing of the document and, if sealed, the sealing of the document, have been done in the presence of a witness who signs the declaration. In some cases, the witness may also sign an affidavit of execution. This is required on some documents, such as wills and some real estate documents. An affidavit of execution is similar to the declaration in the attestation clause, except that the affidavit is a sworn statement.

■ EXAMPLE OF ATTESTATION AND TESTIMONIUM CLAUSES

THE PARTIES ACKNOWLEDGE THAT they have signed and delivered this agreement on the dates set out below:

DATED this 7th day of June 20XX.

HAPHAZARD FABRICATIONS LIMITED

Bozenka Paric

Witness

per: *Daniel Duplicitous*

Daniel Duplicitous, President and duly authorized signing officer of Haphazard Fabrications Limited

DATED this 7th day of June 20XX

Ishtar Amagediou

Witness

Mortimer Moribund

Employee

Schedules and Appendixes

If lists, formulas, examples of calculations, or collateral agreements are referred to in the body of the contract, they should be reproduced and attached as schedules or appendixes to the agreement after the testimonium and attestation clauses. Make sure the name of the schedule or appendix and its number corresponds to its reference in the body of the document. The same rules about drafting contracts apply, with necessary modifications, to drafting schedules and appendixes, which form part of the contract and need to be clear.

Layout and Format

Use a good word-processing software package to draft contracts. Take care with "canned" contract programs—ones that contain a precedent from which you choose and tack on relevant clauses or fill in blanks. These programs may be fast, but they should be used, if at all, like precedents, to help you refine a draft or an outline after you have thought about and organized the terms and provisions of the contract. Most word-processing software allows you to create an automatic table of contents if you ensure that each paragraph and subparagraph of the contract has a heading or subheading. You should use the automatic number or lettering system, so that when you make revisions and amendments, the numbering/lettering sequence is maintained in each draft. Use page numbering on all drafts.

Your aim is also to make the contract easy to read visually. Use a justified left margin, where the words all line up in the same place on the left, and a ragged right margin, where the computer decides when to end a line. Use serif fonts—ones that have short lines on the ends of the letters, such as Times New Roman or Bookman Old Style, since the eye follows these more easily. Font size should be no smaller than 12 points, and line spacing should be one-and-one-half or double spacing.

Make defined terms and headings bold or italic in the text. Cross-references to paragraphs should include the paragraph number and title or heading. A consistent numbering system should be used with paragraphs and subparagraphs and they should be block indented:

1.

    b)

        iii)

Do not split paragraphs over two pages; end a paragraph on the page on which it starts.

SUMMARY

In order to draft a contract it is wise to proceed in a methodical way. The drafter begins by obtaining instructions, identifying issues, identifying key terms, and creating headings and subheadings and determining how they should be sequenced. When drafting the contract, use an outline and prepare a first draft in one sitting, using precedents carefully and with caution. You should be prepared to revise your draft and proofread it carefully.

In drafting, there are a number of language and drafting problems you should avoid. Use the active voice and present tense, and be sure to use words carefully, avoiding some of the more common problems that arise from the use of unclear or ambiguous language. In particular, be careful not to use "legalese" or jargon that you do not understand.

Most contracts, when the draft is complete, should identify the parties and set out recitals, terms, the testimonium and attestation clauses, and the schedules and appendixes, if any.

KEY TERMS

ejusdem generis

expressio unius est exclusio alterius

plain language drafting

recital

terms of art

REVIEW QUESTIONS

1. Is it appropriate to obtain instructions from clients, and then draft a contract and present it to them? Explain.

2. What are the dangers in using a precedent? What are the advantages?

3. When do you need to include a definition section in a contract you are drafting?

4. Describe what you need to do to organize and prepare an outline for a contract you are drafting.

5. Why is checking for internal consistency and cross-references in a draft of a contract important?

6. What is a legal sentence? How does it differ from other types of sentences?

7. What is "active voice," and why is it important to use it in drafting contracts and other legal writing?

8. What is "passive voice"? Is it ever permissible to use passive voice in legal writing? Why or why not?

9. What tense should contracts be written in, and why? Is it ever appropriate to switch to other tenses? Explain.

10. What is the function of a proviso? Give an example of a well-written proviso.

11. Identify three different meanings that the conjunction "and" can have in a legal sentence.

12. Why should you not use "and/or" in legal writing?

13. Show how the conjunction "and" can create ambiguity, and then show how to correct and clarify the sentence to eliminate the ambiguity.

14. Describe three problems you might encounter in expressing periods of time and how those problems can be solved by using good drafting practices. Use examples in your description.

15. What problem might arise by referring to a "calendar month"?

16. "You must be more than 65 years old to receive the employer's pension." What problems might you face in deciding when this pension should begin, and how might you eliminate the problems through better drafting?

17. Give examples of when to use the words "shall," "will," and "may."

18. Why is it a good idea to avoid putting lists in contracts?

19. What is the purpose of a recital in a contract?

20. Why is the choice of language in contract headings important?

21. If you have to include a contract provision to increase pay in accordance with the annual increase in the consumer price index, what problems might you expect to have in drafting this provision? What can you do to solve these problems?

22. Explain the *ejusdem generis* rule. How can you avoid its impact on a contract you are drafting?

23. Explain the *expressio unius est exclusio alterius* rule. How can you avoid its impact on a contract you are drafting?

24. What is plain language drafting? What is legalese? What is the difference between the two? Which is preferred by most writers of contracts, and why?

25. What word(s) can you use to replace "said" and "aforesaid" in a legal sentence?

26. Give an example of inappropriate use of the following words in a legal sentence, and show how you would improve the sentence in each case.

    a. such,

    b. same,

    c. any, each, every, all.

27. Describe the matters you should consider in identifying the parties to a contract.

28. What kinds of information should be included in the recitals to a contract?

29. Should you have a nominal consideration clause that is separate from the terms of the contract? Why or why not?

30. When drafting obligations, what drafting rules or conventions should you observe, and why?

31. If you are acting for a party who wants to minimize the impact of a representation as a term of the contract, what sorts of strategies and drafting techniques might you employ?

32. If you want to limit the impact of a condition precedent in a contract, what approach might you take in drafting the clause?

33. Explain the difference between a contract representation and a contract statement.

DRAFTING EXERCISES

1. TO: Paul Paregoric, Law Clerk

   FROM: Linda Loquacious, Solicitor

   RE: Colnard Blague, purchase of "Slumflowers" painting

   Our client, Colnard Blague, the well-known gourmet restaurant owner, has arranged to buy a newly discovered Van Gogh painting of some rather drab-looking flowers with a decrepit urban area as background. Our client calls it "Slumflowers," which is, I suppose, an accurate description. The painting is in its original 19th-century frame. The current owner is Tentacle Industries Ltd. The company is in difficulty and has had to liquidate its corporate art collection. Our client knows John Eatem, the president of Tentacle, and they have negotiated the main terms, though not everything is settled. Our client has agreed to purchase this painting for $100,000 in its current condition and in its current frame. Tentacle owes our client $50,000, and the debt will also be considered paid when the painting is delivered and has been accepted by Blague. Our client is concerned that he not get stuck with something that was painted-by-numbers, so he wants a provision allowing him to have the painting examined and authenticated by an expert before he accepts it. He also wants to hang it in a particular place in his restaurant with museum lighting and wants to be sure it looks right before he finally has to decide to accept it. Our client has also discovered that Tentacle has let the insurance lapse on the painting and wants some provision so that if the painting is destroyed before he finally accepts it, the parties are restored to their pre-contract position. The seller has said that the painting is original and claims it can trace the painting back through previous owners to Van Gogh himself. Be sure to include something about this in the contract. Our client also wants the painting delivered December 1, 20XX, so he can hang it in his restaurant just before the busy Christmas season to impress his customers, and use it as a reason to raise the prices on his menu.

   a. Please go through the process of creating categories and headings, and organize the headings into an outline to be used as a table of contents for me to approve.

   b. Once I have approved the outline, please prepare a draft of the contract from our client's perspective.

2. TO: Paul Paregoric, Law Clerk

   FROM: Linda Loquacious, Solicitor

   RE: Compensation and bonus provisions for employment contract

   I need you to prepare draft contract provisions for determining base pay and bonus payments for a master employment contract for employees of Tentacle Industries. You do not have to draft the whole contract, just the base pay and bonus provisions.

The scheme is as follows: The employer pays the employee a base salary of $X.XX per hour for a 35-hour week. Payment is made on the first day of each month in roughly equal installments. The employer can adjust the payment in the month before the anniversary of the start date of the employee's employment to be sure that the full annual salary is paid in the year that the employee worked. Increases of base salary are in the discretion of the employer and are based on the employee's performance review, which must be conducted within 90 days of the year-end. All salary paid, whether base, bonus, or both, is subject to the usual statutory deductions.

If the employer's net profit is more than $100,000 in the fiscal year, the employee is entitled to receive a profit-sharing bonus. The net profit is the gross corporate income from all sources minus management fees of $75,000, all other expenses, and taxes. To receive a bonus, the employee must have been working for the employer for two full years by the end of the fiscal year that generates the bonus. If the employee has not worked for the two full years, she or he gets nothing. If the employee has worked for the two full years but has not been at work each day in the last fiscal year, the absence will reduce the amount of bonus on a pro rata basis.

Of the net profit, 10 percent is allocated as a bonus for distribution to employees. This amount is divided by the number of employees eligible for the bonus, and each employee receives, within 90 days of the end of the fiscal year, an equal share of the total bonus. This amount is reduced by the number of days absent divided by 365. Earned vacation is not an absence for the purpose of these calculations, nor are weekends or holidays.

RECOMMENDED TEXTS ON INTERPRETATION AND DRAFTING

Dick, Robert C. *Legal Drafting*. Toronto: Carswell, 1972. This standard Canadian work on legal drafting is often referred to by judges and accepted as authoritative. Clear explanations and good examples are used to illustrate concepts.

Fitzgerald, M.F. *Legal Problem Solving: Reasoning, Research and Writing*. Toronto: Butterworths, 1996. This is a useful introduction to the topic that is used by law students.

"Introduction and Overview of Writing and Drafting." In *Professional Legal Training Course Skills Material*. Vancouver: Continuing Legal Education Society of British Columbia, 1991. These materials are used in practical continuing education programs, and are succinct and useful for lawyers and others who are developing their drafting skills.

O'Brien's Encyclopedia of Forms, 11th ed. Aurora, ON: Canada Law Book (annual supplements). These volumes provide useful precedent forms for various types of contracts and commercial documents used in Canada.

Saunders, J.B., ed. *Words and Phrases Legally Defined*, vols. 1-5, 2d ed. London: Butterworths, 1970. This text, or other words and phrases texts and law dictionaries, can be found in the law reference section of most good libraries and all law libraries. It is a good place to start research on how a particular word, phrase, or term has been interpreted by the courts. It is also useful for checking the language used in precedents for the purpose of eliminating inappropriate or archaic language from the contract you are drafting.

Sullivan, R. *Driedger on the Construction of Statutes*, 3d ed. Toronto: Butterworths, 1994. This is the standard reference work on drafting and interpreting statutes. Elmer A. Driedger was for many years a respected and senior legislative drafter for the federal government.

Appendixes

Business Practices Act

RSO 1990, c. B.18

Current to November 4, 2004

Note: On a day to be named by proclamation of the Lieutenant Governor, this Act is repealed by the Statutes of Ontario, 2002, chapter 30, Schedule E, section 1. See: SO 2002, c. 30, Sched. E, ss. 1, 22.

Definitions

1. In this Act,

…

"consumer" means a natural person but does not include a natural person, partnership or association of individuals acting in the course of carrying on business;

"consumer representation" means a representation, statement, offer, request or proposal,

(a) made respecting or with a view to the supplying of goods or services, or both, to a consumer, or

(b) made for the purpose of or with a view to receiving consideration for goods or services, or both, supplied or purporting to have been supplied to a consumer;

"Director" means the Director under the *Ministry of Consumer and Business Services Act*;

…

"goods" means chattels personal or any right or interest therein other than things in action and money, including chattels that become fixtures but not including securities as defined in the *Securities Act*;

"Minister" means the Minister of Consumer and Business Services;

…

"services" means services,

(a) provided in respect of goods or of real property, or

(b) provided for social, recreational or self-improvement purposes, or

(c) that are in their nature instructional or educational;

"Tribunal" means the Licence Appeal Tribunal.

Unfair practices

2. For the purposes of this Act, the following shall be deemed to be unfair practices:

1. A false, misleading or deceptive consumer representation including, but without limiting the generality of the foregoing,

i. a representation that the goods or services have sponsorship, approval, performance characteristics, accessories, uses, ingredients, benefits or quantities they do not have,

ii. a representation that the person who is to supply the goods or services has sponsorship, approval, status, affiliation or connection the person does not have,

iii. a representation that the goods are of a particular standard, quality, grade, style or model, if they are not,

iv. a representation that the goods are new, or unused, if they are not or are reconditioned or reclaimed, provided that the reasonable use of goods to enable the seller to service, prepare, test and deliver the goods for the purpose of sale shall not be deemed to make the goods used for the purposes of this subparagraph,

v. a representation that the goods have been used to an extent that is materially different from the fact,

vi. a representation that the goods or services are available for a reason that does not exist,

vii. a representation that the goods or services have been supplied in accordance with a previous representation, if they have not,

viii. a representation that the goods or services or any part thereof are available to the consumer when the person making the representation knows or ought to know they will not be supplied,

ix. a representation that a service, part, replacement or repair is needed, if it is not,

x. a representation that a specific price advantage exists, if it does not,

xi. a representation that misrepresents the authority of a salesperson, representative, employee or agent to negotiate the final terms of the proposed transaction,

xii. a representation that the proposed transaction involves or does not involve rights, remedies or obligations if the representation is false or misleading,

xiii. a representation using exaggeration, innuendo or ambiguity as to a material fact or failing to state a material fact if such use or failure deceives or tends to deceive,

xiv. a representation that misrepresents the purpose or intent of any solicitation of or any communication with a consumer.

2. An unconscionable consumer representation made in respect of a particular transaction and in determining whether or not a consumer representation is unconscionable there may be taken into account that the person making the representation or the person's employer or principal knows or ought to know,

i. that the consumer is not reasonably able to protect his or her interests because of physical infirmity, ignorance, illiteracy, inability to understand the language of an agreement or similar factors,

ii. that the price grossly exceeds the price at which similar goods or services are readily available to like consumers,

iii. that the consumer is unable to receive a substantial benefit from the subject-matter of the consumer representation,

iv. that there is no reasonable probability of payment of the obligation in full by the consumer,

v. that the proposed transaction is excessively one-sided in favour of someone other than the consumer,

vi. that the terms or conditions of the proposed transaction are so adverse to the consumer as to be inequitable,

vii. that he or she is making a misleading statement of opinion on which the consumer is likely to rely to his or her detriment,

viii. that he or she is subjecting the consumer to undue pressure to enter into the transaction.

3. Such other consumer representations under paragraph 1 as are prescribed by the regulations made in accordance with section 16.

Unfair practices prohibited

3(1) No person shall engage in an unfair practice.

One act deemed practice

(2) A person who performs one act referred to in section 2 shall be deemed to be engaging in an unfair practice.

Rescission

4(1) Subject to subsection (2), any agreement, whether written, oral or implied, entered into by a consumer after a consumer representation that is an unfair practice and that induced the consumer to enter into the agreement,

(a) may be rescinded by the consumer and the consumer is entitled to any remedy therefor that is at law available, including damages; or

(b) where rescission is not possible because restitution is no longer possible, or because rescission would deprive a third party of a right in the subject-matter of the agreement that the third party has acquired in good faith and for value, the consumer is entitled to recover the amount by which the amount paid under the agreement exceeds the fair value of the goods or services received under the agreement or damages, or both.

Exemplary damages

(2) Where the unfair practice referred to in subsection (1) comes within paragraph 2 of section 2, the court may award exemplary or punitive damages.

…

Time for rescission

(5) A remedy conferred by subsection (1) may be claimed by the giving of notice of the claim by the consumer in writing to each other party to the agreement within six months after the agreement is entered into.

…

Application

(8) This section applies despite any agreement or waiver to the contrary.

…

Order to cease unfair practice

6(1) Where the Director believes on reasonable and probable grounds that any person is engaging or has engaged in an unfair practice, the Director may order such person to comply with section 3 in respect of the unfair practice specified in the order.

…

Investigations by order of Minister

10. The Minister may by order appoint a person to make an investigation into any matter to which this Act applies as may be specified in the Minister's order and the person appointed shall report the result of the investigation to the Minister and, for the pur-

poses of the investigation, the person making it has the powers of a commission under Part II of the *Public Inquiries Act*, which Part applies to such investigation as if it were an inquiry under that Act.

Investigation by Director

11(1) Where, upon a statement made under oath, the Director believes on reasonable and probable grounds that any person is contravening or is about to contravene any of the provisions of this Act or regulations or an order or assurance of voluntary compliance made or given pursuant to this Act, the Director may by order appoint one or more persons to make an investigation as to whether such a contravention of the Act, regulation, order or assurance of voluntary compliance has occurred and the person appointed shall report the result of the investigation to the Director.

...

Offences

17(1) Every person who, knowingly,

    (a) furnishes false information in an investigation under this Act;

    (b) contravenes a regulation;

    (c) fails to comply with any order or assurance of voluntary compliance made or entered into under this Act; or

    (d) obstructs a person making an investigation under section 10 or 11,

is guilty of an offence and on conviction is liable to a fine of not more than $25,000 or to imprisonment for a term of not more than one year, or to both.

Idem

(2) Every person who engages in an unfair practice other than an unfair practice prescribed by a regulation made under clause 16(1)(c), knowing it to be an unfair practice is guilty of an offence and on conviction is liable to a fine of not more than $25,000 or to imprisonment for a term of not more than one year, or to both.

Corporation

(3) Where a corporation is convicted of an offence under subsection (1) or (2), the maximum penalty that may be imposed upon the corporation is $100,000 and not as provided therein.

Directors and officers

(4) Where a corporation has been convicted of an offence under subsection (1) or (2),

    (a) each director of the corporation; and

    (b) each officer, servant or agent of the corporation who was in whole or in part responsible for the conduct of that part of the business of the corporation that gave rise to the offence,

is a party to the offence unless the director, officer, servant or agent satisfies the court that he, she or it did not authorize, permit or acquiesce in the offence.

Limitation period

(5) No proceeding under this section shall be commenced more than two years after the time when the subject-matter of the proceeding arose.

Collection Agencies Act

RSO 1990, c. C.14

Current to November 4, 2004

Definitions

1(1) In this Act,

...

"collection agency" means a person other than a collector who obtains or arranges for payment of money owing to another person, or who holds out to the public as providing such a service or any person who sells or offers to sell forms or letters represented to be a collection system or scheme;

"collector" means a person employed, appointed or authorized by a collection agency to collect debts for the agency or to deal with or trace debtors for the agency;

...

"Tribunal" means the License Appeal Tribunal ("Tribunal")

...

Application of Act

2. This Act does not apply,

(a) to a barrister or solicitor in the regular practice of his or her profession or to his or her employees;

(b) to an insurer or agent licensed under the *Insurance Act* or broker registered under the *Registered Insurance Brokers Act*, to the extent of the business authorized by such licence or registration, or to the employees of the insurer, agent or broker;

(c) to an assignee, custodian, liquidator, receiver, trustee or other person licensed or acting under the *Bankruptcy Act (Canada)*, the *Corporations Act*, the *Business Corporations Act*, the *Courts of Justice Act* or the *Winding-up Act (Canada)* or a person acting under the order of any court;

(d) to a broker or salesperson registered under the Real Estate and Business Brokers Act, or an official or other employee of such a broker to the extent of the business authorized by the registration;

(e) to a bank listed in Schedule I or II to the *Bank Act (Canada)*, the Province of Ontario Savings Office, a loan corporation or trust corporation registered under the *Loan and Trust Corporations Act*, or an employee thereof in the regular course of his or her employment;

(f) to an isolated collection made by a person whose usual business is not collecting debts for other persons; or

(g) to a credit union incorporated under the *Credit Unions and Caisses Populaires Act* or any employee thereof acting in the regular course of his or her employment.

…

Registration

4(1) No person shall carry on the business of a collection agency or act as a collector unless the person is registered by the Registrar under this Act.

Name and place of business

(2) A registered collection agency shall not carry on business in a name other than the name in which it is registered or invite the public to deal at a place other than that authorized by the registration.

Use of name to collect debts

5. No creditor shall deal with the debtor for payment of the debt except under the name in which the debt is lawfully owing or through a registered collection agency.

Registration

6(1) An applicant is entitled to registration or renewal of registration by the Registrar except where,

(a) having regard to the applicant's financial position, the applicant cannot reasonably be expected to be financially responsible in the conduct of business; or

(b) the past conduct of the applicant affords reasonable grounds for belief that the applicant will not carry on business in accordance with law and with integrity and honesty; or

(c) the applicant is a corporation and,

(i) having regard to its financial position, it cannot reasonably be expected to be financially responsible in the conduct of its business, or

(ii) the past conduct of its officers or directors affords reasonable grounds for belief that its business will not be carried on in accordance with law and with integrity and honesty; or

(d) the applicant is carrying on activities that are, or will be, if the applicant is registered, in contravention of this Act or the regulations.

…

Refusal to renew, suspend or revoke

(2) Subject to section 8, the Registrar may refuse to renew or may suspend or revoke a registration for any reason that would disentitle the registrant to registration under section 6 if the registrant were an applicant, or where the registrant is in breach of a term or condition of the registration.

…

Practices prohibited

22. No collection agency or collector shall,

(a) collect or attempt to collect for a person for whom it acts any money in addition to the amount owing by the debtor;

(b) send any telegram or make any telephone call, for which the charges are payable by the addressee or the person to whom the call is made, to a debtor for the purpose of demanding payment of a debt;

Note: On a day to be named by proclamation of the Lieutenant Governor, clause (b) is repealed by the Statutes of Ontario, 2002, chapter 18, Schedule E, subsection 3(1) and the following substituted:

(b) communicate or attempt to communicate with a person for the purpose of collecting, negotiating or demanding payment of a debt by a means that enables the charges or costs of the communication to be payable by that person;

See: SO 2002, c. 18, Sched. E, ss. 3(1), 11(1).

(c) receive or make an agreement for the additional payment of any money by a debtor of a creditor for whom the collection agency acts, either on its own account or for the creditor and whether as a charge, cost, expense or otherwise, in consideration for any forbearance, favour, indulgence, intercession or other conduct by the collection agency;

(d) deal with a debtor in a name other than that authorized by the registration; or

(e) engage in any prohibited practice or employ any prohibited method in the collection of debts.

...

Use of unregistered collection agency

24(1) No person shall knowingly engage or use the services of a collection agency that is not registered under this Act.

Employment of unregistered collectors

(2) No collection agency shall employ a collector or appoint or authorize a collector to act on its behalf unless the collector is registered under this Act.

Collection Agencies Act Regulations

GENERAL

RRO 1990, Reg. 74

Amended to O. Reg. 467/01

Current to November 4, 2004

...

Prohibited Practices and Methods in the Collection of Debts

20. No collection agency or collector shall,

(a) attempt to collect payment of a debt from a debtor unless the collection agency or the collector has notified or has attempted to notify the debtor in writing by letter addressed to the debtor's last known address that the collection agency or collector has been engaged by the creditor to act in respect of the collection of the debt;

(b) commence a legal proceeding with respect to the collection of a debt, or recommend to a creditor that a legal proceeding be commenced with respect to the collection of a debt, unless the collection agency or collector first gives notice to the debtor that the collection agency or the collector intends to commence the proceeding or recommend that a proceeding be commenced, as the case may be;

(c) directly or indirectly threaten or state an intention to proceed with any action for which the collection agency or the collector does not have lawful authority;

(d) make telephone calls or personal calls of such nature or with such frequency as to constitute harassment of the debtor, his or her spouse or same-sex partner or any member of his or her family or household;

(e) make a telephone call or personal call for the purpose of demanding payment of a debt,

(i) on a Sunday, or

(ii) on a statutory holiday,

or on any other day except between the hours of 7 o'clock in the forenoon and 9 o'clock in the afternoon;

(f) give any person, directly or indirectly, by implication or otherwise, any false or misleading information that may be detrimental to a debtor, his or her spouse or same-sex partner or any member of his or her family;

(g) make a demand by telephone, by personal call or by writing for payment of a debt without indicating the name of the creditor, the balance of the moneys owing and the identity and authority of the person making the demand;

(h) where a person has informed the collection agency or the collector that the person is not in fact the debtor, continue to communicate with that person in respect of the collection of the debt unless the collection agency or the collector first takes all reasonable precautions to ensure that the person is in fact the debtor;

(i) commence or continue a court action in the name of the collection agency or collector for the recovery of the debt of a client unless the debt has been assigned to the collection agency or collector, as the case may be, in good faith by instrument in writing for valuable consideration and notice of such assignment has been given to the debtor; or

(j) commence a court action for the collection of the debt of a client in the name of the client unless the collection agency or collector has received express written authority from the client to commence such action.

21. Except for the purpose of obtaining the debtor's address or telephone number, no collection agency or collector shall contact a debtor's employer, spouse, same-sex partner, relatives, neighbours or friends unless,

(a) the person contacted has guaranteed to pay the debt and is being contacted in respect of such guarantee;

(b) the person contacted is the employer of the debtor and the collection agency or collector is contacting the employer in respect of payments pursuant to a wage assignment or an order or judgment made by a court in favour of the collection agency or of a creditor who is a client of the collection agency; or

(c) the person contacted is the employer of the debtor and the collection agency or collector is contacting the employer for the purpose of verifying the employment of the debtor.

Competition Act

RSC 1985, c. C-34

An Act to provide for the general regulation of trade and commerce in respect of conspiracies, trade practices and mergers affecting competition

Current to August 31, 2004

…

False or misleading representations

52(1) No person shall, for the purpose of promoting, directly or indirectly, the supply or use of a product or for the purpose of promoting, directly or indirectly, any business interest, by any means whatever, knowingly or recklessly make a representation to the public that is false or misleading in a material respect.

…

Representations accompanying products

(2) For the purposes of this section, a representation that is

(a) expressed on an article offered or displayed for sale or its wrapper or container,

(b) expressed on anything attached to, inserted in or accompanying an article offered or displayed for sale, its wrapper or container, or anything on which the article is mounted for display or sale,

(c) expressed on an in-store or other point-of-purchase display,

(d) made in the course of in-store, door-to-door or telephone selling to a person as ultimate user, or

(e) contained in or on anything that is sold, sent, delivered, transmitted or made available in any other manner to a member of the public, is deemed to be made to the public by and only by the person who causes the representation to be so expressed, made or contained, subject to subsection (2.1).

…

Deemed representation to public

(3) Subject to subsection (2), a person who, for the purpose of promoting, directly or indirectly, the supply or use of a product or any business interest, supplies to a wholesaler, retailer or other distributor of a product any material or thing that contains a representation of a nature referred to in subsection (1) is deemed to have made that representation to the public.

General impression to be considered

(4) In a prosecution for a contravention of this section, the general impression conveyed by a representation as well as its literal meaning shall be taken into account in determining whether or not the representation is false or misleading in a material respect.

Offence and punishment

(5) Any person who contravenes subsection (1) is guilty of an offence and liable

(a) on conviction on indictment, to a fine in the discretion of the court or to imprisonment for a term not exceeding five years or to both; or

(b) on summary conviction, to a fine not exceeding $200,000 or to imprisonment for a term not exceeding one year, or to both.

Reviewable conduct

(6) Nothing in Part VII.1 shall be read as excluding the application of this section to a representation that constitutes reviewable conduct within the meaning of that Part.

...

Definition of "telemarketing"

52.1(1) In this section, "telemarketing" means the practice of using interactive telephone communications for the purpose of promoting, directly or indirectly, the supply or use of a product or for the purpose of promoting, directly or indirectly, any business interest.

Required disclosures

(2) No person shall engage in telemarketing unless

(a) disclosure is made, in a fair and reasonable manner at the beginning of each telephone communication, of the identity of the person on behalf of whom the communication is made, the nature of the product or business interest being promoted and the purposes of the communication;

(b) disclosure is made, in a fair, reasonable and timely manner, of the price of any product whose supply or use is being promoted and any material restrictions, terms or conditions applicable to its delivery; and

(c) disclosure is made, in a fair, reasonable and timely manner, of such other information in relation to the product as may be prescribed by the regulations.

Deceptive telemarketing

(3) No person who engages in telemarketing shall

(a) make a representation that is false or misleading in a material respect;

(b) conduct or purport to conduct a contest, lottery or game of chance, skill or mixed chance and skill, where

(i) the delivery of a prize or other benefit to a participant in the contest, lottery or game is, or is represented to be, conditional on the prior payment of any amount by the participant, or

(ii) adequate and fair disclosure is not made of the number and approximate value of the prizes, of the area or areas to which they relate and of any fact within the person's knowledge, that affects materially the chances of winning;

(c) offer a product at no cost, or at a price less than the fair market value of the product, in consideration of the supply or use of another product, unless fair, reasonable and timely disclosure is made of the fair market value of the first product and of any restrictions, terms or conditions applicable to its supply to the purchaser; or

(d) offer a product for sale at a price grossly in excess of its fair market value, where delivery of the product is, or is represented to be, conditional on prior payment by the purchaser.

General impression to be considered

(4) In a prosecution for a contravention of paragraph (3)(a), the general impression conveyed by a representation as well as its literal meaning shall be taken into account in determining whether or not the representation is false or misleading in a material respect.

Exception

(5) The disclosure of information referred to in paragraph (2)(b) or (c) or (3)(b) or (c) must be made during the course of a telephone communication unless it is established by the accused that the information was disclosed within a reasonable time before the communication, by any means, and the information was not requested during the telephone communication.

…

Offence and punishment

(9) Any person who contravenes subsection (2) or (3) is guilty of an offence and liable

(a) on conviction on indictment, to a fine in the discretion of the court or to imprisonment for a term not exceeding five years, or to both; or

(b) on summary conviction, to a fine not exceeding $200,000 or to imprisonment for a term not exceeding one year, or to both.

Sentencing

(10) In sentencing a person convicted of an offence under this section, the court shall consider, among other factors, the following aggravating factors:

(a) the use of lists of persons previously deceived by means of telemarketing;

(b) characteristics of the persons to whom the telemarketing was directed, including classes of persons who are especially vulnerable to abusive tactics;

(c) the amount of the proceeds realized by the person from the telemarketing;

(d) previous convictions of the person under this section or under section 52 in respect of conduct prohibited by this section; and

(e) the manner in which information is conveyed, including the use of abusive tactics.

Deceptive notice of winning a prize

53(1) No person shall, for the purpose of promoting, directly or indirectly, any business interest or the supply or use of a product, send or cause to be sent by electronic or regular mail or by any other means a document or notice in any form, if the document or notice gives the general impression that the recipient has won, will win, or will on doing a particular act win, a prize or other benefit, and if the recipient is asked or given the option to pay money, incur a cost or do anything that will incur a cost.

Non-application

(2) Subsection (1) does not apply if the recipient actually wins the prize or other benefit and the person who sends or causes the notice or document to be sent

(a) makes adequate and fair disclosure of the number and approximate value of the prizes or benefits, of the area or areas to which they have been allocated and of any fact within the person's knowledge that materially affects the chances of winning;

(b) distributes the prizes or benefits without unreasonable delay; and

(c) selects participants or distributes the prizes or benefits randomly, or on the basis of the participants' skill, in any area to which the prizes or benefits have been allocated.

...

Offence and punishment

(6) Any person who contravenes this section is guilty of an offence and liable

(a) on conviction on indictment, to a fine in the discretion of the court or to imprisonment for a term not exceeding five years, or to both; or

(b) on summary conviction, to a fine not exceeding $200,000 or to imprisonment for a term not exceeding one year, or to both.

Double ticketing

54(1) No person shall supply a product at a price that exceeds the lowest of two or more prices clearly expressed by him or on his behalf, in respect of the product in the quantity in which it is so supplied and at the time at which it is so supplied,

(a) on the product, its wrapper or container;

(b) on anything attached to, inserted in or accompanying the product, its wrapper or container or anything on which the product is mounted for display or sale; or

(c) on an in-store or other point-of-purchase display or advertisement.

Offence and punishment

(2) Any person who contravenes subsection (1) is guilty of an offence and liable on summary conviction to a fine not exceeding ten thousand dollars or to imprisonment for a term not exceeding one year or to both.

Definition of "multi-level marketing plan"

55(1) For the purposes of this section and section 55.1, "multi-level marketing plan" means a plan for the supply of a product whereby a participant in the plan receives compensation for the supply of the product to another participant in the plan who, in turn, receives compensation for the supply of the same or another product to other participants in the plan.

Representations as to compensation

(2) No person who operates or participates in a multi-level marketing plan shall make any representations relating to compensation under the plan to a prospective participant in the plan unless the representations constitute or include fair, reasonable and timely disclosure of the information within the knowledge of the person making the representations relating to

(a) compensation actually received by typical participants in the plan; or

(b) compensation likely to be received by typical participants in the plan, having regard to any relevant considerations, including

    (i) the nature of the product, including its price and availability,

    (ii) the nature of the relevant market for the product,

    (iii) the nature of the plan and similar plans, and

    (iv) whether the person who operates the plan is a corporation, partnership, sole proprietorship or other form of business organization.

Idem

(2.1) A person who operates a multi-level marketing plan shall ensure that any representations relating to compensation under the plan that are made to a prospective participant in the plan by a participant in the plan or by a representative of the person who operates the plan constitute or include fair, reasonable and timely disclosure of the information within the knowledge of the person who operates the plan relating to

    (a) compensation actually received by typical participants in the plan; or

    (b) compensation likely to be received by typical participants in the plan, having regard to any relevant considerations, including those specified in paragraph (2)(b).

...

Offence and punishment

(3) Any person who contravenes subsection (2) or (2.1) is guilty of an offence and liable

    (a) on conviction on indictment, to a fine in the discretion of the court or to imprisonment for a term not exceeding five years or to both; or

    (b) on summary conviction, to a fine not exceeding $200,000 or to imprisonment for a term not exceeding one year, or to both.

Definition of "scheme of pyramid selling"

55.1(1) For the purposes of this section, "scheme of pyramid selling" means a multi-level marketing plan whereby

    (a) a participant in the plan gives consideration for the right to receive compensation by reason of the recruitment into the plan of another participant in the plan who gives consideration for the same right;

    (b) a participant in the plan gives consideration, as a condition of participating in the plan, for a specified amount of the product, other than a specified amount of the product that is bought at the seller's cost price for the purpose only of facilitating sales;

    (c) a person knowingly supplies the product to a participant in the plan in an amount that is commercially unreasonable; or

    (d) a participant in the plan who is supplied with the product

        (i) does not have a buy-back guarantee that is exercisable on reasonable commercial terms or a right to return the product in saleable condition on reasonable commercial terms, or

        (ii) is not informed of the existence of the guarantee or right and the manner in which it can be exercised.

Pyramid selling

(2) No person shall establish, operate, advertise or promote a scheme of pyramid selling.

Offence and punishment

(3) Any person who contravenes subsection (2) is guilty of an offence and liable

(a) on conviction on indictment, to a fine in the discretion of the court or to imprisonment for a term not exceeding five years or to both; or

(b) on summary conviction, to a fine not exceeding $200,000 or to imprisonment for a term not exceeding one year, or to both.

Consumer Packaging and Labelling Act

RSC 1985, c. C-38

An Act respecting the packaging, labelling, sale, importation and advertising of prepackaged and certain other products

Current to August 31, 2004

...

INTERPRETATION

Definitions

2(1) In this Act,

"advertise"

"advertise" means make any representation to the public by any means whatever, other than a label, for the purpose of promoting directly or indirectly the sale of a product;

...

"container"

"container" means a receptacle, package, wrapper or confining band in which a product is offered for sale but does not include package liners or shipping containers or any outer wrapping or box that is not customarily displayed to the consumer;

"dealer"

"dealer" means a person who is a retailer, manufacturer, processor or producer of a product, or a person who is engaged in the business of importing, packing or selling any product;

"inspector"

"inspector" means any person designated as an inspector

(a) for the enforcement of this Act under the *Department of Industry Act*, or

(b) for the enforcement of this Act as it relates to food, as defined in section 2 of the *Food and Drugs Act*, under the *Canadian Food Inspection Agency Act*;

"label"

"label" means any label, mark, sign, device, imprint, stamp, brand, ticket or tag;

...

"prepackaged product"

"prepackaged product" means any product that is packaged in a container in such a manner that it is ordinarily sold to or used or purchased by a consumer without being re-packaged;

…

"sell"

"sell" includes

(a) offer for sale, expose for sale and have in possession for sale, and

(b) display in such manner as to lead to a reasonable belief that the substance or product so displayed is intended for sale.

…

APPLICATION OF ACT

Application notwithstanding other Acts

3(1) Subject to subsection (2) and any regulations made under section 18, the provisions of this Act that are applicable to any product apply notwithstanding any other Act of Parliament.

Exemption

(2) This Act does not apply to any product that is a device or drug within the meaning of the *Food and Drugs Act*.

PROHIBITIONS

Prohibition respecting labels

4(1) No dealer shall sell, import into Canada or advertise any prepackaged product unless that product has applied to it a label containing a declaration of net quantity of the product in the form and manner required by this Act or prescribed and in terms of either

(a) numerical count, or

(b) a unit of measurement set out in Schedule I to the *Weights and Measures Act*, as may be prescribed.

Declaration of net quantity to be readily distinguishable

(2) A declaration of net quantity referred to in subsection (1) shall be located on the principal display panel of the label and shall be clearly and prominently displayed, easily legible and in distinct contrast to any other information or representation shown on the label.

Prohibition respecting advertising

5. No dealer shall, in advertising any prepackaged product, make any representation with respect to the net quantity of the product except in accordance with this Act and the regulations.

Prohibition respecting packaging

6. No dealer shall sell or import into Canada any prepackaged product that is packaged in such a manner that it does not meet the packaging requirements established in relation to that product by regulations made pursuant to subsection 11(1).

Representations relating to prepackaged products

7(1) No dealer shall apply to any prepackaged product or sell, import into Canada or advertise any prepackaged product that has applied to it a label containing any false or misleading representation that relates to or may reasonably be regarded as relating to that product.

Definition of "false or misleading representation"

(2) For the purposes of this section, "false or misleading representation" includes

(a) any representation in which expressions, words, figures, depictions or symbols are used, arranged or shown in a manner that may reasonably be regarded as qualifying the declared net quantity of a prepackaged product or as likely to deceive a consumer with respect to the net quantity of a prepackaged product;

(b) any expression, word, figure, depiction or symbol that implies or may reasonably be regarded as implying that a prepackaged product contains any matter not contained in it or does not contain any matter in fact contained in it; and

(c) any description or illustration of the type, quality, performance, function, origin or method of manufacture or production of a prepackaged product that may reasonably be regarded as likely to deceive a consumer with respect to the matter so described or illustrated.

Where, within prescribed tolerances, net quantity not less than declared

(3) Where a declaration of net quantity shows the purported net quantity of the prepackaged product to which it is applied, that declaration shall be deemed not to be a false or misleading representation if the net quantity of the prepackaged product is, subject to the prescribed tolerance, not less than the declared net quantity of the prepackaged product and the declaration otherwise meets the requirements of this Act and the regulations.

Labels on edible and potable prepackaged products

8. No dealer shall apply to any edible or potable prepackaged product a label that contains any representation with respect to the number of servings contained in the container of the prepackaged product unless that label contains a declaration of net quantity of each serving in the form and manner prescribed and in terms of either

(a) numerical count, or

(b) a unit of measurement set out in Schedule I to the *Weights and Measures Act,*
as may be prescribed.

Containers of prepackaged products

9(1) No dealer shall sell, import into Canada or advertise any prepackaged product that is packaged in a container that has been manufactured, constructed or filled or is displayed in such a manner that a consumer might reasonably be misled with respect to the quality or quantity of the product.

Recognized and accepted production practice, if necessary for packaging, a defence

(2) No dealer is guilty of the offence of selling, importing into Canada or advertising a prepackaged product that is packaged in a container that has been filled in such a manner that a consumer might reasonably be misled with respect to the quality or quantity of the product if the dealer establishes that the container was filled in accordance with a recognized and accepted production practice that is reasonably necessary for the purpose of packaging the product.

LABELS

Label containing declaration of net quantity

10. Each label containing a declaration of net quantity of the prepackaged product to which it is applied shall

(a) be applied to the prepackaged product in such form and manner as may be prescribed; and

(b) show, in such form and manner and in such circumstances as may be prescribed,

(i) the identity and principal place of business of the person by or for whom the prepackaged product was manufactured or produced for resale,

(ii) the identity of the prepackaged product in terms of its common or generic name or in terms of its function, and

(iii) such information respecting the nature, quality, age, size, material content, composition, geographic origin, performance, use or method of manufacture or production of the prepackaged product as may be prescribed.

...

OFFENCES AND PUNISHMENT

Contraventions of sections 4 to 9

20(1) Subject to subsection (2.1), every dealer who contravenes any of sections 4 to 9 is guilty of an offence and liable

(a) on summary conviction, to a fine not exceeding $5,000; or

(b) on conviction on indictment, to a fine not exceeding $10,000.

Contravention of other provisions or regulations

(2) Subject to subsection (2.1), every person who contravenes any provision of this Act, other than any of sections 4 to 9, or any regulation made under paragraph 18(1)(d), (e) or (h), is guilty of an offence and liable

(a) on summary conviction, to a fine not exceeding $1,000 or to imprisonment for a term not exceeding six months or to both; or

(b) on conviction on indictment, to a fine not exceeding $3,000 or to imprisonment for a term not exceeding one year or to both.

Offences relating to food

(2.1) Every person who contravenes a provision referred to in subsection (1) or (2) as that provision relates to food, as defined in section 2 of the *Food and Drugs Act*, is guilty of an offence and liable

(a) on summary conviction, to a fine not exceeding $50,000 or to imprisonment for a term not exceeding six months or to both; or

(b) on conviction on indictment, to a fine not exceeding $250,000 or to imprisonment for a term not exceeding two years or to both.

Criminal liability of officers, etc., of corporations

(3) Where a corporation commits an offence under this Act, any officer, director or agent of the corporation who directed, authorized, assented to, acquiesced in or participated in the commission of the offence is a party to and guilty of the offence and is liable on conviction to the punishment provided for the offence whether or not the corporation has been prosecuted or convicted.

...

Consumer Protection Act

RSO 1990, c. C.31

Current to November 4, 2004

Note: On a day to be named by proclamation of the Lieutenant Governor, this Act is repealed by the Statutes of Ontario, 2002, chapter 30, Schedule E, section 3. See: SO 2002, c. 30, Sched. E, ss. 3, 22.

Definitions

1. In this Act,

"actually received" means the sum of money received by the borrower from the lender that can be used by the borrower without any restrictions on its use imposed by the lender;

"borrower" means a person who receives credit;

"buyer" means a person who purchases goods for consumption or services under an executory contract and includes his or her agent, but does not include a person who buys in the course of carrying on business or an association of individuals, a partnership or a corporation;

"cost of borrowing" means,

    (a) in the case of credit other than variable credit, the amount by which,

      (i) the total sum that the borrower is required to pay if the payments required are made as they become due, including all such sums regardless of the purpose or reason for the payment or the time of the payment, exceeds,

      (ii) the sum actually received in cash by the borrower or, where the lender is a seller, the amount of the cash price of the goods or services less the sums, if any, actually paid as a down payment or credited in respect of a trade-in or paid or credited for any other reason plus, in each case, insurance or official fees, if any, actually paid by the lender,

    (b) in the case of variable credit, the charges made in respect of the extension of the variable credit;

"credit" means credit for which the borrower incurs a cost of borrowing and,

    (a) given under an agreement between a seller and a buyer to purchase goods or services by which all or part of the purchase price is payable after the agreement is entered into, or

(b) given by the advancement of money,

but does not include credit given on the security of a mortgage of real property;

"executory contract" means a contract between a buyer and a seller for the purchase and sale of goods or services in respect of which delivery of the goods or performance of the services or payment in full of the consideration is not made at the time the contract is entered into;

"goods" means personal property;

"lender" means a person who extends credit;

"purchase price" means the total obligation payable by the buyer under an executory contract;

"seller" means a person who is in the business of selling goods or services to buyers, and includes an agent of the seller;

...

Marketers of gas, retailers of electricity

(2) Despite subsection (1), this Act applies to a sale by,

(a) a gas marketer who is a seller and who sells to a buyer; and

(b) a retailer of electricity who is a seller and who sells to a buyer.

Definitions

(3) In this section,

"gas marketer" means a gas marketer as defined in Part IV of the *Ontario Energy Board Act, 1998*;

...

"retailer of electricity" means a retailer as defined in the *Electricity Act, 1998*.

...

PART II

EXECUTORY CONTRACTS

Application of Part

18. This Part applies to executory contracts for the sale of goods or services where the purchase price, excluding the cost of borrowing, exceeds $50.

Form of executory contract

19(1) Every executory contract, other than an executory contract under an agreement for variable credit, shall be in writing and shall contain,

(a) the name and address of the seller and the buyer;

(b) a description of the goods or services sufficient to identify them with certainty;

(c) the itemized price of the goods or services and a detailed statement of the terms of payment;

(d) where credit is extended, a statement of any security for payment under the contract, including the particulars of any negotiable instrument, conditional sale agreement, chattel mortgage or any other security;

(e) where credit is extended, the statement required to be furnished by section 24;

(f) any warranty or guarantee applying to the goods or services and, where there is no warranty or guarantee, a statement to this effect; and

(g) any other matter required by the regulations.

Validity

(2) An executory contract is not binding on the buyer unless the contract is made in accordance with this Part and the regulations and is signed by the parties, and a duplicate original copy thereof is in the possession of each of the parties thereto.

…

Rescission of certain executory contracts within two days

21(1) Where a seller solicits, negotiates or arranges for the signing by a buyer of an executory contract at a place other than the seller's permanent place of business, the buyer may rescind the contract by delivering a notice of rescission in writing to the seller within two days after the duplicate original copy of the contract first comes into the possession of the buyer, and the buyer is not liable for any damages in respect of such rescission.

Duties upon rescission

(2) Where a buyer rescinds a contract under subsection (1),

(a) the buyer shall immediately return any goods received under the contract and the seller shall bear the expense of the return, not exceeding the expense of returning the goods from the place where the buyer received their delivery; and

(b) the seller shall return any money received or realized in respect of the contract, whether from the buyer or any other person, and shall return any trade-in received under the contract.

…

Delivery of notice

(4) A notice of rescission may be delivered personally or sent by registered mail addressed to the person to whom delivery is required to be made at the address shown in the contract, and delivery by registered mail shall be deemed to have been made at the time of mailing.

…

No repossession after two-thirds paid except by leave of judge

23(1) Where a buyer under an executory contract has paid two-thirds or more of the purchase price of the goods as fixed by the contract, any provision in the contract, or in any security agreement incidental thereto, under which the seller may retake possession of or resell the goods upon default in payment by the buyer is not enforceable except by leave of a judge of the Ontario Court (General Division).

Powers of judge

(2) Upon an application for leave under subsection (1), the judge may, in his or her absolute discretion, grant or refuse leave or grant leave upon such terms and conditions as he or she considers advisable.

PART III

CREDIT TRANSACTIONS

Disclosure of cost of borrowing

24. Except as provided in section 25, every lender shall furnish to the borrower, before giving the credit, a clear statement in writing showing,

(a) the sum,

(i) expressed as one sum in dollars and cents, actually received in cash by the borrower, plus insurance or official fees, if any, actually paid by the lender, or

(ii) where the lender is a seller, being the amount of the cash price of the goods or services, including any insurance or official fees;

(b) where the lender is a seller, the sums, if any, actually paid as a down payment or credited in respect of a trade-in, or paid or credited for any other reason;

(c) where the lender is a seller, the amount by which the sum stated under subclause (a)(ii) exceeds the sum stated under clause (b);

(d) the cost of borrowing expressed as one sum in dollars and cents;

(e) the percentage that the cost of borrowing bears to the sum stated,

(i) under subclause (a)(i), where the lender is not a seller, or

(ii) under clause (c), where the lender is a seller, expressed as an annual rate applied to the unpaid balance thereof from time to time, calculated and expressed in the manner prescribed by the regulations;

(f) the amount, if any, charged for insurance;

(g) the amount, if any, charged for official fees; and

(h) the basis upon which additional charges are to be made in the event of default.

Definition

25(1) In this section, "period" means a period of time of not less than four weeks and not more than five weeks in duration.

Variable credit

(2) A lender extending variable credit shall,

(a) before agreeing to extend variable credit, furnish the borrower with a clear statement in writing setting forth the cost of borrowing in respect of the unpaid balances from time to time,

(i) stated as an annual percentage, or scale of annual percentages, of such balance charged at the end of each period, subject to a minimum dollars-and-cents charge, if any, and

(ii) stated in dollars and cents in a schedule of fixed amounts of outstanding balances, and the corresponding charges for the cost of borrowing; and

(b) at the end of each period during the extension of credit, furnish the borrower with a clear statement in writing showing,

(i) the outstanding balance in the account of the borrower at the beginning of the period,

(ii) the amount and date of each extension of credit to the borrower during the period and the identity of the goods or services in respect of which the credit was extended,

(iii) the amount of each sum received or credited to the account of the borrower during the period, and the date and occasion thereof,

(iv) the cost of borrowing, expressed as one sum in dollars and cents, charged during the period,

(v) the outstanding balance in the account of the borrower at the end of the period, and

(vi) the statement referred to in clause (a).

Manner of applying percentage rate

26. The percentage rate by which the cost of borrowing is expressed shall be applied in the manner prescribed by the regulations.

When costs of borrowing not recoverable

27. A borrower is not liable to pay a lender as the cost of borrowing any sum in excess of the sum shown in the statement required by section 24 or 25 in respect of the transaction.

Prepayment

28. Where the sum remaining to be paid under an agreement for credit is paid in full before the term of the agreement has expired,

(a) the borrower is entitled to a proportionate credit in respect of the cost of borrowing; and

(b) the lender is entitled to a proportionate part of the cost of lending,

in an amount determined in the manner prescribed by the regulations.

Advertising of cost of borrowing

29(1) Subject to the regulations, no lender shall represent, either orally or in print, or by radio or television broadcast, the lender's charge for credit or cause such charge to be so represented unless the representation includes the full cost of borrowing and is expressed in the manner required by section 24 or 25.

Advertising of other terms of credit

(2) Subject to the regulations, where a lender represents or causes to be represented in a printing, broadcast or other publication any terms of the credit agreement other than that referred to in subsection (1), the lender shall also include or cause to be included all other relevant terms of the credit transaction, including,

(a) the sum to be actually received in cash by the borrower or the actual cash price of the goods;

(b) the amount of the down payment;

(c) the amount of each instalment; and

(d) the number of instalments required to repay the total indebtedness, including the cost of borrowing.

Assignment of negotiable instrument

30(1) Where a lender assigns a negotiable instrument given to secure credit, the lender shall deliver to the assignee with the negotiable instrument a copy of the statement required by section 24 and, where the lender is a seller, a copy of the contract of sale.

Reassignment of negotiable instrument

(2) Every assignee of a negotiable instrument who reassigns the instrument shall deliver to his, her or its assignee the statement and contract of sale, if any, received by him, her or it in respect of the instrument.

...

PART IV

GENERAL

Agreements and waivers contrary to Act

33. This Act applies despite any agreement or waiver to the contrary.

Definition

34(1) In this section, "consumer sale" means a contract for the sale of goods made in the ordinary course of business to a purchaser for the purchaser's consumption or use, but does not include a sale,

(a) to a purchaser for resale;

(b) to a purchaser whose purchase is in the course of carrying on business;

(c) to an association of individuals, a partnership or a corporation;

(d) by a trustee in bankruptcy, a receiver, a liquidator or a person acting under the order of a court.

Implied warranties

(2) The implied conditions and warranties applying to the sale of goods by virtue of the *Sale of Goods Act* apply to goods sold by a consumer sale and any written term or acknowledgment, whether part of the contract of sale or not, that purports to negative or vary any of such implied conditions and warranties is void and, if a term of a contract, is severable therefrom, and such term or acknowledgment shall not be evidence of circumstances showing an intent that any of the implied conditions and warranties are not to apply.

Rights of buyer and borrower preserved

35. The rights of a buyer or borrower under this Act are in addition to any rights of the buyer or borrower under any other Act or by the operation of law, and nothing in this Act shall be construed to derogate from such rights.

Definitions

36(1) In this section,

"credit" means the advancing of money, goods or services to or on behalf of another for repayment at a later time, whether or not there is a cost of borrowing, and includes variable credit;

"unsolicited goods" means personal property furnished to a person who did not request it and a request shall not be inferred from inaction or the passing of time alone, but does not include,

(a) personal property that the recipient knows or ought to know is intended for another person, or

(b) personal property supplied under a contract in writing to which the recipient is a party that provides for the periodic supply of personal property to the recipient without further solicitation.

Credit arrangement

(2) No action shall be brought by which to charge any person upon any arrangement for the extension of credit evidenced by a credit card unless the person to whom credit is to be extended requested or accepted the credit arrangement and card in writing, and the

obtaining of credit by the person named in the credit card shall be deemed to constitute such written acceptance by the person.

Use of unsolicited goods

(3) No action shall be brought by which to charge any person for payment in respect of unsolicited goods notwithstanding their use, misuse, loss, damage or theft.

Relief from legal obligations

(4) Except as provided in this section, the recipient of unsolicited goods or of a credit card that has not been requested or accepted in accordance with subsection (2) has no legal obligation in respect of their use or disposal.

Definitions

37(1) For the purposes of this section in addition to the meanings defined in section 1 for "buyer" and "seller,"
"buyer" includes a person who hires or leases goods for consumption where,

    (a) the person has an option to purchase the goods, or

    (b) upon compliance with agreed terms, the person will become the owner of the goods or will be entitled to keep them without further payment;
"seller" includes a person who is in the business of letting goods, by hire or lease, to buyers.

Order if false advertising

38(1) If the Director believes on reasonable and probable grounds that a seller or lender is making false, misleading or deceptive statements in an advertisement, circular, pamphlet or similar material, the Director may make an order for the immediate cessation of the use of that material.

Order effective

(2) The order takes effect immediately upon being made.

. . .

Offence

39(1) Every person who contravenes this Act or the regulations and every director or officer of a corporation who knowingly concurs in a contravention of this Act or the regulations is guilty of an offence and on conviction is liable to a fine of not more than $25,000 or to imprisonment for a term of not more than one year, or to both.

Corporations

(2) Where a corporation is convicted of an offence under subsection (1), the maximum penalty that may be imposed upon the corporation is $100,000 and not as provided therein.

Limitation

(3) No proceeding under this section shall be instituted more than three years after the time when the subject-matter of the proceeding arose.

Consumer Protection Bureau Act

RSO 1990, c. C.32

Current to November 4, 2004

Note: On a day to be named by proclamation of the Lieutenant Governor, this Act is repealed by the Statutes of Ontario, 2002, chapter 30, Schedule E, section 4. See: SO 2002, c. 30, Sched. E, ss. 4, 22.

Consumer Protection Bureau

1. There shall be a branch of the Ministry of Consumer and Business Services, to be known in English as the Consumer Protection Bureau and in French as Office de protection du consommateur.

Registrar

2. The Consumer Protection Bureau shall consist of the Registrar of the Consumer Protection Bureau and such other persons as are considered necessary.

Duties of Consumer Protection Bureau

3. The Consumer Protection Bureau shall,

(a) disseminate information for the purpose of educating and advising consumers respecting consumer protection and lending and borrowing practices;

(b) receive and investigate complaints of conduct in contravention of legislation for the protection of consumers;

(c) enforce legislation for the protection of consumers; and

(d) perform any other duties given to it by any Act.

Consumer Reporting Act

RSO 1990, c. C.33

Current to November 4, 2004

Definitions

1(1) In this Act,

"consumer" means a natural person but does not include a person engaging in a transaction, other than relating to employment, in the course of carrying on a business, trade or profession;

"consumer report" means a written, oral or other communication by a consumer reporting agency of credit information or personal information, or both, pertaining to a consumer for consideration in connection with a purpose set out in clause 8(1)(d);

"consumer reporting agency" means a person who for gain or profit or on a regular cooperative non-profit basis furnishes consumer reports;

"credit information" means information about a consumer as to name, age, occupation, place of residence, previous places of residence, marital status, spouse's name and age, number of dependants, particulars of education or professional qualifications, places of employment, previous places of employment, estimated income, paying habits, outstanding debt obligations, cost of living obligations and assets;

...

"employment purposes" means the purposes of taking into employment, granting promotion, reassigning employment duties or retaining as an employee;

"file," when used as a noun, means all of the information pertaining to a consumer that is recorded and retained by a consumer reporting agency, regardless of the manner or form in which the information is stored;

...

"personal information" means information other than credit information about a consumer's character, reputation, health, physical or personal characteristics or mode of living or about any other matter concerning the consumer;

"personal information investigator" means a person who obtains or reports personal information to a consumer reporting agency for hire or reward;

...

Agreements to waive

(2) This Act applies despite any agreement or waiver to the contrary.

Registrar

2(1) The Deputy Minister shall appoint a person as the Registrar of Consumer Reporting Agencies.

...

Registration required

3. No person shall conduct or act as a consumer reporting agency or act as a personal information investigator unless registered by the Registrar under this Act.

Registration of agencies

4(1) An applicant is entitled to registration or renewal of registration as a consumer reporting agency by the Registrar except where,

(a) having regard to the applicant's financial position, the applicant cannot reasonably be expected to be financially responsible in the conduct of business; or

(b) the past conduct of the applicant affords reasonable grounds for belief that the applicant will not carry on business in accordance with law and with integrity and honesty; or

(c) the applicant is a corporation and,

(i) having regard to its financial position, it cannot reasonably be expected to be financially responsible in the conduct of business, or

(ii) the past conduct of its officers or directors affords reasonable grounds for belief that its business will not be carried on in accordance with law and with integrity and honesty; or

(d) the applicant is carrying on activities that are, or will be, if the applicant is registered, in contravention of this Act or the regulations.

Registration of investigators

(2) An applicant is entitled to registration or renewal of registration as a personal information investigator by the Registrar except where the past conduct of the applicant affords reasonable grounds for belief that the applicant will not carry out the applicant's duties in accordance with law and with integrity and honesty.

...

Refusal to register

5(1) Subject to section 6, the Registrar may refuse to register an applicant where in the Registrar's opinion the applicant is disentitled to registration under section 4.

Revocation and refusal to renew

(2) Subject to section 6, the Registrar may refuse to renew or may suspend or revoke a registration for any reason that would disentitle the registrant to registration under section 4 if the registrant were an applicant, or where the registrant is in breach of a term or condition of the registration.

...

To whom reports may be given

8(1) No consumer reporting agency and no officer or employee thereof shall knowingly furnish any information from the files of the consumer reporting agency except,

(a) in response to the order of a court having jurisdiction to issue such an order;

(b) in accordance with the written instructions of the consumer to whom the information relates;

(c) in response to an order or direction made under this Act; or

(d) in a consumer report given to a person who it has reason to believe,

(i) intends to use the information in connection with the extension of credit to or the purchase or collection of a debt of the consumer to whom the information pertains,

(ii) intends to use the information in connection with the entering into or renewal of a tenancy agreement,

(iii) intends to use the information for employment purposes,

(iv) intends to use the information in connection with the underwriting of insurance involving the consumer,

(v) intends to use the information to determine the consumer's eligibility for any matter under a statute or regulation where the information is relevant to the requirement prescribed by law,

(vi) otherwise has a direct business need for the information in connection with a business or credit transaction involving the consumer, or

(vii) intends to use the information for the purpose of up-dating the information in a consumer report previously given to the person for one of the reasons referred to in subclauses (i) to (vi).

Idem

(2) No person shall knowingly obtain any information from the files of a consumer reporting agency respecting a consumer except for the purposes referred to in subsection (1).

Information as to identities

(3) 0Despite subsections (1) and (2), a consumer reporting agency may furnish identifying information respecting any consumer, limited to his or her name, address, former addresses, places of employment, or former places of employment, to the Government of Ontario or of Canada or any province thereof or of any agency of such government or the government of any municipality in Canada or any agency thereof or to any police officer acting in the course of his or her duties, even though such information is not to be used for a purpose mentioned in subsection (1).

Sale of files

(4) No person who is or has been registered as a consumer reporting agency shall sell, lease or transfer title to its files or any of them except to a consumer reporting agency registered under this Act.

Procedures of agencies

9(1) Every consumer reporting agency shall adopt all procedures reasonable for ensuring accuracy and fairness in the contents of its consumer reports.

Information included in consumer report

(2) A consumer reporting agency shall not report,

(a) any information that is not stored in a form capable of being produced under section 12;

(b) any information that is not extracted from information appearing in files stored or collected in a repository located in Canada regardless of whether or not the information was obtained from a source outside Canada, except where the consumer report is in writing and contains the substance of any prior information orally acquired that conforms to the requirements of this Act.

Idem

(3) A consumer reporting agency shall not include in a consumer report,

(a) any credit information based on evidence that is not the best evidence reasonably available;

(b) any unfavourable personal information unless it has made reasonable efforts to corroborate the evidence on which the personal information is based, and the lack of corroboration is noted with and accompanies the information;

(c) information as to judgments after seven years after the judgment was given, unless the creditor or the creditor's agent confirms that it remains unpaid in whole or in part, and such confirmation appears in the file;

(d) information as to any judgment against the consumer unless mention is made of the name and, where available, the address of the judgment creditor or the creditor's agent as given at the date of entry of the judgment and the amount;

(e) information as to the bankruptcy of the consumer after seven years from the date of the discharge except where the consumer has been bankrupt more than once;

(f) information regarding any collection or debt after seven years following the commencement of the debt obligation, unless the creditor or the creditor's agent confirms that the debt obligation is not barred under the *Limitations Act, 2002* and the confirmation appears in the file;

(g) information as to the payment or non-payment of taxes or lawfully imposed fines after seven years;

(h) information as to convictions for crimes, after seven years from the date of conviction or, where the conviction resulted in imprisonment, from the date of release or parole, provided information as to convictions for crimes shall not be reported if at any time it is learned that after a conviction an absolute discharge or a full pardon has been granted;

(i) information regarding writs or actions that are more than seven years old or writs that were issued or actions commenced against the consumer more than twelve months prior to the making of the report unless the consumer reporting agency has ascertained the current status of the writ or action and has a record of this on file;

(j) information regarding any criminal charges against the consumer where the charges have been dismissed, set aside or withdrawn;

(k) any other adverse item of information where more than seven years have expired since the information was acquired or last reaffirmed;

(l) information as to race, creed, colour, sex, ancestry, ethnic origin, or political affiliation; or

(m) any information given orally in the consumer report unless the content of the oral report is recorded in the file.

Maintenance of files

(4) Every consumer reporting agency shall maintain in its file respecting a person all the material and information of which the person is entitled to disclosure under section 12.

Disclosure of report on request

10(1) Every person shall, where requested by a consumer in writing or personally, inform the consumer whether or not a consumer report respecting him or her has been or is to be referred to in connection with any specified transaction or matter in which such person is engaged, and, if so, of the name and address of the consumer reporting agency supplying the report.

…

Right of consumer to disclosure

12(1) Every consumer reporting agency shall, at the written request of a consumer and during normal business hours, clearly and accurately disclose to the consumer, without charge,

(a) the nature and substance of all information in its files pertaining to the consumer at the time of the request;

(b) the sources of credit information;

(c) the name and address of every person on whose behalf the file has been accessed;

(d) the names of the recipients of any consumer report pertaining to the consumer that it has furnished,

(i) containing personal information, within the one year period preceding the request, and

(ii) containing credit information, within the six month period preceding the request;

(e) copies of any written consumer report pertaining to the consumer made to any other person or, where the report was oral, particulars of the content of such oral report, furnished,

(i) where the report contains personal information, within the one year period preceding the request, and

(ii) where the report contains credit information, within the six month period preceding the request,

and shall inform the consumer of his or her right to protest any information contained in the file under sections 13 and 14 and the manner in which a protest may be made.

…

Correction of errors

13(1) Where a consumer disputes the accuracy or completeness of any item of information contained in his or her file, the consumer reporting agency within a reasonable time shall use its best endeavours to confirm or complete the information and shall correct, supplement or delete the information in accordance with good practice.

Idem

(2) Where a consumer reporting agency corrects, supplements or deletes information under subsection (1), the consumer reporting agency shall furnish notification of the correction, supplement or deletion to,

(a) all persons who have been supplied with a consumer report based on the unamended file within sixty days before the correction, supplement or deletion is made; and

(b) the persons specifically designated by the consumer from among those who have been supplied with a consumer report based on the unamended file,

    (i) where the report contains personal information, within the one year period preceding the correction, supplement or deletion, and

    (ii) where the report contains credit information, within the six month period preceding the correction, supplement or deletion.

...

Offences

23(1) Every person who,

(a) knowingly, furnishes false information in any application under this Act or in any statement or return required to be furnished under this Act or the regulations;

(b) fails to comply with any order, direction or other requirement made under this Act; or

(c) contravenes any provision of this Act or the regulations,

and every director or officer of a corporation who knowingly concurs in such furnishing, failure or contravention is guilty of an offence and on conviction is liable to a fine of not more than $25,000 or to imprisonment for a term of not more than one year, or to both.

Corporations

(2) Where a corporation is convicted of an offence under subsection (1), the maximum penalty that may be imposed upon the corporation is $100,000 and not as provided therein.

Criminal Code

RSC 1985, c. C-46

An Act respecting the Criminal Law

Current to August 31, 2004

…

Criminal interest rate

347(1) Notwithstanding any Act of Parliament, every one who

(a) enters into an agreement or arrangement to receive interest at a criminal rate, or

(b) receives a payment or partial payment of interest at a criminal rate,

is guilty of

(c) an indictable offence and is liable to imprisonment for a term not exceeding five years, or

(d) an offence punishable on summary conviction and is liable to a fine not exceeding twenty-five thousand dollars or to imprisonment for a term not exceeding six months or to both.

Definitions

(2) In this section,

"criminal rate" means an effective annual rate of interest calculated in accordance with generally accepted actuarial practices and principles that exceeds sixty per cent on the credit advanced under an agreement or arrangement;

"interest" means the aggregate of all charges and expenses, whether in the form of a fee, fine, penalty, commission or other similar charge or expense or in any other form, paid or payable for the advancing of credit under an agreement or arrangement, by or on behalf of the person to whom the credit is or is to be advanced, irrespective of the person to whom any such charges and expenses are or are to be paid or payable, but does not include any repayment of credit advanced or any insurance charge, official fee, overdraft charge, required deposit balance or, in the case of a mortgage transaction, any amount required to be paid on account of property taxes;

Presumption

(3) Where a person receives a payment or partial payment of interest at a criminal rate, he shall, in the absence of evidence to the contrary, be deemed to have knowledge of the nature of the payment and that it was received at a criminal rate.

Food and Drugs Act

RSC 1985, c. F-27

An Act respecting food, drugs, cosmetics and therapeutic devices

Current to August 31, 2004

...

INTERPRETATION

Definitions

2. In this Act,

"advertisement"

"advertisement" includes any representation by any means whatever for the purpose of promoting directly or indirectly the sale or disposal of any food, drug, cosmetic or device;

...

"contraceptive device"

"contraceptive device" means any instrument, apparatus, contrivance or substance other than a drug, that is manufactured, sold or represented for use in the prevention of conception;

"cosmetic"

"cosmetic" includes any substance or mixture of substances manufactured, sold or represented for use in cleansing, improving or altering the complexion, skin, hair or teeth, and includes deodorants and perfumes;

...

"device"

"device" means any article, instrument, apparatus or contrivance, including any component, part or accessory thereof, manufactured, sold or represented for use in

    (a) the diagnosis, treatment, mitigation or prevention of a disease, disorder or abnormal physical state, or its symptoms, in human beings or animals,

    (b) restoring, correcting or modifying a body function or the body structure of human beings or animals,

    (c) the diagnosis of pregnancy in human beings or animals, or

    (d) the care of human beings or animals during pregnancy and at and after birth of the offspring, including care of the offspring, and includes a contraceptive device but does not include a drug;

"drug"

"drug" includes any substance or mixture of substances manufactured, sold or represented for use in

(a) the diagnosis, treatment, mitigation or prevention of a disease, disorder or abnormal physical state, or its symptoms, in human beings or animals,

(b) restoring, correcting or modifying organic functions in human beings or animals, or

(c) disinfection in premises in which food is manufactured, prepared or kept;

"food"

"food" includes any article manufactured, sold or represented for use as food or drink for human beings, chewing gum, and any ingredient that may be mixed with food for any purpose whatever;

...

"sell"

"sell" includes offer for sale, expose for sale, have in possession for sale and distribute, whether or not the distribution is made for consideration;

"unsanitary conditions"

"unsanitary conditions" means such conditions or circumstances as might contaminate with dirt or filth, or render injurious to health, a food, drug or cosmetic.

...

PART I

FOODS, DRUGS, COSMETICS AND DEVICES

General

Prohibited advertising

3(1) No person shall advertise any food, drug, cosmetic or device to the general public as a treatment, preventative or cure for any of the diseases, disorders or abnormal physical states referred to in Schedule A.

Prohibited label or advertisement where sale made

(2) No person shall sell any food, drug, cosmetic or device

(a) that is represented by label, or

(b) that the person advertises to the general public as a treatment, preventative or cure for any of the diseases, disorders or abnormal physical states referred to in Schedule A.

Unauthorized advertising of contraceptive device prohibited

(3) Except as authorized by regulation, no person shall advertise to the general public any contraceptive device or any drug manufactured, sold or represented for use in the prevention of conception.

Food

Prohibited sales of food

4. No person shall sell an article of food that

(a) has in or on it any poisonous or harmful substance;

(b) is unfit for human consumption;

(c) consists in whole or in part of any filthy, putrid, disgusting, rotten, decomposed or diseased animal or vegetable substance;

(d) is adulterated; or

(e) was manufactured, prepared, preserved, packaged or stored under unsanitary conditions.

Deception, etc., regarding food

5(1) No person shall label, package, treat, process, sell or advertise any food in a manner that is false, misleading or deceptive or is likely to create an erroneous impression regarding its character, value, quantity, composition, merit or safety.

…

Unsanitary manufacture, etc., of food

7. No person shall manufacture, prepare, preserve, package or store for sale any food under unsanitary conditions.

Drugs

Prohibited sales of drugs

8. No person shall sell any drug that

(a) was manufactured, prepared, preserved, packaged or stored under unsanitary conditions; or

(b) is adulterated.

Deception, etc., regarding drugs

9(1) No person shall label, package, treat, process, sell or advertise any drug in a manner that is false, misleading or deceptive or is likely to create an erroneous impression regarding its character, value, quantity, composition, merit or safety.

Drugs labelled or packaged in contravention of regulations

(2) A drug that is not labelled or packaged as required by, or is labelled or packaged contrary to, the regulations shall be deemed to be labelled or packaged contrary to subsection (1).

…

Samples

14(1) No person shall distribute or cause to be distributed any drug as a sample.

Exception

(2) Subsection (1) does not apply to the distribution, under prescribed conditions, of samples of drugs to physicians, dentists, veterinary surgeons or pharmacists.

…

Cosmetics

Prohibited sales of cosmetics

16. No person shall sell any cosmetic that

(a) has in or on it any substance that may cause injury to the health of the user when the cosmetic is used,

(i) according to the directions on the label or accompanying the cosmetic, or

(ii) for such purposes and by such methods of use as are customary or usual therefor;

(b) consists in whole or in part of any filthy or decomposed substance or of any foreign matter; or

(c) was manufactured, prepared, preserved, packaged or stored under unsanitary conditions.

...

Unsanitary conditions

18. No person shall manufacture, prepare, preserve, package or store for sale any cosmetic under unsanitary conditions.

Devices

Prohibited sales of devices

19. No person shall sell any device that, when used according to directions or under such conditions as are customary or usual, may cause injury to the health of the purchaser or user thereof.

Deception, etc., regarding devices

20(1) No person shall label, package, treat, process, sell or advertise any device in a manner that is false, misleading or deceptive or is likely to create an erroneous impression regarding its design, construction, performance, intended use, quantity, character, value, composition, merit or safety.

Devices labelled or packaged in contravention of regulations

(2) A device that is not labelled or packaged as required by, or is labelled or packaged contrary to, the regulations shall be deemed to be labelled or packaged contrary to subsection (1).

...

Offences and Punishment

Contravention of Act or regulations

31. Subject to section 31.1, every person who contravenes any of the provisions of this Act or of the regulations made under this Part is guilty of an offence and liable

(a) on summary conviction for a first offence to a fine not exceeding five hundred dollars or to imprisonment for a term not exceeding three months or to both and, for a subsequent offence, to a fine not exceeding one thousand dollars or to imprisonment for a term not exceeding six months or to both; and

(b) on conviction on indictment to a fine not exceeding five thousand dollars or to imprisonment for a term not exceeding three years or to both.

Offences relating to food

31.1 Every person who contravenes any provision of this Act or the regulations, as it relates to food, is guilty of an offence and liable

(a) on summary conviction, to a fine not exceeding $50,000 or to imprisonment for a term not exceeding six months or to both; or

(b) on conviction by indictment, to a fine not exceeding $250,000 or to imprisonment for a term not exceeding three years or to both.

Limitation period

32(1) A prosecution for a summary conviction offence under this Act may be instituted at any time within two years after the time the subject-matter of the prosecution becomes known to the Minister or, in the case of a contravention of a provision of the Act that relates to food, to the Minister of Agriculture and Agri-Food.

...

SCHEDULE A

(Section 3)

Alcoholism	Gout
Alopecia	Heart disease
Anxiety state	Hernia
Appendicitis	Hypertension
Arteriosclerosis	Hypotension
Arthritis	Impetigo
Asthma	Kidney disease
Bladder disease	Leukemia
Cancer	Liver disease
Convulsions	Nausea and vomiting of pregnancy
Depression	Obesity
Diabetes	Pleurisy
Disease of the prostate	Rheumatic fever
Disorder of menstrual flow	Septicemia
Dysentery	Sexual impotence
Edematous state	Thrombotic and Embolic disorders
Epilepsy	Thyroid disease
Gall bladder disease	Tumor
Gangrene	Ulcer of the gastro-intestinal tract
Glaucoma	Venereal disease

Hazardous Products Act

RSC 1985, c. H-3

An Act to prohibit the advertising, sale and importation of hazardous products

Current to August 31, 2004

...

INTERPRETATION

Definitions

...

"controlled product"

"controlled product" means any product, material or substance specified by the regulations made pursuant to paragraph 15(1)(a) to be included in any of the classes listed in Schedule II;

"hazardous product"

"hazardous product" means any prohibited product, restricted product or controlled product;

...

"prohibited product"

"prohibited product" means any product, material or substance included in Part I of Schedule I;

"restricted product"

"restricted product" means any product, material or substance included in Part II of Schedule I;

...

PART I

PROHIBITED AND RESTRICTED PRODUCTS

Application

Restrictions on application

3(1) This Part does not apply in respect of the advertising, sale or importation of any

(a) explosive within the meaning of the *Explosives Act*;

(b) cosmetic, device, drug or food within the meaning of the *Food and Drugs Act*;

(c) control product as defined in subsection 2(1) of the *Pest Control Products Act*; or

(d) prescribed substance within the meaning of the *Nuclear Safety and Control Act*, that is radioactive.

Restrictions on application

(2) This Part does not apply to the advertising, sale or importation of a tobacco product as defined in section 2 of the *Tobacco Act* or the advertising of lighters or matches that display a tobacco product-related brand element.

…

Prohibitions

Prohibited products

4(1) No person shall advertise, sell or import a prohibited product.

Restricted products

(2) No person shall advertise, sell or import a restricted product except as authorized by the regulations made under section 5.

…

PART II

CONTROLLED PRODUCTS

Interpretation

Definitions

11(1) In this Part,

…

"hazard symbol"

"hazard symbol" includes any design, mark, pictogram, sign, letter, word, number, abbreviation or any combination thereof that is to be displayed on a controlled product, or a container in which a controlled product is packaged, in order to show the nature of the hazard of the controlled product;

…

Application

Restrictions on application

12. This Part does not apply in respect of the sale or importation of any
    (a) explosive within the meaning of the *Explosives Act*;
    (b) cosmetic, device, drug or food within the meaning of the *Food and Drugs Act*;
    (c) control product as defined in subsection 2(1) of the *Pest Control Products Act*;
    (d) prescribed substance within the meaning of the *Nuclear Safety and Control Act*, that is radioactive;
    (e) hazardous waste;
    (f) product, material or substance included in Part II of Schedule I and packaged as a consumer product;
    (g) wood or product made of wood;
    (h) tobacco or a tobacco product as defined in section 2 of the *Tobacco Act*; or
    (i) manufactured article.

…

Prohibitions

Prohibition re sale

13. Subject to the *Hazardous Materials Information Review Act*, no supplier shall sell to any person a controlled product intended for use in a work place in Canada unless

(a) on the sale of the controlled product, the supplier transmits to that person a material safety data sheet with respect to the controlled product that discloses the following information, namely,

(i) where the controlled product is a pure substance, the chemical identity of the controlled product and, where the controlled product is not a pure substance, the chemical identity of any ingredient thereof that is a controlled product and the concentration of that ingredient,

(ii) where the controlled product contains an ingredient that is included in the Ingredient Disclosure List and the ingredient is in a concentration that is equal to or greater than the concentration specified in the Ingredient Disclosure List for that ingredient, the chemical identity and concentration of that ingredient,

(iii) the chemical identity of any ingredient thereof that the supplier believes on reasonable grounds may be harmful to any person and the concentration of that ingredient,

(iv) the chemical identity of any ingredient thereof the toxicological properties of which are not known to the supplier and the concentration of that ingredient, and

(v) such other information with respect to the controlled product as may be prescribed; and

(b) the controlled product or container in which the controlled product is packaged has applied to it a label that discloses prescribed information and has displayed on it all applicable prescribed hazard symbols.

...

PART III

ADMINISTRATION AND ENFORCEMENT

Inspectors and Analysts

Inspectors and analysts

21(1) The Minister may designate as an inspector or analyst for the purposes of this Act any person who, in the Minister's opinion, is qualified to be so designated.

Certificate to be produced

(2) The Minister shall furnish every inspector with a certificate of designation and, on entering any place pursuant to subsection 22(1), an inspector shall, if so required, produce the certificate to the person in charge of that place.

Search, Seizure and Forfeiture

Powers of inspectors

22(1) An inspector may at any reasonable time enter any place where the inspector believes on reasonable grounds any hazardous product is manufactured, prepared, preserved, processed, packaged, sold or stored for sale, processing or packaging and

(a) examine any product, material or substance that the inspector believes on reasonable grounds is a hazardous product and take samples thereof, and examine any other thing that the inspector believes on reasonable grounds is used or is capable of being used for the manufacture, preparation, preservation, processing, packaging, sale or storage of a hazardous product;

(b) open and examine any receptacle or package that the inspector believes on reasonable grounds contains any hazardous product;

(c) examine any books, records or other documents that the inspector believes on reasonable grounds contain any information relevant to the enforcement of this Act and make copies thereof or of any portion thereof;

(d) where the inspector believes on reasonable grounds that any computer system on the premises contains data relevant to the enforcement of this Act or that such data is available to the computer system, use the computer system or cause it to be used to search any data contained in or available to the computer system, reproduce any record or cause it to be reproduced from the data in the form of a printout or other intelligible output and seize the printout or other output for examination or copying; and

(e) seize any product, material or substance, or any labelling, advertising material or other thing, by means of or in relation to which the inspector believes on reasonable grounds any provision of this Act or of any regulation made under this Act has been contravened or has not been complied with.

Assistance to inspectors

(2) The owner or person in charge of a place entered by an inspector pursuant to subsection (1) and every person found therein shall give the inspector such assistance and furnish the inspector with such information as the inspector may, for the purpose of exercising the powers referred to in paragraphs (1)(a) to (e), reasonably require them to give or furnish.

...

Offence, Punishment and Procedure

Contravening or not complying with Act or regulation

28(1) Every person who contravenes or fails to comply with any provision of this Act or of any regulation made under this Act

(a) is guilty of an offence punishable on summary conviction and liable to a fine not exceeding one hundred thousand dollars or to imprisonment for a term not exceeding six months or to both; or

(b) is guilty of an indictable offence and liable to a fine not exceeding one million dollars or to imprisonment for a term not exceeding two years or to both.

Officers, etc., of corporations

(2) Where a corporation commits an offence under subsection (1), any officer, director or agent of the corporation who directed, authorized, assented to, acquiesced in or participated in the commission of the offence is a party to and guilty of the offence and is liable on conviction to the punishment provided for the offence, whether or not the corporation has been prosecuted or convicted.

Limitation period

(3) Proceedings by way of summary conviction in respect of an offence under paragraph (1)(a) may be instituted at any time within but not later than twelve months after the time when the subject-matter of the proceedings arose.

Exception, etc., need not be mentioned

29(1) No exception, exemption, excuse or qualification prescribed by law is required to be set out or negatived, as the case may be, in an information or indictment for an offence under section 28 of this Act or under section 463, 464 or 465 of the *Criminal Code* in respect of an offence under section 28.

Burden of proof

(2) In any prosecution for an offence mentioned in subsection (1), the burden of proving that an exception, exemption, excuse or qualification prescribed by law operates in favour of the accused is on the accused and the prosecutor is not required, except by way of rebuttal, to prove that the exception, exemption, excuse or qualification does not operate in favour of the accused, whether or not it is set out in the information or indictment.

...

Motor Vehicle Repair Act

RSO 1990, c. M.43

Current to November 4, 2004

Note: On a day to be named by proclamation of the Lieutenant Governor, this Act is repealed by the Statutes of Ontario, 2002, chapter 30, Schedule E, section 13. See: SO 2002, c. 30, Sched. E, ss. 13, 22.

Definitions

1. In this Act,

"customer" means an individual who contacts a repairer for an estimate, work or repairs to a vehicle;

"estimate" means an estimate of the total cost of work on and repairs for a vehicle;

"repairer" means a person who works on or repairs vehicles for compensation;

"vehicle" means a motor vehicle as defined in the *Highway Traffic Act.*

Estimates

2(1) Where a customer asks for a written estimate, no repairer shall charge for any work on or repairs to a vehicle unless the repairer first gives the customer an estimate, in writing, of the cost of the work on or repairs to the customer's vehicle.

Idem

(2) An estimate given under subsection (1) must include,

(a) the name and address of both the customer and repairer;

(b) the make, model, vehicle identification number and licence number of the vehicle;

(c) a description of the work or repairs to be made to the vehicle;

(d) the parts to be installed and a statement as to whether they will be new, used or reconditioned;

(e) the price of the parts to be installed;

(f) the number of hours to be billed, the hourly rate and the total cost of labour;

(g) the total amount to be billed; and

(h) the date the estimate is given and the date after which it ceases to apply.

Estimate fee

3(1) No person shall charge a fee for an estimate unless the customer is told in advance that a fee will be charged and the amount of the fee.

...

Idem

(3) No person shall charge a fee for an estimate if the work or repairs in question are authorized and carried out.

...

Authorization required

4(1) No person shall charge for any work on or repairs to a vehicle unless the customer authorizes the work or repairs.

Idem

(2) No person shall charge, for work or repairs for which an estimate was given, an amount that exceeds the estimate by more than 10 per cent.

Authorization by telephone

5. An authorization for work or repairs that is given by telephone is not effective for the purpose of this Act unless the person receiving the authorization records,

    (a) the name and telephone number of the person giving the authorization; and

    (b) the date and time of the authorization.

Disclosure

6(1) Every repairer shall post signs in a conspicuous place clearly visible to prospective customers stating,

    (a) that written estimates are available on request;

    (b) whether there is a charge for an estimate;

    (c) the cost of computing labour charges including,

        (i) the hourly rate,

        (ii) whether a rate predetermining the length of time required for the work or repairs will be applied, and

        (iii) whether any commissions are payable;

    (d) that replaced parts will be available to the customer after the work or repairs; and

    (e) the telephone number of the Ministry of Consumer and Business Services where complaints may be directed.

...

Return of parts

7(1) Every repairer shall offer to return to the customer all parts removed from the vehicle in the course of work or repairs unless advised when the work or repairs are authorized that the customer does not require their return.

...

Invoice

8(1) The repairer shall, on completion of work or repairs, provide the customer with an invoice showing,

(a) the name and address of both customer and repairer;

(b) the make, model, vehicle identification number and licence number of the vehicle;

(c) the date the vehicle is returned to the customer;

(d) the odometer reading at the time of return;

(e) a description of the work or repairs made to the vehicle;

(f) the parts installed and whether they are new, used or reconditioned;

(g) the price of the parts installed;

(h) the number of hours billed, the hourly rate and the total cost of labour;

(i) the total amount billed; and

(j) the terms of the warranty.

...

Warranty

9(1) Every repairer warrants all new or reconditioned parts installed and the labour required to install them for a minimum of ninety days or 5,000 kilometres, whichever comes first.

...

Idem

(3) The person having charge of a vehicle that becomes inoperable or unsafe to drive because of the failure or inadequacy of work or repairs to which a warranty under this section applies may, where it is not reasonable to return the vehicle to the original repairer, have the failure or inadequacy repaired at the closest facility available for the work or repairs.

Idem

(4) Where work or repairs are made under subsection (3), the person entitled to a warranty under this section is entitled, in addition to any other rights or recourse available at law, to recover from the repairer the original cost of the work or repairs and reasonable towing charges.

Loss of warranty

(5) A customer who subjects any part to misuse or abuse is not entitled to the benefit of the warranty on that part.

Idem

(6) No repairer shall refuse to reimburse a customer because of the operation of subsection (5) unless the repairer has reasonable and probable grounds to believe that the part under warranty was subjected to misuse or abuse.

Return of parts

(7) A customer who seeks to recover costs under this section shall return, upon the request and at the expense of the original repairer, the defective parts to the original repairer unless, in the circumstances, it is not reasonably possible for the customer to do so.

Reimbursement

(8) An original repairer who is required to make a payment under this section is entitled to recover from the supplier of a defective part any amount paid to the customer under subsection (4).

Consistent cost

10. No person shall give an estimate or charge an amount for work or repairs that is greater than that usually given or charged by that person for the same work or repairs merely because the cost is to be paid, directly or indirectly, by an insurance company registered under the *Insurance Act*.

Illegal charges not payable

11(1) No charge made in contravention of this Act is collectable or payable.

Idem

(2) Any payment of a charge that was levied in contravention of this Act or any entitlement under subsection 9(4) is recoverable by the person that made the payment or by the warranty holder in a court of competent jurisdiction.

Offence

12(1) Every person who contravenes this Act is guilty of an offence and on conviction is liable to a fine of not more than $2,000 or to imprisonment for a term of not more than one year, or to both.

Idem

(2) Where a corporation is convicted of an offence under this Act, the maximum penalty that may be imposed upon the corporation is $25,000 and not as provided in subsection (1).

Idem

(3) Where a corporation has been convicted of an offence under this Act,
    (a) each director of the corporation; and
    (b) each officer, employee or agent of the corporation who was in whole or in part responsible for the contravention,
is a party to the offence unless he or she satisfies the court that he or she did not authorize, permit or acquiesce in the offence.

...

Motor Vehicle Safety Act

SC 1993, c. 16

[Unofficially, RSC 1985, c. M-10.01]

Assented to May 6, 1993

An Act to regulate the manufacture and importation of motor vehicles and motor vehicle equipment to reduce the risk of death, injury and damage to property and the environment

Current to August 31, 2004

Her Majesty, by and with the advice and consent of the Senate and House of Commons of Canada, enacts as follows:

…

INTERPRETATION

Definitions

2. In this Act,

…

"equipment"

"equipment" means any equipment set out in Schedule I that is designed for use in or on a vehicle;

…

"manufacture"

"manufacture," in relation to a vehicle, includes any process of assembling or altering the vehicle prior to its sale to the first retail purchaser;

…

"national safety mark"

"national safety mark" means the expression "Canada Motor Vehicle Safety Standard" or "Norme de sécurité des véhicules automobiles du Canada," the abbreviation "CMVSS" or "NSVAC," or the symbol set out in Schedule II;

…

"sell"

"sell" includes to offer for sale or lease, have in possession for sale or lease and deliver for sale or lease;

"standard"

"standard" means a standard that governs the design, construction, functioning or marking of vehicles or equipment for the purpose of reducing the risk of death, injury or property damage from vehicle use;

"vehicle"

"vehicle" means any vehicle that is capable of being driven or drawn on roads by any means other than muscular power exclusively, but does not include any vehicle designed to run exclusively on rails.

NATIONAL SAFETY MARKS

National trade-marks

3(1) The national safety marks are hereby declared to be national trade-marks and, except as provided in this Act, the exclusive property in and right to the use of those marks are vested in Her Majesty in right of Canada.

Use of marks

(2) A company authorized by the Minister in the prescribed manner may, subject to the provisions of this Act, apply a national safety mark, in the prescribed form and manner and on the prescribed place, to a vehicle or equipment of a prescribed class.

Prohibition

(3) No person shall use a national safety mark except as authorized by this Act.

...

VEHICLE AND EQUIPMENT STANDARDS

Compliance by companies

5(1) No company shall apply a national safety mark to any vehicle or equipment, sell any vehicle or equipment to which a national safety mark has been applied, or import into Canada any vehicle or equipment of a prescribed class unless

    (a) the vehicle or equipment conforms to the standards prescribed for vehicles or equipment of its class at the time the main assembly of the vehicle was completed or the equipment was manufactured;

    (b) evidence of such conformity has been obtained and produced in the prescribed form and manner or, where the regulations so provide, in a form and manner satisfactory to the Minister;

    (c) in the case of a vehicle, prescribed information relating to standards for emissions has been obtained and submitted to the Minister in the prescribed manner;

    (d) prescribed information is marked on the vehicle or equipment in the prescribed form and manner and on the prescribed place;

    (e) where required by the regulations, prescribed documentation or prescribed accessories accompany the vehicle or equipment;

    (f) prescribed information relating to the operation of the vehicle or equipment is disseminated in the prescribed form and manner;

(g) records are maintained and furnished in the prescribed form and manner in relation to the design, manufacture, testing and field performance of the vehicle or equipment, for the purpose of

    (i) enabling an inspector to determine whether the vehicle or equipment conforms to all prescribed standards applicable to it, and

    (ii) facilitating the identification and analysis of defects referred to in subsection 10(1); and

(h) in the case of equipment, the company maintains a registration system in the prescribed form and manner by which any person who has purchased equipment manufactured, imported or sold by the company and who wishes to be identified may be identified.

…

NOTICE OF SAFETY DEFECTS

Obligation to give notice

10(1) A company that manufactures, sells or imports any vehicle or equipment of a class for which standards are prescribed shall, on becoming aware of a defect in the design, construction or functioning of the vehicle or equipment that affects or is likely to affect the safety of any person, cause notice of the defect to be given in the prescribed manner to

    (a) the Minister;

    (b) each person who has obtained such a vehicle or equipment from the company; and

    (c) each current owner of such a vehicle or equipment as determined

        (i) from any warranty issued by the company with respect to the functioning of the vehicle or equipment that has, to its knowledge, been given, sold or transferred to the current owner,

        (ii) in the case of a vehicle, from provincial motor vehicle registration records, or

        (iii) in the case of equipment, from a registration system referred to in paragraph 5(1)(h).

Where notice previously given

(2) A company is not required to cause notice to be given of a defect of which notice has already been given under this section by another company that manufactured, sold or imported the vehicle or equipment.

Publication of notice

(3) Where the Minister is satisfied that the name of the current owner of a vehicle or equipment cannot reasonably be determined by a company in accordance with paragraph (1)(c),

    (a) the Minister may order the company to give notice of the defect by publication in the prescribed form for a period of five consecutive days in two major daily newspapers in each of the following six regions, namely, the Atlantic provinces, Quebec, Ontario, the Prairie provinces, British Columbia and the Territories, or by dissemination in an alternative medium for such period as the Minister determines; or

    (b) the Minister may order that the current owner need not be notified.

Contents of notice

(4) A notice required to be given under subsections (1) and (3) shall contain, in the form and to the extent prescribed, a description of the defect, an evaluation of the safety risk arising from it and directions for correcting it.

...

OFFENCES AND PUNISHMENT

Offence and punishment

17(1) Every corporation that contravenes any provision of this Act

(a) is guilty of an offence punishable on summary conviction and is liable to a fine not exceeding one hundred thousand dollars; or

(b) is guilty of an indictable offence and is liable to a fine not exceeding one million dollars.

Idem

(2) Every individual who contravenes any provision of this Act

(a) is guilty of an offence punishable on summary conviction and is liable to a fine not exceeding two thousand dollars or to imprisonment for a term not exceeding six months, or to both; or

(b) is guilty of an indictable offence and is liable to a fine not exceeding ten thousand dollars or to imprisonment for a term not exceeding two years, or to both.

Defence where more than one manufacturer

(3) In a prosecution for a contravention of section 4 or subsection 5(1) by a company engaged in the business of assembling or altering vehicles, it is a defence for the company to establish that the contravention occurred as a result of work previously done on a vehicle by another person engaged in the manufacture of the vehicle.

Offence by employee or agent

18(1) In a prosecution under this Act, it is sufficient proof of an offence to establish that it was committed by an employee or agent of the accused whether or not the employee or agent is identified or has been prosecuted for the offence, unless the accused establishes that the offence was committed without the knowledge or consent of the accused and that the accused exercised all due diligence to prevent its commission.

Time limit

(2) A prosecution by way of summary conviction under this Act may not be instituted later than two years after the time when the subject-matter of the prosecution arose.

Sale of Goods Act

RSO 1990, c. S.1

Current to November 4, 2004

Definitions

1(1) In this Act,

"buyer" means the person who buys or agrees to buy goods;

...

"goods" means all chattels personal, other than things in action and money, and includes emblements, industrial growing crops, and things attached to or forming part of the land that are agreed to be severed before sale or under the contract of sale;

...

"quality of goods" includes their state or condition;

"sale" includes a bargain and sale as well as a sale and delivery;

"seller" means a person who sells or agrees to sell goods;

...

"warranty" means an agreement with reference to goods that are the subject of a contract of sale but collateral to the main purpose of the contract, the breach of which gives rise to a claim for damages but not to a right to reject the goods and treat the contract as repudiated.

...

When condition to be treated a warranty

12(1) Where a contract of sale is subject to a condition to be fulfilled by the seller, the buyer may waive the condition or may elect to treat the breach of the condition as a breach of warranty and not as a ground for treating the contract as repudiated.

Stipulation which may be condition or warranty

(2) Whether a stipulation in a contract of sale is a condition the breach of which may give rise to a right to treat the contract as repudiated or a warranty the breach of which may give rise to a claim for damages but not to a right to reject the goods and treat the contract as repudiated depends in each case on the construction of the contract, and a stipulation may be a condition, though called a warranty in the contract.

Where breach of condition to be treated as breach of warranty

(3) Where a contract of sale is not severable and the buyer has accepted the goods or part thereof, or where the contract is for specific goods the property in which has passed to the buyer, the breach of any condition to be fulfilled by the seller can only be treated as a breach of warranty and not as a ground for rejecting the goods and treating the con-

tract as repudiated, unless there is a term of the contract, express or implied, to that effect.

Fulfillment excused by impossibility

(4) Nothing in this section affects the case of a condition or warranty, fulfillment of which is excused by law by reason of impossibility or otherwise.

Implied conditions and warranties

13. In a contract of sale, unless the circumstances of the contract are such as to show a different intention, there is,

(a) an implied condition on the part of the seller that in the case of a sale the seller has a right to sell the goods, and that in the case of an agreement to sell the seller will have a right to sell the goods at the time when the property is to pass;

(b) an implied warranty that the buyer will have and enjoy quiet possession of the goods; and

(c) an implied warranty that the goods will be free from any charge or encumbrance in favour of any third party, not declared or known to the buyer before or at the time when the contract is made.

Sale by description

14. Where there is a contract for the sale of goods by description, there is an implied condition that the goods will correspond with the description, and, if the sale is by sample as well as by description, it is not sufficient that the bulk of the goods corresponds with the sample if the goods do not also correspond with the description.

Implied conditions as to quality or fitness

15. Subject to this Act and any statute in that behalf, there is no implied warranty or condition as to the quality or fitness for any particular purpose of goods supplied under a contract of sale, except as follows:

1. Where the buyer, expressly or by implication, makes known to the seller the particular purpose for which the goods are required so as to show that the buyer relies on the seller's skill or judgment, and the goods are of a description that it is in the course of the seller's business to supply (whether the seller is the manufacturer or not), there is an implied condition that the goods will be reasonably fit for such purpose, but in the case of a contract for the sale of a specified article under its patent or other trade name there is no implied condition as to its fitness for any particular purpose.

2. Where goods are bought by description from a seller who deals in goods of that description (whether the seller is the manufacturer or not), there is an implied condition that the goods will be of merchantable quality, but if the buyer has examined the goods, there is no implied condition as regards defects that such examination ought to have revealed.

3. An implied warranty or condition as to quality or fitness for a particular purpose may be annexed by the usage of trade.

4. An express warranty or condition does not negative a warranty or condition implied by this Act unless inconsistent therewith.

Sale by sample

16(1) A contract of sale is a contract for sale by sample where there is a term in the contract, express or implied, to that effect.

Implied conditions

(2) In the case of a contract for sale by sample, there is an implied condition,

(a) that the bulk will correspond with the sample in quality;

(b) that the buyer will have a reasonable opportunity of comparing the bulk with the sample; and

(c) that the goods will be free from any defect rendering them unmerchantable that would not be apparent on reasonable examination of the sample.

Textile Labelling Act

RSC 1985, c. T-10

An Act respecting the labelling, sale, importation and advertising of consumer textile articles

Current to August 31, 2004

...

INTERPRETATION

Definitions

2. In this Act,

"advertise"

"advertise" means make any representation to the public by any means whatever, except a representation on a label, for the purpose of promoting directly or indirectly the sale of a textile fibre product;

...

"consumer textile article"

"consumer textile article" means

(a) any textile fibre, yarn or fabric, or

(b) any product made in whole or in part from a textile fibre, yarn or fabric that is in the form in which it is or is to be sold to any person for consumption or use, other than consumption or use in the manufacturing, processing or finishing of any product for sale;

...

"fabric"

"fabric" means any material woven, knitted, crocheted, knotted, braided, felted, bonded, laminated or otherwise produced from, or in combination with, a textile fibre;

...

"sell"

"sell" includes

(a) offer for sale, expose for sale and have in possession for sale, and

(b) display in such manner as to lead to a reasonable belief that the product so displayed is intended for sale;

"textile fibre"

"textile fibre" means any natural or manufactured matter that is capable of being made into a yarn or fabric and, without limiting the generality of the foregoing, includes human hair, kapok, feathers and down and animal hair or fur that has been removed from an animal skin;

"textile fibre product"

"textile fibre product" means

    (a) any consumer textile article, or

    (b) any textile fibre, yarn or fabric used or to be used in a consumer textile article.

...

PROHIBITIONS

Prohibition respecting consumer textile articles

3. No dealer shall sell, import into Canada or advertise

    (a) a prescribed consumer textile article unless the article has applied to it a label containing a representation with respect to the textile fibre content of the article; or

    (b) any consumer textile article that has applied to it a label containing a representation with respect to the textile fibre content of the article unless the label is applied to it in accordance with and complies with all applicable provisions of this Act.

Prohibition respecting advertising

4. No dealer shall, in advertising a consumer textile article, make any representation with respect to the textile fibre content of the article except in accordance with the regulations.

Representations relating to consumer textile articles

5(1) No dealer shall apply to a consumer textile article a label, or sell, import into Canada or advertise a consumer textile article that has applied to it a label containing any false or misleading representation that relates to or may reasonably be regarded as relating to the article.

Representations relating to textile fibre products

(2) No dealer shall, by means of a label, advertising or otherwise, make any false or misleading representation that relates to or may reasonably be regarded as relating to a textile fibre product.

Definition of "false or misleading representation"

(3) For the purposes of this section, "false or misleading representation" includes

    (a) any representation in which expressions, words, figures, depictions or symbols are arranged or shown in a manner that may reasonably be regarded as likely to deceive any person with respect to textile fibre content;

    (b) any expression, word, figure, depiction or symbol that implies or may reasonably be regarded as implying that a textile fibre product contains any fibre, fur or hair not contained in the product; and

    (c) any description of the type, quality, performance, origin or method of manufacture or production of a textile fibre product that may reasonably be regarded as likely to deceive any person with respect to the matter so described.

LABELS

Label containing representation respecting textile fibre content

6. Each label containing a representation with respect to the textile fibre content of the consumer textile article to which it is applied shall

(a) be applied to the article in such form and manner as may be prescribed; and

(b) show, in such form and manner as may be prescribed,

(i) the generic name of each textile fibre comprising five per cent or more by mass of the total fibre mass of the article,

(ii) subject to the regulations, such percentage by mass of the total fibre mass of the article as each textile fibre named pursuant to subparagraph (i) comprises,

(iii) the identity of the person by or for whom the consumer textile article was manufactured or made, and

(iv) such other information and representations as may be required by the regulations to be included in the label.

...

OFFENCE AND PUNISHMENT

Contravention of sections 3 to 5

12(1) Every dealer who contravenes section 3, 4 or 5 is guilty of an offence and liable

(a) on summary conviction, to a fine not exceeding five thousand dollars; or

(b) on conviction on indictment, to a fine not exceeding ten thousand dollars.

Contravention of other provisions, or regulations

(2) Every person who contravenes any provision of this Act, other than section 3, 4 or 5, or of the regulations is guilty of an offence and liable,

(a) on summary conviction, to a fine not exceeding one thousand dollars or to imprisonment for a term not exceeding six months or to both; or

(b) on conviction on indictment, to a fine not exceeding three thousand dollars or to imprisonment for a term not exceeding one year or to both.

...

Limitation period

(2) Proceedings by way of summary conviction under this Act may be instituted at any time within but not later than twelve months after the time when the subject-matter of the proceedings arose.

Unconscionable Transactions Relief Act

RSO 1990, c. U.2

Current to November 4, 2004

Definitions

1. In this Act,

"cost of the loan" means the whole cost to the debtor of money lent and includes interest, discount, subscription, premium, dues, bonus, commission, brokerage fees and charges, but not actual lawful and necessary disbursements made to a land registrar, a local registrar of the Ontario Court (General Division), a sheriff or a treasurer of a municipality;

"court" means a court having jurisdiction in an action for the recovery of a debt or money demand to the amount claimed by a creditor in respect of money lent;

"creditor" includes the person advancing money lent and the assignee of any claim arising or security given in respect of money lent;

"debtor" means a person to whom or on whose account money lent is advanced and includes every surety and endorser or other person liable for the repayment of money lent or upon any agreement or collateral or other security given in respect thereof;

"money lent" includes money advanced on account of any person in any transaction that, whatever its form may be, is substantially one of money-lending or securing the repayment of money so advanced and includes and has always included a mortgage within the meaning of the Mortgages Act.

2. Where, in respect of money lent, the court finds that, having regard to the risk and to all the circumstances, the cost of the loan is excessive and that the transaction is harsh and unconscionable, the court may,

    (a) reopen the transaction and take an account between the creditor and the debtor;

    (b) despite any statement or settlement of account or any agreement purporting to close previous dealings and create a new obligation, reopen any account already taken and relieve the debtor from payment of any sum in excess of the sum adjudged by the court to be fairly due in respect of the principal and the cost of the loan;

    (c) order the creditor to repay any such excess if the same has been paid or allowed on account by the debtor;

(d) set aside either wholly or in part or revise or alter any security given or agreement made in respect of the money lent, and, if the creditor has parted with the security, order the creditor to indemnify the debtor.

Exercise of powers of court

3. The powers conferred by section 2 may be exercised,

(a) in an action or proceeding by a creditor for the recovery of money lent;

(b) in an action or proceeding by the debtor despite any provision or agreement to the contrary, and despite the fact that the time for repayment of the loan or any instalment thereof has not arrived;

(c) in an action or proceeding in which the amount due or to become due in respect of money lent is in question.

Relief by way of originating notice

4(1) In addition to any right that a debtor may have under this or any other Act or otherwise in respect of money lent, the debtor may apply for relief under this Act to the Ontario Court (General Division) which may exercise any of the powers of the court under section 2.

Appeal

(2) An appeal lies to the Divisional Court from any order made under subsection (1).

Saving holder for value, and existing jurisdiction

5. Nothing in this Act affects the rights of a assignee or holder for value without notice, or derogates from the existing powers or jurisdiction of any court.

Glossary of Terms

acceptance
when there has been acceptance of an offer made by one party in the bargaining process, the parties are assumed to have reached an agreement on contract terms, and a binding contract exists from that time

accord and satisfaction
a means of discharging a contract whereby the parties agree to accept some form of compromise or settlement instead of performance of the original terms of the contract

ad idem
see consensus ad idem

adequate notice
the requirement for a party who wants to rely on an exclusion clause in a contract to bring the clause to the other party's attention and explain its legal implications before the contract is signed

adhesion contract
a standardized contract for goods or services offered to consumers on a non-negotiable or "take it or leave it" basis, without offering consumers the opportunity to bargain over the terms of the contract

affidavit of execution
a sworn statement in writing, signed by the witness to a contract, stating that the witness was present and saw the person signing the contract actually sign it; the affidavit can be used to prove that a party to a contract actually signed it

agreement
a binding contract

anticipatory breach
an express repudiation that occurs before the time of performance of a contract

arm's-length transaction
a transaction negotiated by unrelated parties, each acting in his or her own independent self-interest; "unrelated" in this context usually means not related as family members by birth or marriage, and not related by business interests

assignee
a party to whom rights under a contract have been assigned by way of an assignment

assignment
a transfer by one party of his or her rights under a contract to a third party

assignor
a party who assigns his or her rights under a contract to a third party

beneficiary
a person who is entitled to the benefits of an agreement entered into between two or more other parties

breach of contract
failure, without legal excuse, to perform any promise that forms part of a contract

chattel mortgage
a contract that grants one party a security interest in goods or personal property to secure payment of money, often the purchase price of the goods

chattels
items of personal property

chose in action/thing in action
an intangible right of ownership in a tangible thing that carries the right to take legal action on it—for example, debts, insurance policies, negotiable instruments, contract rights, patents, and copyrights

common mistake

both parties to a contract are mistaken and make the same mistake

condition precedent

an event (or non-event) that must occur (or not occur) before a contract can be enforced

condition subsequent

an event that, if it occurs, will terminate an existing contract

condition

an essential term of a contract, the breach of which denies the innocent party of the benefit of the contract, or defeats the purpose of the contract

conditional sale contract

a contract for the sale and purchase of goods in which title to the goods does not pass to the buyer unless conditions are fulfilled

consensus ad idem

when there has been acceptance by the offeree of an offer, the parties have reached an agreement on terms, and they have an intention to be bound by those terms; they are said to have reached a *consensus ad idem* (a "meeting of the minds"); sometimes a shorter form is used, and the parties are said to be *ad idem*

consequential damages

secondary damages that do not flow from the breach of contract but from the consequences of the breach, such as loss of future profits

consideration

the price, which must be something of value, paid in return for a promise

constructive trust

a trust created by the operation of law, as distinguished from an express trust

consumer

an individual who purchases goods or services, generally for his or her own use

consumer goods

goods purchased by a consumer that are intended only for personal, household, or family use

contra proferentem

a rule used in the interpretation of contracts when dealing with ambiguous terms according to which a court will choose the interpretation that favours the party who did not draft the contract

contract

an agreement made between two or more persons that the law recognizes and will enforce

counteroffer

a response to an offer by an offeree that does not unconditionally accept the terms of the offer but proposes to add to or modify the terms

deed

a written contract, made under seal by the promisor(s); also called a formal contract

discharged

released, extinguished; a discharge of a contract occurs when the parties have complied with their obligations or other events have occurred that release one or both parties from performing their obligations

doctrine of frustration of contract

a legal doctrine that permits parties to a contract to be relieved of the contractual obligations because of the occurrence of some event beyond their control that makes it impossible for them to perform the contract

doctrine of laches

a common law doctrine that states that the neglect or failure to institute an action or lawsuit within a reasonable time period, together with prejudice suffered by the other party as a result of the delay, will result in the barring of the action

due diligence

the attention and care that a reasonable person would exercise with respect to his or her concerns; the obligation to make every reasonable effort to meet one's obligations

duress

an unlawful threat or coercion used by one person to induce another to perform some act against his or her will

easement

an interest in land that permits certain uses without interruption or interference by the person who has legal title to the land

ejusdem generis

a rule of contract construction that requires that general words following specific words take their meaning from the specific words and are confined to the same category as the specific words

equitable remedies

remedies developed by the court of equity that are based on fairness instead of the strict application of common law

estopped
stopped or prevented

exclusion/exemption clause
a clause in a contract that limits the liability of the parties

executory contract
a contract between a buyer and seller in which full payment is not made at the time of the contract; a contract to buy on credit

exemplary or punitive damages
damages awarded to an injured party over and above compensation for actual loss to punish the wrongdoer or to act as a deterrent to other wrongdoers

expectancy damages
damages that are based on a loss of expected profits

express repudiation/express breach
the failure or refusal to perform the obligations of a contract when they become due

express trust
a trust that arises as a result of an agreement, usually in writing, that is created in express terms

expressio unius est exclusio alterius
"to express one thing and exclude another"; a rule of contract construction that requires that the use of one word implies the exclusion of another

fiduciary
a relationship where one person is in a position of trust to another and has a duty to safeguard the other's interests ahead of his or her own interests

force majeure
a major event that the parties to a contract did not foresee or anticipate that prevents performance of the contract and thus terminates the contract; such an event, for example, a natural disaster or war, is outside the control of the parties and cannot be avoided with due diligence

formal contract
a contract that is in writing and sealed by any party who is a promisor (which may be one or both parties); formal contracts are also called "deeds," and in English law are sometimes referred to as "covenants"

fraud
false or misleading allegations for the purpose of inducing another to part with something valuable or to give up some legal right

fraudulent misrepresentation
a false statement made to induce a party to enter into a contract that the maker knows is false

fundamental breach
the failure to perform a primary obligation under a contract, which has the effect of depriving the other party of substantially the whole benefit of the contract

gratuitous promise
a promise made by someone who does not receive consideration for it

guarantee
a promise by a third party to pay the debt of another person if that person fails to pay the debt when it is due

guarantor
a third party who gives a guarantee to the creditor of another person

implied repudiation
repudiation that is not express and must be implied or deduced from the circumstances

injunction
a court order that prohibits someone from doing some act or compels someone to do some act

innocent misrepresentation
a false statement made to induce a party to enter into a contract that the maker of the statement does not know is false

inquiry
questioning by the offeree as to whether the offeror will consider other terms or is willing to modify the terms of the offer; an inquiry does not constitute a counteroffer and is not a rejection of the original offer

intangible property
personal property where the interest in it or its value rests in rights it confers rather than in its physical properties

interlocutory/interim injunction
a temporary injunction granted by a court before the final determination of a lawsuit for the purpose of preventing irreparable injury

judicial interventionism
an approach to the interpretation of law that draws on social, economic, and political values in interpreting the meaning and application of legal rules and principles

lapse

the termination or failure of an offer through the neglect to accept it within some time limit or through failure of some contingency

legal tender

notes (bills) issued by the Bank of Canada and coins issued by the Royal Canadian Mint, subject to certain restrictions

licence

a grant of a right; in real property law, a grant of a right to some use of land that does not amount to a grant of an interest in the land

life estate

a transfer of interest in land for a term of years measured by the life of the transferee or by the life of another person; when the person dies, the life estate ends, and the property goes back to the transferor or other persons designated to receive the interest in land

liquidated damages

damages that are easily determined from a fixed or measurable standard, or can be assessed by calculating the amount owing from a mathematical formula or from circumstances where no subjective assessment has to be made

liquidated damages clause

a term in a contract that attempts to reasonably estimate the damages that will be suffered if the contract is breached

lost opportunity damages

damages that are based on a longer-term loss of business

mandatory injunction

an injunction that commands a person to do a certain thing

material alteration

a change in a contract that changes its legal meaning and effect; a change that goes to the heart or purpose of the contract

material inducement

a statement made before a contract is made that influences a party to enter into the contract

material representation

a statement of fact, not opinion, made by one party, of sufficient weight to induce the other party to enter into the contract

merger

the discharge of one contract by its replacement with, or absorption into, an identical contract

minor

at common law, an individual under the age of 21; minority status has also been defined by statute law, lowering the age of majority to 18 or 19 in most provinces

mitigate

to take steps to minimize or reduce the damages one will suffer as a result of another's breach of contract

multilevel marketing scheme

a plan for the supply of a product whereby a participant in the plan receives compensation for the supply of the product to another participant in the plan who, in turn, receives compensation for the supply of the product to other participants in the plan

mutual mistake

both parties to a contract are mistaken but each makes a different mistake

negative covenant

a promise in a contract to refrain from doing a certain thing

negotiable instrument

a promise in writing and signed to pay a specific sum of money to the bearer—for example, a cheque or promissory note

non est factum

Latin for "I did not make this"; a defence used by one who appears to be a party to a contract but who did not intend to enter into this type of contract; in effect, the party is denying that he or she consented to this contract

novation

a requirement that the parties to a contract agree to substitute a new contract for an existing contract—terminating the existing contract

null and void

of no force, validity, or effect

nullity

nothing; something that has no legal force or effect

offer

a promise to do something or give something of value to another person; if the other accepts the offer, a binding contract exists

offeree

a person to whom an offer is made during the bargaining process

offeror

a person who, during the bargaining process that precedes making a contract, agrees to do something for the other party; once the offer is accepted, the bargain is concluded and the parties have made an agreement

onus

the burden of responsibility or proof

option to terminate

a term in a contract that allows one or both parties to discharge or terminate the contract before performance has been fully completed

parol evidence

if a contract is in writing and is clear, no other written or oral evidence is admissible to contradict, vary, or interpret the agreement

past consideration

an act done or something given before a contract is made, which by itself is not consideration for the contract

penalty clause

a term in a contract that imposes a penalty for default or breach

persons under mental disability

a general term that includes persons who are delusional and insane so as to be a danger to themselves and others, and those who, while not insane and dangerous, lack the ability to manage their own affairs

plain language drafting

the modern style of drafting legal documents that employs plain, ordinary language and emphasizes clarity, precision, and brevity

positivism

an approach to the interpretation of law that states that the meaning to be given to the words in legal rules should be the ordinary, dictionary meaning without resorting to social, economic, or political values to aid in interpretation

precedent

an essential doctrine of common law that requires judges to follow the rule in a previously decided case when that case deals with similar facts or issues to the case currently being decided

presumption of law

an inference in favour of a particular fact; a rule of law whereby a finding of a basic fact gives rise to the existence of a presumed fact or state of affairs unless the presumption can be rebutted, or proven false, by the party seeking to deny the presumed fact

privity

the relationship that exists between the parties to a contract

prohibitory injunction

an injunction that directs a person not to do a certain thing

promisee

the party to a contract who receives the benefit of a promise made by another party to the contract

promisor

the party to a contract who undertakes to do something

promissory estoppel

a rule whereby a person is prevented from denying the truth of a statement of fact made by him or her where another person has relied on that statement and acted accordingly

pyramid selling scheme

a multilevel marketing plan whereby a participant in the plan pays for the right to receive compensation for recruiting into the plan another participant who pays for the same right

quantum meruit

an equitable doctrine that states that no one should unjustly benefit from the labour and materials of another; under those circumstances, the law implies a promise to pay a reasonable amount, even in the absence of a contractual term for price; loosely translated as "as much as is deserved"

quiet possession

the right to possess and use goods without interference or disturbance from other parties

recital

a part of a contract, at the beginning, that recites facts that establish the background and purpose of the parties in entering into the contract

representation

a statement made to induce someone to enter into a contract

repudiate

to renounce or reject an obligation

rescission

the cancellation, nullification, or revocation of a contract; the "unmaking" of a contract

restitution

a remedy in which one seeks to rescind a contract; if granted, restitution restores the party, as far as possible, to a pre-contract position

restraint of trade

practices that are designed to artificially maintain prices, eliminate competition, create a monopoly, or otherwise obstruct the course of trade and commerce

restrictive covenant

a provision in a contract that prohibits certain activities or uses of property

revoke

to annul or make void by recalling or taking back; to cancel or rescind

setoff

in an action for debt, a defence where the debtor admits that he or she owes a debt to the creditor but also claims that the creditor owes a debt to him or her, and uses this to cancel or reduce the debt owed to the creditor

simple contract

a contract that can be oral or in writing and that is not a formal contract

specific goods

specific, identifiable chattels that have been singled out for contract purposes

specific performance

a remedy requiring the party who is in breach of a contract to perform his or her obligations under the contract

substantial performance

performance of contractual obligations that does not entirely meet the terms of the contract but nevertheless confers a benefit on a party

tender of performance

offering to perform that which the contracted party is obligated to perform under a contract

term

a provision of a contract; terms are either conditions or warranties

terms of art

words, phrases, or technical terms that have a fairly precise, specific legal meaning, often as a result of being interpreted and defined in previous court decisions

tort

a civil wrong done by one party to another for which the law awards damages; the law of torts is much older than the law of contracts, and it is from tort law that modern contract law developed

trust

a legal entity created by a grantor for a beneficiary whereby the grantor transfers property to a trustee to manage for the benefit of the beneficiary

trustee

a person who holds property in trust for, or to the benefit of, another person

uberrimae fidei contracts

a class of contracts where full disclosure is required because one party must rely on the power and authority of another, who must behave with utmost good faith and not take advantage of the weaker party

under seal

to bear an impression made in wax, a gummed paper wafer, or an impression made directly on paper

undue influence

persuasion, pressure, or influence short of actual force that overpowers a weaker party's judgment and free will and imposes the will of the stronger party

unilateral mistake

one party to a contract is mistaken about a fundamental element of the contract

unjust enrichment doctrine

principle that a person should not be permitted to inequitably gain a profit or benefit at the expense of another

unliquidated damages

damages that cannot be fixed by a mathematical or measured calculation but require information from a source outside the contract

vicarious performance

the performance of obligations under a contract by a third party in circumstances in which the original party remains responsible for proper performance

void ab initio

a contract that is invalid from the beginning; no rights can arise under it

void contract

a contract that does not exist at law because one or more essential elements of the contract are lacking; an unenforceable contract

voidable contract

a contract that may be avoided or declared void at the option of one party to the contract; once it is declared invalid no further rights can be obtained under it, but benefits obtained before the declaration are not forfeit

waiver

a voluntary agreement to relinquish a right, such as a right under a contract

warranty

a minor term of a contract, the breach of which does not defeat the purpose of the contract

Index